7AM6

The Illustrated Book of
Signs & Symbols

DIAMOND
CADUCEUS
BROOCH

RED ROSE OF
LOVE AND BEAUTY

MEDUSA, WITH HAIR
OF SNAKES

VISHNU, EMBODIMENT
OF LOVE, TRUTH,
AND MERCY

RAVEN TOTEM

The Illustrated Book of
Signs & Symbols

Miranda Bruce-Mitford

THE LION AND THE UNICORN TAPESTRY, C.1500

DORLING KINDERSLEY
LONDON • NEW YORK • STUTTGART

IVY, SACRED TO DIONYSUS

A DORLING KINDERSLEY BOOK

SHAMROCK

SENIOR EDITOR *Emma Foa*

SENIOR ART EDITOR *Sarah Ponder*

MANAGING EDITOR *Anna Kruger*

MANAGING ART EDITOR *Peter Bailey*

ART EDITORS *Joanna Pocock, Martin Wilson*

EDITOR *Shirin Patel*

ASSISTANT DESIGNER *Ali Cobb*

DTP DESIGNER *Nicola Studdart*

PICTURE RESEARCH *Sharon Southren*

PRODUCTION *Katy Holmes*

INDEX & GLOSSARY *Joanna Lane*

EGYPTIAN FUNERARY STELA (DETAIL)

PALMISTRY

First published in Great Britain in 1996
by Dorling Kindersley Limited,
9 Henrietta Street, London, WC2E 8PS

ISBN 0 7513 5428 7

Colour reproduction by Colourscan, Singapore
Printed and bound in Italy by A. Mondadori Editore, Verona

ISLAMIC EYE OF WISDOM

SHIVA, LORD OF THE DANCE

DANCE OF DEATH

CONTENTS

UROBOROS

INTRODUCTION

IT IS A FUNDAMENTAL PART OF HUMAN NATURE not only to survive and reproduce but also to seek explanations for the mysteries of life. Because these mysteries are in fact beyond explanation we use the language of symbolism to represent them. Whether we live in commercialized societies or communities relatively unchanged by time, we are surrounded by signs, images, and ideas that are often highly symbolic.

Signs in a familiar context

Most of us are largely unaware of the meaning and significance – even the presence – of much of this symbolism, and an area of great richness is closed to us. This book sets out to examine the nature of symbolism, and to present in simple terms both familiar and unfamiliar symbols.

Alchemical symbol showing the serpent of Arabia, the triple sun, and the moon

SIGNS OR SYMBOLS?

A sign is an object or idea which in a fairly straightforward way represents or points to something else. An advertisement, for example, reminds us of the product it is promoting; a road sign indicates conditions ahead; and a gesture expresses a mood. As the modern world challenges our sense of identity, we often adopt signs to define ourselves, for example by donning badges or brand-name clothing.

A symbol is clearly linked in function to a sign, and the two words are often used interchangeably, but the symbol generally has a deeper meaning. A symbol is something that through its nature or appearance reflects or represents something more profound than itself. A fire, for instance, may symbolize the flames of the sun, which itself has qualities of warmth, light, and creative power, and is therefore equated with the life force and masculine creative strength. The creator gods of mythology, who possess these very qualities, are usually linked to the sun. On a small scale, objects such as the candle or lamp can also be related to the imagery of the sun, and thus to the masculine realm and the life force.

Paul Delvaux' surreal painting seems to be a hymn to the goddess within her temple. The moon, night sky, the sea, flowers, and statue-head are all of the feminine realm, and the lamp signifies the divine spark.

ANCIENT SYMBOLS

Symbols grow in meaning and complexity over hundreds of years, changing according to their cultural context. But the subjects which have preoccupied mankind from the earliest times have remained relatively constant: fertility, both of the soil and of the human race, birth, life, and death.

Throughout the world, symbols have always been recognized as significant because of qualities they possess which relate in some way to deeper truths. The moon is as powerful a symbol as the sun. It controls the tidal waters and passes through stages from new moon to full moon. It is thus symbolic of water, pregnancy, and birth. Women, sea creatures, the dark, and creatures of the night all belong to the

Christ's sacrifice bears fruit of redemption for the faithful

sphere of the moon. *The Temple* by Delvaux combines much of this lunar imagery, with the full moon shining down on a mysterious goddess figure.

Animals, birds, and trees all have their individual associations. A tree may represent life and growth, for example, and the Tree of Life is a symbol the world over. In the 16th-century engraving above, Christ is actually seen crucified on the Tree of Life, and his crucifixion can be viewed as a symbol of sacrifice. The death or sacrifice of a god or king is a common theme – the shedding of divine blood to ensure the wellbeing of mankind.

Egyptian carving of bird in combat with snake

LOCKED IN COMBAT

The image of two creatures that represent opposing forces is widespread. One form found almost universally is the bird of prey doing battle with the serpent, perhaps the most symbolic of all creatures. Here, the bird represents the sun and the heavens while the serpent, which writhes on the ground and

In Henri Pierre Picou's Homage to Nature, *summer revellers take their pleasures at the feet of the goddess*

Fate, or Fortuna, presides over the random turning of the wheel

in the water, symbolizes the earth and the life-giving waters. The two together represent creation and fertility, and the precariously balanced forces of nature.

MOTHER GODDESSES AND THE WHEEL OF FORTUNE

The theme of the goddess or Earth Mother permeates world mythology and dates back thousands of years. Clay figurines as early as 20,000 BC have been found depicting large-breasted women in their nurturing, procreative role. All human life sprang from this symbolic mother figure and depended on her. The earth itself is regarded as feminine and nurturing because it is fertilized by the rains, and life springs from its soil.

15th-century cherub with skull

Perplexed by the random, often cruel nature of fate, some cultures chose to personify fate in the form of a woman. She is sometimes shown blindfolded to symbolize the arbitrary nature of her decisions.

Along with the randomness of life, the inevitability of death is also a common theme. This takes many forms, from a cherub juxtaposed with a human skull, to the more familiar image of sand ebbing out of an hourglass – all stark reminders of the fate that must befall us all.

However, although certain images are recognized as symbolic by many societies, the symbolism of a particular image may vary from place to place and over time. The forest, for example, is symbolic of retreat and meditation to many Indians, a place in which the soul may draw nearer to Brahman, the one true totality. However, in the West, the forest tends to be a sinister place harbouring dangerous animals and robbers, its shadows representing the dark places of the unconscious.

In The Cat that Walked by Himself, *the cat is "neither a friend nor a servant" to humankind*

CATS IN MYTHOLOGY AND THE IMAGINATION

The cat has captured the imagination from ancient Egyptian times to the present day, although like the forest its symbolism has varied enormously. In farming communities the cat has always been a working animal used to kill rats and mice, and there has been little mystique about it; however, something in the cat's nature and appearance has

Ancient Egyptian cat goddess Bastet

Tuesday, *by Leonora Carrington, combines bizarre, cat-like creatures in a personal dream sequence*

given it a symbolism which is to do with the night, mystery, and aloofness. Black cats, now considered lucky, were once associated with witchcraft, for example. And cats feature prominently in children's stories. Both the Cheshire cat from *Alice's Adventures in Wonderland* and Kipling's *Cat that Walked by Himself* emanate enigma and mockery.

In Ancient Egypt cats were worshipped and the cult of Bastet centered around a cat goddess. Images of cats were revered, and domestic cats were mummified on death so that, like people, they could enter an afterlife.

THE SYMBOLISM OF DREAMS

In many parts of the world dream symbolism is treated with respect. Wise men interpret dream images, often thought to be sent by the gods, and people act on these interpretations. In the West however, dreams are nowadays thought to be relatively unimportant, and the urgings of the unconscious mind go largely ignored by most people. The psychologist

Lewis Carroll's Alice meets the enigmatic Cheshire cat

Goya's The Sleep of Reason Produces
Monsters *shows how daytime fears
can produce night-time terrors*

Sigmund Freud studied the symbolism of dreams and found much of it to be related to wish-fulfilment. He believed that dreams reflected our deepest desires, often rooted in infancy, and thought many had sexual or erotic overtones. His pupil Carl Jung believed that the symbolism went deeper than the purely sexual to include a spiritual dimension.

Jung was fascinated by the way in which ordinary objects or people appear in a strange, often distressing, context in people's dreams and sought to understand why. Many images, he believed, appear in our dreams as a direct product of the individual unconscious, which is a highly personal amalgam of memories and emotions buried deep within us. Often we are not conscious of these impulses and they can only surface in dreams. A hairbrush, for instance, might trigger memories of one's hair being brushed by one's mother in childhood, so symbolizing the caring mother image; however another individual might have been struck with a hairbrush in childhood, triggering quite different associations. In Magritte's painting *The Reckless Sleeper*, a figure dreams about a series of mundane and apparently unrelated objects which are somehow linked meaningfully in his unconscious.

In this Indian miniature, men grapple with a giant trapped in a well, representing "the shadow", or base desires we try to bury in the unconscious.

The images in Magritte's Restless Sleeper *seem disconcertingly simple*

UNIVERSAL DREAM SYMBOLS

After analyzing the dreams of many patients, Jung concluded that certain images appear as symbols universally and are therefore part of what he called the collective unconscious, built on the cultural experiences and memories of our ancestors. Images such as being pursued by some huge monster, a yearning for safety, or dangers lurking in the darkness, are very commonly experienced in dreams in all parts of the world, and these images seem to be universal.

Jung termed these universal images "archetypes", which appear in the unconscious of millions. There is the "anima", or female principle, which can manifest as the goddess, the queen, princess, or witch; and the "animus", or male principle, which could be the god, the king, prince, wizard, or demon character. These figures symbolize for us our image of male and female and could represent either an aspect of ourselves, a parent, or loved one.

Other archetypes include the shadow, embodiment of feelings of guilt or fear, particularly about our hidden and unacknowledged feelings or desires.

MODERN SYMBOLISM

Neil Armstrong makes "a giant leap for mankind"

In today's world, symbols retain their power to affect us, although we are perhaps less aware of their effects than in the past. Some symbols have remained constant for centuries, some have evolved different meanings, and yet others are quite new. One dramatic symbol to have emerged during the course of the twentieth century is the mushrooming cloud of the atomic bomb. This surely is the ultimate image of the great shadow of destruction that mankind has brought upon himself – by opening the Pandora's box of knowledge.

The film star is often literally larger than life

A more positive image was the American moon landing in 1969. Witnessed by 600 million people throughout the world, it became the ultimate symbol of man's indomitable spirit and urge for conquest.

TODAY'S GODS, GODDESSES, AND SUPERHEROES

Some modern fictitious characters assume semi-godlike status similar to that of the ancient Greek heroes. Creations such as Superman are not thought of as real, yet they embody the classic male archetype of the powerful and heroic force for good. In righting the wrongs of the world, such figures appeal to an innate need in all of us.

Also appealing to this need are the pop, sports, and film stars who, for some, have largely supplanted the gods of old. Since the death of "the King" Elvis Presley, for example, his home, Graceland, has become a shrine and place of pilgrimage for his millions of devoted followers.

Sporting heroes, too, attract a huge following, especially among men. The sense of group identity – and passion – they inspire is evident at any football stadium as hordes of fans cheer their heroes on in moments of shared admiration. Similar, instinctual urges can be seen at rock concerts when members of the audience strike matches, light lighters, and hold up candles to express their devotion to their idols. The resultant sea of flickering flames harks back to the symbolism of fire in religions and cultures throughout history.

Audiences at rock concerts show their admiration and reverence by holding flames up to their heroes

Superman is today's superhero – embodying all that is good and powerful

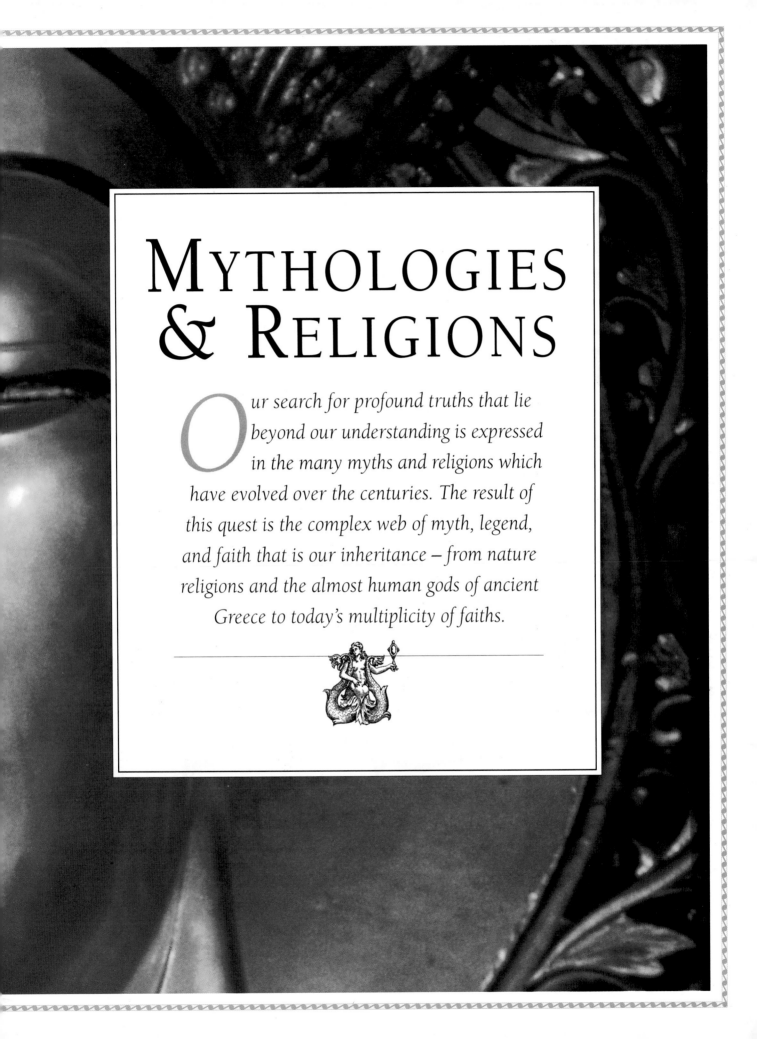

MYTHOLOGIES & RELIGIONS

*O*ur search for profound truths that lie
beyond our understanding is expressed
in the many myths and religions which
have evolved over the centuries. The result of
this quest is the complex web of myth, legend,
and faith that is our inheritance – from nature
religions and the almost human gods of ancient
Greece to today's multiplicity of faiths.

ANCIENT DEITIES

THE CLASSICAL RELIGIONS of Europe and Egypt no longer exist as belief systems although their mythology survives. Like modern-day Hinduism these religions were centred around a family of gods who more or less controlled the lives of humans, and much of human activity involved the worship and placation of those gods. Many of these ancient gods live on in our imagination, and their symbolism has been absorbed into our language, our music, poetry, and art. Today song writers still pay tribute to Venus, universal symbol of feminine beauty, and to Cupid's arrow piercing a lover's heart.

EGYPTIAN

Egyptian gods developed from the merging of two earlier cultures, one with gods in human form and one with animal-shaped gods. Gradually a remarkable religion evolved that focused on the cult of the dead.

ISIS AND HORUS
Isis was the mother goddess, queen and sister of Osiris. She is here shown suckling her son Horus. Her crown is in the form of a throne, suggesting that she was originally a personification of the throne of the pharaohs.

THOTH
Depicted variously as an ibis-headed man and a baboon (the two animals sacred to him), Thoth is lord of the moon, lord of time, and reckoner of the years. He is the helper of the dead and protector of Osiris, ruler of the underworld.

OSIRIS
Originally a powerful fertility god, Osiris was drowned in the river Nile. His body was dismembered and scattered over the Nile valley, ensuring the growth of crops, which sprang from his flesh. He was later restored to life and became a symbol of resurrection, as well as the god of the underworld. He is often depicted in a mummy-like posture.

AMUN-RE
The creator god Amun was merged with Re, the sun god, to form Amun-Re. Known as "the hidden one", Amun-Re was the power of the invisible wind and the soul of all things. Even the other gods were unable to penetrate his mysterious nature.

ANUBIS
Originally the jackal-headed god of the dead, Anubis was supplanted by Osiris. He was nevertheless the protector of the dead and was often carved on rock tombs.

SKY GODDESS NUT
Nut was the sky goddess of Egyptian mythology and she is often depicted touching the earth with her toes and fingers, her body arching to represent the arc of heaven. The stars on her body denote the Milky Way, and she is sometimes surrounded by astrological signs.

GREEK

In the second millennium BC, Aegean religion revolved around the cult of a mother goddess, but later the centre of civilization moved to the mainland, and the Greeks worshipped many divinities who fought, squabbled, and loved, just like humans.

Zeus' thunderbolt, symbol of his power

ZEUS
Zeus was king of the gods and god of the skies. His well-known amorous conquests reflect the Greek conquest of many outlying regions, and the absorption of their mother goddess cults.

APOLLO
Apollo, son of Zeus, was the sun god who caused the fruits of the earth to ripen. His arrows were the sun's rays. He was also a shepherd god and god of music.

ATHENA
The daughter of Zeus, Athena was the goddess of wisdom and learning but also of warfare (hence her helmet). Often depicted with an owl, she was the patron of Athens and her owl is the emblem of that city.

EROS
Known to the Romans as Cupid, Eros was a symbol of earthly love. He was the son of Venus, and carried a bow and arrows with which he pierced the hearts of his victims, causing them to fall passionately in love.

POSEIDON
Brother of Zeus and god of the sea, Poseidon (the Roman Neptune) was symbolic of the power of the waters. He carried a trident, symbol of creation, and could protect those at sea.

ROMAN

The Romans absorbed elements of all the cultures they came into contact with. They adopted the Greek gods as well as those of other peoples they conquered, and had hundreds of different gods, goddesses, demi-gods, and spirits governing virtually every aspect of life. They honoured and worshipped them in order to safeguard themselves – in this life and the next.

MINERVA
The warlike Minerva often wears armour. Like her Greek counterpart Athena, she represents the arts, wisdom, and learning.

MARS
The son of Jupiter and Juno, Mars was the much-respected god of war. He is usually depicted with a spear in one hand and a shield in the other. The month of March comes from his name.

MERCURY, JUPITER, JUNO, APOLLO
Mercury was the god of commerce who appeared late in the pantheon, at a time when trade flourished. He is sometimes equated with the Greek god Hermes, messenger of the Gods. Here he weighs Trojan against Greek to decide the victor of the Trojan War. With him are: Jupiter (the Greek Zeus); Juno, wife of Jupiter and goddess of light, marriage, and childbirth; and Apollo, son of Jupiter.

FLORA
Flora was the goddess of spring, the vine, fruit, flowers, and grain, and she symbolized fertility. Festivals in her honour were often wild events.

BACCHUS
Usually depicted as a beautiful youth, Bacchus was the god of wine, and his worship featured much drunken revelry.

GREEK SCULPTURE OF APHRODITE

THE BIRTH OF APHRODITE/VENUS

The name Aphrodite means "born from the foam", and in Greek myth the goddess was said to have appeared from the sea, emerging from a scallop shell. The image has captured the imagination of poets and painters through the ages: English poet Alfred Lord Tennyson wrote of "Aphrodite beautiful, fresh as the foam". Then, as now, Aphrodite symbolized love and beauty. Her Roman equivalent, Venus, is equally renowned. Below, in Botticelli's famous painting, the god of the West Wind is gently blowing the beautiful Venus towards the shore, where a nymph awaits ready to cloak her.

ROMAN BRONZE STATUE OF VENUS

The nymph wears a garland of myrtle, the tree of Venus

THE BIRTH OF VENUS, SANDRO BOTTICELLI, C.1482

CELTIC

Although the pre-Roman Celts of Europe and the British Isles adopted some of the gods of the conquering Romans, they had their own beliefs in a creator god, a mother goddess, and nature gods. A trio of mother or fertility goddesses are sometimes presented together.

Antler-headed god

CERNUNNOS
The horned god Cernunnos is found throughout the Celtic lands. Here he is shown with antlers, surrounded by animals. In his left hand he holds a ram-headed serpent, symbol of fertility.

NORSE

The Nordic people, who lived in a harsh climate, worshipped gods of the elements and nature. By respecting and honouring the gods, they hoped to exert some control over the fierceness of the weather.

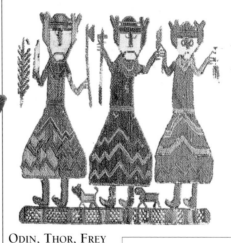

ODIN, THOR, FREY
This 12th-century tapestry depicts three Norse deities. Odin, god of war and intelligence, could transform himself into whatever shape he wanted. Thor was feared as the god of thunder, whose hammer, when thrown, caused lightning. Frey was a god of fertility and birth.

JUDAISM

JUDAISM EMERGED IN ABOUT THE 14TH CENTURY BC and has evolved into a strongly monotheistic religion based on a dialogue between God, or Yahweh, and his chosen people, the Jews. The patriarchs of Judaism are the ancient leaders, Abraham, his son Isaac, and grandson Jacob, whose deeds are recorded in Genesis, the first book of the Bible. Today Jews are scattered throughout the world, but all are linked by a culture centred on Jewish history, law, and family life.

The two triangles symbolize the balance of the universe

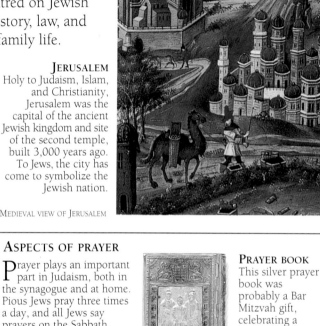

MEDIEVAL VIEW OF JERUSALEM

STAR OF DAVID
The main symbol of Judaism and the Jewish state, the star of David is also allied to Jewish mysticism. Its triangles represent the sun, fire, and masculine energy interlocked with the moon, water, and female energy.

"Servant candle" used to light the others

HANUKKAH
This 8-armed menorah is used to celebrate Hanukkah, the festival of lights. Candles are lit on 8 consecutive nights to mark the miracle of a day's supply of sacramental oil lasting 8 days, when the eternal light in the temple of Jerusalem was relit in 164 BC.

JERUSALEM
Holy to Judaism, Islam, and Christianity, Jerusalem was the capital of the ancient Jewish kingdom and site of the second temple, built 3,000 years ago. To Jews, the city has come to symbolize the Jewish nation.

MEZUZAH
Traditionally the mezuzah is positioned on the front door post. It contains a tiny scroll, or *shema*, with words from the Bible. This calls on God's people to love him totally, and sums up the heart of the Jewish faith.

SHOFAR
The shofar horn signals Rosh Hashanah, the Jewish New Year, and calls on the Jews to repent their sins before the Day of Atonement. The shofar is a ram's horn and serves as a reminder of the animal God gave to Abraham to sacrifice in place of Isaac.

SHOFAR

ASPECTS OF PRAYER

Prayer plays an important part in Judaism, both in the synagogue and at home. Pious Jews pray three times a day, and all Jews say prayers on the Sabbath, their holy day, which starts at sunset on Friday. The day of rest marks the Israelites' liberation from slavery and the forming of a Jewish nation.

SILVER PRAYER BOOK

PRAYER BOOK
This silver prayer book was probably a Bar Mitzvah gift, celebrating a boy's official coming of age at thirteen.

WESTERN WALL
This is the only wall that survives from the Temple of Jerusalem, destroyed by the Romans in AD 70. It is a symbol both of the temple itself and of the Jewish nation, and is the most holy place of pilgrimage and worship.

KIPPAH

TEFILLIN

KIPPAH & TEFILLIN
Male Jews wear a skull-cap, or *kippah*, as a sign of respect for God. The small leather boxes, or *tefillin*, contain passages from the Torah and are also worn while praying.

BOY AT PRAYER
This boy has the ritual tefillin strapped around his arm and on his forehead. The wearing of "God's words" in this way is thought to foster humility. The boy also wears a *tallit*, or prayer shawl, which has a tassle at each corner symbolizing the four corners of the earth.

TORAH
The Torah is the Jewish law, and contains 613 commandments – God's instructions to the people of Israel. Because the Torah scrolls represent the word of God, they are considered so sacred that no-one may touch them. They may be unrolled only by means of the handles.

Woven leaves of palm, myrtle, and willow, representing the spine, the eyes, and the mouth

TORAH SCROLL

YAD, OR POINTER

The crown is a symbol of the Torah because the Torah is the crowning glory of Jewish life

TORAH MANTLE
Torah scrolls are often traditionally covered in an embroidered mantle. This both protects them and reinforces their aura of preciousness.

Lulav is carried around the temple seven times at Sukkot

CITRUS FRUIT (ETROG), SYMBOL OF THE HEART

MOSES DESCENDING FROM MOUNT SINAI, AFTER DORE, 1865

THE BIRTH OF JEWISH LAW
During the Jewish people's long journey from Egypt, where they had been slaves, God spoke to Moses, their leader, and made a pact, or covenant, with them. His Ten Commandments to the Jews were written in fire on tablets of stone and set out a moral and religious code of conduct for his chosen people.

SUKKOT
The festival of Sukkot commemorates the way God provided for the Jews as they wandered in the wilderness on their way to the Promised Land. Festive huts are built, and leaves of palms, myrtle, and willow are woven into a lulav to symbolize the tents that gave them shelter.

PASSOVER
The Passover festival commemorates the Exodus of the Jews from Egypt, when the angel of death "passed over" the Israelites, sparing their lives. At the Passover *seder*, or ritual meal, all the foods eaten are symbolic of that journey.

Egg is reminder of spring and rebirth

Fresh lettuce for frugal meals eaten in slavery

Shankbone of lamb recalls lambs killed at the first Passover

SALT WATER
A dish of salt water represents the tears shed by the Jews during their long years in captivity.

Bitter herbs such as horseradish represent the bitterness of slavery

Nut and fruit paste represent bricks and mortar used to build cities in Egypt

"Pesach", Hebrew for Passover

MATZAH
The flat, unleavened matzah bread is eaten as a reminder of the haste with which the Israelites fled Egypt.

MATZAH

PASSOVER PLATE
The seder plate forms the centrepiece of the table in a Passover meal. It contains portions of all the ceremonial foods that play a part in the story of the Exodus of the Jews from Egypt.

HOLY ARK
The Ark of the Covenant was a portable wooden chest overlaid with gold that contained the original Torah. The Jews carried it from the desert to the Temple in Jerusalem. Today Torah scrolls are housed in a symbolic "holy ark" behind a curtain in that wall of the synagogue that faces Jerusalem.

CHRISTIANITY

CHRISTIANITY HAS ITS ROOTS in the Jewish faith: the Old Testament of the Bible has prophecies of a Messiah (saviour). Christians believe these prophesies were fulfilled in the life of Jesus, who they believe is the Son of God. His teachings, recorded in the gospels of the New Testament, stress brotherly love and compassion, and are rich in symbolic meaning. Since its birth 2,000 years ago the Christian church has split into many denominations, but all Christians are united in the central belief that Christ died to redeem the sins of the world and that his resurrection offers salvation.

JESUS CHRIST
This modern Russian icon shows Christ blessing in the manner of the Eastern church. The thumb forms a circle with the fourth finger and the middle and index fingers are crossed. This represents Chi and Rho, the first two Greek letters of his name. Icons are seen as embodying spiritual truths.

THE VIRGIN MARY
In the Eastern and Roman Catholic churches, Mary, Jesus' mother, is worshipped in her own right. She intercedes between man and God, and is often called Mother of God. The cult of Mary is similar to some mother goddess cults, and arose out of the need for a mother figure.

SACRED LAMB
The sacrificial lamb is a symbol of Christ. John the Baptist described him as "the lamb of God that taketh away the sins of the world". In this crozier (bishop's crook) the lamb stands for the salvation of the faithful.

FISH
The fish is a symbol of Christ, because in Greek the first letters of the words Jesus Christ, Son of God, Saviour, spell Ichthus, or fish. Three fish together represent the Trinity: the Father, the Son, and the Holy Spirit.

ROSARY
The rosary is both the repetition of the prayer "Hail Mary" and also the string of beads used to count each incantation. It takes its name from the rose, symbol of Mary.

DOVE
John the Baptist saw the Holy Spirit enter Jesus in the form of a dove.

CROWN OF THORNS
The crown of thorns Christ was made to wear is a symbol of his crucifixion.

THE CROSS

DANISH CRUCIFIX, GILDED COPPER OVER CARVED OAK

The cross has many forms: St Peter was crucified upside down; Constantine's combines Chi Rho, the first two letters for Christ in Greek; the anchor combines the cross and the crescent, a symbol of Mary; and the Russian cross includes the inscription and the footrest of the crucifix.

CRUCIFIX
The image of Christ on the cross, the crucifix, is an object of Christian devotion. It is the most powerful symbol of Christianity, a reminder that although Jesus died on the cross, he rose again, triumphing over death.

ST PETER'S CROSS

CONSTANTINE'S CROSS

ANCHOR CROSS

RUSSIAN CROSS

CELTIC CROSS
The ring on the Celtic cross, symbol of Irish Christianity, stands for the sun and eternity.

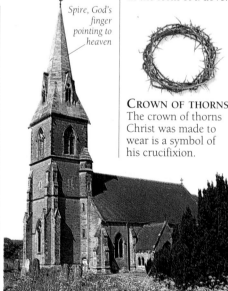

Spire, God's finger pointing to heaven

Circle of sun and eternity

CHURCH
The Church refers both to Christian believers and also to a place of worship. The central part of a church, the nave, is named after the Latin for ship, symbol of the Church itself.

SAINTS

Christian saints were particularly devout people who lived – and often died – for the Christian cause and have since been canonized by the Church. There are thousands of saints, and many of them are depicted in sculpture and paintings carrying attributes related to their life or manner of death. St Francis, for instance, is seen with birds or animals, and St Catherine sometimes carries a wheel. St John the Baptist carries his severed head on a platter.

SERBIAN ICON PAINTING, 1645

PERUVIAN NATIVITY SCENE

JOHN THE BAPTIST
John the Baptist was the last of the Old Testament prophets and Jesus' first disciple. He foretold the coming of Christ and baptized him. He was beheaded at the wish of Herod's wife and her daughter, Salome, and his head was presented to them on a plate.

MARY MAGDALENE
A former prostitute, St Mary Magdalene represents the penitent sinner.

ST CHRISTOPHER
St Christopher carried a child across a river – the child was Christ, or the world itself. St Christopher is the patron of travellers.

NATIVITY
Jesus was born in a humble stable, and his whole life was lived in simplicity. Such humble beginnings emphasize the spiritual richness of his teachings, which set little store by material riches.

COMMUNION
At his last supper with his disciples, Jesus broke bread and poured wine, which he blessed and shared among them, saying that the bread was his body and the wine was his blood. By imitating this at communion, Christians partake ritually of the body and blood of Christ.

BREAD
Bread symbolizes the body of Christ. In communion it takes the form of a wafer.

WINE
The wine drunk at communion is the blood of Christ, shed for mankind.

CATHERINE'S WHEEL
St Catherine died for her Christian beliefs, crucified on four flaming wheels – hence the firework, the Catherine Wheel.

THE FOUR APOSTLES, ALBRECHT DÜRER, 1523-26

FOUR APOSTLES
The Apostles were sent out by Christ to preach the Gospel. St John (left), one of the writers of the Gospel, carries his book. Next to him, Peter holds the keys to the kingdom of Heaven. Paul holds a sword and a letter, symbolizing his manner of martyrdom and letters to the churches he had founded, and on the right Mark, like John, holds his Gospel.

FRANCIS OF ASSISI
St Francis embodies purity and simplicity. He is said to have preached to the birds.

MEDIEVAL BOOK OF HOURS

RELIGIOUS BOOKS
The Bible consists of the Old and the New Testaments, the latter dealing with the life and teachings of Jesus and his apostles. For some, the Bible is the direct word of God. Books of Hours were meditations, often on religious themes, for different times of the day.

SEE ALSO
JESUS CHRIST ☞ UNICORN 28; PHOENIX 31; WHEAT 46; SEA CREATURES 54; ANCHOR 97

THE VIRGIN MARY ☞ THE LANGUAGE OF THE ROSE 51; THE LILY AND CHRISTIANITY 53, 106; STARFISH 55; BEES IN CHRISTIANITY 56

HINDUISM

HINDUISM IS THE MAJOR RELIGION OF INDIA. It has evolved over millennia and encompasses a complex range of traditions, religious beliefs, philosophy, and mythology. The roots of Hinduism can be traced to the Aryans who arrived in India with their pantheon of male gods in the second millennium BC. The indigenous Indus valley peoples already had strong religious beliefs centred on fertility cults and a Mother Goddess. The Aryans adopted many of their beliefs, including the Goddess. All the gods and goddesses of Hinduism, including Brahma (creator), Vishnu (preserver), Shiva (destroyer), and the Goddess are aspects of Brahman, the one eternal principle.

Brahma's four heads face the four points of the compass

The conch, symbolizing creation and transience

The chakra, wheel of existence

Lotus, symbol of creation and purity

Many signs represent the universe, contained within the god

Club, symbol of authority

KRISHNA
An incarnation of Vishnu, Krishna embodies divine love. His adventures are recorded in the *Bhagvat Purana*. Here he is a naughty child stealing butter.

HANUMAN
Hanuman, the mighty monkey general of the epic *Ramayana*, represents loyalty, religious devotion, and courage.

DURGA
Durga is the ferocious form of the Mother Goddess and wields various weapons in her many hands. She stands for the more active, destructive aspects of feminine nature.

BRAHMA
The four heads of Brahma, the creator, symbolize the four quarters, the four Vedas, or religious texts, and the four castes of Hinduism. Brahma has become less important than Vishnu, Shiva, and the Goddess.

The many hands symbolize the many aspects of the deity

SHIVA
Originally a mountain god, Shiva, meaning auspicious, is the god of destruction. But, in a world of endless rebirths, destruction precedes creation. He may be worshipped as a *linga*, or phallic symbol, as an ascetic, as a teacher, or in his form as dancer in the great dance of creation and destruction.

GANESHA
Ganesha overcomes all obstacles and is the god of new ventures. He has the head of an elephant, which can forge through the thickest jungle. In myth Shiva mistakenly beheaded the god, and only an elephant's head could be found as a replacement.

VISHNU
Originally connected with the sun, Vishnu is the preserver of the universe and the embodiment of love, truth, order, and mercy. To his worshippers he is the supreme being, from whom everything emanates. He rides on Garuda, the fabulous bird, or rests on Ananta, the cosmic serpent. In order to restore the cosmic balance Vishnu has been incarnated on earth in nine *avatars*, or incarnations, some human, some animal. The tenth incarnation, the horse avatar, is yet to come.

OM
This is a sacred syllable and thought to be the "seed" of all *mantras*, divine and powerful words or sounds. The sound A-U-M is thought to be the one eternal syllable, in which the past, present, and future exist.

SWASTIKA
In India the swastika is an auspicious mark worn as jewellery or marked on objects as a symbol of wellbeing. Counter-clockwise swastikas are sometimes considered inauspicious. The symbol, which predates Hinduism, is associated with the sun and the wheel of birth and rebirth, and is an emblem of Vishnu.

SACRED COW
The cow is sacred to Hindus, and even the lowliest specimen must not be harmed. Valued for its milk and its dung, which is used as fuel, the cow probably represents Mother Earth.

SHRINE
The household shrine is an important focus of daily *puja*, or worship. This is where the gods are invited, welcomed, and worshipped. Offerings of fresh flowers, fruit, and cooked food are placed before an image of the god, and incense may be burned.

APSARAS
Sensuous nymphs like this are found on temple walls. They personify rain clouds and mists and are associated with fertility and growth.

DIVALI
The autumn festival of Divali, the festival of light, is celebrated in honour of Lakshmi, consort of Vishnu and goddess of abundance and good fortune. It celebrates the return from exile of the hero Rama, an avatar of Vishnu, when lamps were relit all over the kingdom.

HOLY MAN
This *sadhu*, or ascetic, is a follower of Shiva, indicated by the horizontal lines on his forehead and the buffalo horns on his staff. A Hindu ideal in later life is to live like a holy man.

OBJECTS OF WORSHIP
In Hindu worship, or *puja*, offerings representing and involving the various elements and senses are made in the form of fire, water, sweet scented air, and clarified butter. Ritual objects are used for sprinkling rose-water and scent, burning incense, or for other religious purposes.

SCENT SHAKER
This ivory scent shaker is shaped like the headily perfumed lotus, symbol of creation.

INCENSE BURNER
The incense burner is waved back and forth in the shrine. Wafting the aroma around welcomes the god into his image with sweet smells.

ROSE-WATER SPRINKLER
The water sprinkler, shaped like a flower, is used to sprinkle rose-water around the shrine in a symbolic purification.

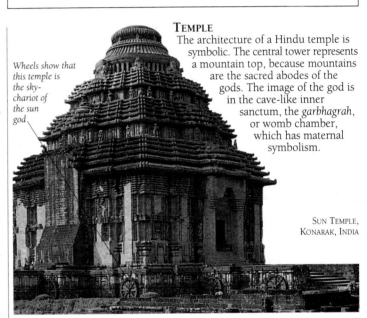

TEMPLE
The architecture of a Hindu temple is symbolic. The central tower represents a mountain top, because mountains are the sacred abodes of the gods. The image of the god is in the cave-like inner sanctum, the *garbhagrah*, or womb chamber, which has maternal symbolism.

Wheels show that this temple is the sky-chariot of the sun god

SUN TEMPLE, KONARAK, INDIA

GANGES
The holiest of the rivers of India, the Ganges, rises in the Himalayas, home of the gods. It is personified by the goddess Ganga. Pilgrims come to the Ganges to visit holy sites, such as Benares, birthplace of Shiva. To die on the banks of the Ganges and to have one's ashes float away on its current is the best of deaths for a Hindu.

The Purana being extracted

ANCIENT TEXT
The Puranas, literally, old stories, contain traditional Hindu lore told in popular verse. Here the sage Vyasa is milking the Puranas out of Kamadhenu, the cow that grants wishes. The Puranas tell of the popular beliefs of Hinduism.

VYASA MILKING THE PURANA OUT OF KAMADHENU, DURGARATNA BETHA, 1836

SEE ALSO
BRAHMA ☞ LOTUS 52
GANESHA ☞ ELEPHANT 63
KRISHNA ☞ KRISHNA'S LOVE 82; BLUE GOD 107
SHIVA ☞ LINGA AND YONI 70; LORD OF DANCE 76
SWASTIKA ☞ SWASTIKA 105
VISHNU ☞ GARUDA 31; MILK 49; FEET 75

BUDDHISM

BUDDHISM IS BASED ON NON-VIOLENCE, compassion, and charity. Its goal is Enlightenment, which ends the round of birth and rebirth and leads to *Nirvana*, literally, blowing out, or absorption into the cosmos. Buddhism developed from the teachings of Gautama Buddha, born Prince Siddhartha in northeast India in the mid-6th century BC. Siddhartha renounced his worldly life in search of an existence free of suffering. When he achieved this goal, through meditation and asceticism, he was called the Buddha, or the Enlightened.

Vase holds wisdom

BUDDHA, CONFUCIUS, AND LAO TZU, WANG SHU-KU, 18TH CENTURY

Bodhi tree   *Mara on elephant*   *Rays of enlightenment*

Mara and troops defeated

FOOTPRINT
The Footprint of the Buddha is marked with auspicious signs, often 108 in number. These include the swastika; the mace, symbol of the force that breaks lust; fish, for freedom from all restraint; the flower vase, for supreme intelligence; the conch, for the voice of the Buddha; the wheel of law or life; and the crown of Brahma, for Buddha's supremacy.

FOLDING BOOK
In Burma books that fold up, called *parabaiks*, tell the story of the Buddha with words and pictures. From left to right, this parabaik depicts the Buddha on his way to the Bodhi tree where he attained enlightenment; Buddha meditating and worshipped by the gods; the approach of Mara, the evil spirit, on an elephant, and his defeat; the Buddha radiating enlightenment and being worshipped by gods and creatures.

THREE GREAT TRUTHS
The great Chinese sages Confucius and Lao Tzu, founder of Taoism, welcome in their midst the infant Buddha, symbolically representing the acceptance of Buddhism in China during the 4th century. Confucianism, Taoism, and Buddhism are known as the Three Great Truths and together have moulded Chinese thought over thousands of years.

ASPECTS OF BUDDHA

Buddhists do not worship the Buddha but pay homage to his teachings and example in front of his effigies. These portray various postures, or *asanas*, with a number of *mudras*, or hand gestures. They all have a particular significance, appropriate for teaching, meditation, or blessing.

The great snake Muchalinda protecting the Buddha

WHEEL OF LAW
With his first sermon, the Buddha is said to have set the wheel of *dharma*, or law, in motion. The wheel, therefore, represents the teachings of Buddha and the eight spokes the Eightfold Path that leads to enlightenment.

RECLINING BUDDHA
After a lifetime of teaching, the Buddha died and entered Nirvana, never to be reborn. This is usually symbolized by the Parinirvana asana, in which the Buddha is shown reclining on his right side.

LAUGHING BUDDHA
Mi Lo Fo is a form of Maitreya, the future Buddha. The name means Friendly One who laughs at fate, and his obesity contains the wisdom of the universe.

MARBLE RECLINING BUDDHA, BURMESE, 19TH CENTURY

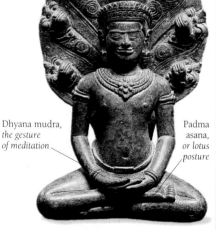

Dhyana mudra, the gesture of meditation

Padma asana, or lotus posture

BUDDHA MUCHALINDA
While the Buddha was engaged in deep meditation there was a violent storm and torrential rain. The great serpent Muchalinda raised the Holy One onto his coils and protected him from the rain with his many hoods.

SHRINE AT BUDDHIST TEMPLE, LONDON

SHRINE
This Buddhist shrine shows Buddha images surrounded by candles and incense, both part of the act of devotion in Buddhism, as in other religions. The light produced is the light of the doctrine and the smoke from the incense wafts the truth of the doctrine towards the devotees, carrying their devotions into the heavens.

SACRED SYMBOLS
An architectural motif combines sacred symbols that stand for the Eightfold Path and also figure on the Footprint of the Buddha.

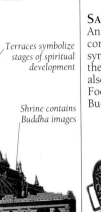

CHORTEN
A miniature shrine, this Tibetan silver box with mystic symbols is worn to keep evil spirits at bay. It holds a a tablet moulded from the ashes of a lama.

BODHISATTVA OF COMPASSION

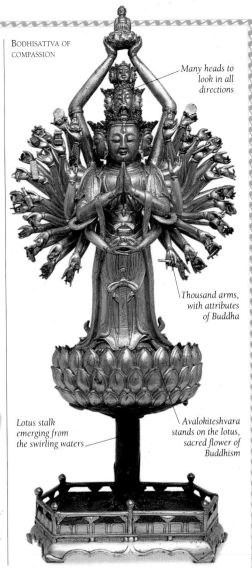

Many heads to look in all directions

Thousand arms, with attributes of Buddha

Avalokiteshvara stands on the lotus, sacred flower of Buddhism

Lotus stalk emerging from the swirling waters

Pagoda finial represents enlightenment

Terraces symbolize stages of spiritual development

Shrine contains Buddha images

SHWE ZIGON PAGODA, PAGAN, BURMA, 11TH CENTURY

BURMESE PAGODA
Pagodas are *stupas*, originally burial mounds erected over the remains of important men in India. After the Buddha's death his ashes were divided and placed within stupas, and later his few possessions were similarly enshrined. Stupas act as a symbol of the Buddha's entry into Nirvana and as a reminder to all of the possibility of enlightenment. In Burma, as in China, the stupa is known as a pagoda.

BODHISATTVA
According to one school of Buddhism, Bodhisattvas are enlightened beings who put off Nirvana to assist others to enlightenment – the ultimate act of compassion. Avalokiteshvara, the Bodhisattva of compassion, is shown here with eleven heads and a thousand arms, so he can reach out to all conscious beings. Each hand holds an object that symbolizes an attribute of the Buddha.

BUDDHIST MONKS
The Buddha established the *sangha*, or monastic order, so that people could devote themselves to his teachings. The majority of Buddhists think that enlightenment can only be attained by following the monastic, meditative life – free from distractions – on the path to complete awareness.

ZEN MONK
This monk from Japan holds the traditional alms bowl in which people place food as an act of merit. Zen Buddhism emphasizes enlightenment gained through meditation.

THAI MONK
A Thai monk sits in the window of a monastic building. He is probably studying *sutras*, Buddhist texts which young monks have to master.

PRAYER WHEEL
Mantras, or sacred verses, are inscribed on prayer wheels. Each rotation of the cylinder stands for one recitation of the mantra. Some large wheels are powered by windmills.

STONE CARVING, ANANDA TEMPLE, PAGAN, BURMA, 11TH CENTURY

THE GREAT DEPARTURE
Prince Siddhartha, the future Buddha, leaves the palace (left), having renounced the worldly life and determined on a life of meditation and asceticism. This Burmese boy (right) symbolically re-enacts the momentous scene before donning the monk's robes and entering the monastery as a novice monk.

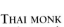

TIBETAN PRAYER WHEEL

ISLAM

ISLAM IS THE FAITH of about one-fifth of the world's population. It is based on the revelations uttered by the Prophet Mohammed who lived in Arabia (*c.*AD 570-632). These were later recorded in the volume called the Koran. Followers of Islam are Muslims. Like Jews and Christians, they worship one god, whom they call Allah, and they see their faith as an act of surrender to the will of Allah. Actions of devout Muslims are dictated by the Five Pillars, which call upon the faithful to declare their faith publicly, pray five times a day, give alms, fast during the month of Ramadan, and make a pilgrimage to Mecca.

PRAYER RUG
A Muslim usually performs *salat*, or prays, on a prayer rug. This 16th-century Ottoman example has Islamic pillars woven into the design.

STAR & CRESCENT
Thought originally to have signified the waxing moon, and once associated with the goddess Diana, the crescent was adopted as a symbol of Islam in the 14th century. The star, a symbol of sovereignty and divinity, was added later.

ASCENT OF PROPHET MOHAMMED TO HEAVEN, AGA MIRAK, 16TH CENTURY

HAND OF GOD
Known as the Hand of Fatima, after Mohammed's daughter, this represents the Five Pillars of Islam.

THE NIGHT JOURNEY
In a dream Mohammed was led to heaven by the Archangel Gabriel. His face is veiled, according to Muslim conventions, and he rides the half-human steed Al Borak, symbol of light and truth.

MUSLIMS AT PRAYER
Adult males pray side by side in the mosque. As they kneel, facing Mecca, they touch their foreheads to the ground and intone the words "Allah is great", their actions symbolically mirroring their spiritual submission to God.

The cube-like shrine is built around the sacred stone, probably a meteorite

KA'BAH
The Ka'bah in Mecca is the central shrine of Islam, to which the faithful must turn in prayer wherever they are in the world. Thus it acts as a point of communion between God and man. Muslims are enjoined to make the pilgrimage here at least once in a lifetime if they are able. They symbolically circle the shrine seven times, each circuit signifying an attribute of God.

Five fingers stand for the five essential practices of Islam

HAND OF FATIMA

THE KA'BAH, MECCA

COMPASS
Since Muslims need to face Mecca when they pray, they often use a *qiblah*, or special compass, to find the direction. Many modern prayer mats have integral compasses, with an image of the Ka'bah at the centre.

MOSQUE LAMP
The interior of a mosque is lit up by lamps. The light of the lamps indicates the presence of the divine within the mosque. It is wisdom and truth and lightens the darkness of ignorance.

Verses from the Koran

Ornamental border to decorate verses

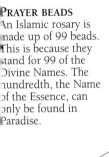

PRAYER BEADS
An Islamic rosary is made up of 99 beads. This is because they stand for 99 of the Divine Names. The hundredth, the Name of the Essence, can only be found in Paradise.

CALLIGRAPHY
Beautifully inscribed Koranic verses are used to decorate any number of objects – a symbolic and constant reminder of the word of God, as in this steel plaque.

KORAN
Some Islamic countries reject the portrayal of living creatures in art, as this is thought to challenge the perfection of Allah. As a result of this prohibition, the word itself has been immortalized in art in the form of Koranic texts. Exquisite examples of calligraphy have been produced, one of Islam's greatest contributions to art. They are usually in Arabic, the language of Islam. These texts, often surrounded by beautiful borders and scrollwork, illustrate the authority and truth of the word of God.

Muezzin calls Muslims to prayer from top of the minaret

CERAMIC TILE
The star is a symbol of divinity and supremacy in Islam. Islamic decoration is characterized by the use of ornamented tiles, many of them star-shaped.

MINARET
The minaret is attached to the mosque, and from its summit the *muezzin*, or crier, calls the faithful to prayer five times a day. Muslims believe that one morning the dawn prayer will be called by the Angel of the Resurrection.

Dome stands for heaven

DOME OF THE ROCK
The Dome of the Rock was erected where the Temple of Solomon once stood in Jerusalem, making the site sacred to Jews, Christians, and Muslims. For the Muslims it enshrines the spot to which Mohammed was brought miraculously by the angel Gabriel for his ascent to heaven. Its great dome represents the arc of the heavens and by passing through the arched gateways around it, one symbolically passes into another state of being.

ANCESTOR & NATURE SPIRITS

IN EVERY PART of the world, at some time or other, there has been a belief that everything in nature possesses a soul or spirit. The spirits of the trees, mountains, crops, rivers, and rocks are ever present, and are honoured, so that man and nature can exist in harmony. Ancestral spirits, too, are central to the beliefs of many people. When someone dies they join the ancestors and watch over the community's links with the past. Some spirits have a protective character and serve to guard a community or individual in times of danger. They may appear on the prow of a boat, on a shield, spear, or helmet, and may be very fierce-looking in order to frighten away evil or the enemy in battle.

ALASKAN MASK
This Alaskan mask represents the essences of various beings. During divination rituals a shaman would wear this to assume the power of the spirits.

ZAIREAN MASK
Grass-skirted masks, such as this, represent the spirits of the ancestors among the Kuba of Zaire. During initiation rites young boys symbolically meet this ancestor for the first time.

ELEPHANT SPIRIT
African masks represent sacred spirits brought to life for rituals. The sacred powers are symbolized by stylized features. This elephant spirit mask from Nigeria represents ugliness.

NATIVE AMERICAN
TOTEM POLE,
CANADA

TOTEM POLE
The totem pole symbolizes the relationship between a tribe or clan and its ancestor. Human and animal ancestor figures are carved on the pole and offerings are made to these sacred figures. This shows respect for the ancestors and solidarity with the clan, all of whom are descended from one ancestor.

ANCESTOR FIGURE
This male ancestor figure from Papua New Guinea, painted in sacred colours, stands for the clan father.

WAR GOD
This Hawaiian war god, with his threatening and terrifying appearance, would protect a particular group in war.

THE DREAMING

Australian Aboriginals call the spiritual and natural order of all existence the Dreaming or Dreamtime. It covers all time, and includes stories of ancestors who created human and animal life. Australian Aboriginals feel at one with nature, and ritual music and art are a vital expression of the spirit essences of the Dreamtime.

BARK PAINTING
Paintings of ancestors are filled in with markings known as *rarrk*. Australian Aboriginals believe these patterns, created by Dreamtime spirits, can release fertility.

WAIJARA SPIRIT, WALLY MANDARRK,
20TH CENTURY

ULURU
Named Ayers Rock by European settlers, Uluru is sacred to Australian Aboriginals, who imbue such sites with special powers. They perform rites to acquire this power and also to renew it.

SHINTO

Shinto, which means "Way of the Kami", is the oldest religion in Japan. According to Shinto belief the world is populated by millions of Kami, spirits that inhabit any person, place, or object that possesses strange transcendent qualities. Spirits inhabit rivers, rocks, trees, and animals, and all nature is thus regarded with awe and respect. In the sixth century Shinto blended with Buddhist philosophy to produce a vast pantheon of gods, including a mixture of nature spirits, guardian deities, and Buddha incarnations.

GOD OF WEALTH
A god of abundance and thus fertility, Daikoku grants a good harvest and brings prosperity.

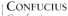

GATEWAY
The *torii* is the gateway to a Shinto shrine. Some shrines may be approached through more than one torii. The ends of the horizontal bars reach towards heaven.

SUN'S RAYS
Ama Terasu, goddess of the sun, is the supreme Shinto god. Japan's emperors claim descent from her. Legend says that, angered by the Storm God, she hid in a cave. The other gods tried to lure her out with jewels and a mirror, hung on a tree outside. Fascinated by her own reflection, she emerged towards it, symbolizing the daily coming of dawn after night.

INARI
The white fox is the messenger and symbol of Inari, the Japanese god of crops and wealth. Offerings of soybean curd, thought to be his favourite food, are made to him, and his bib signifies thanks for prayers answered.

VIEW OF MOUNT FUJI, Hiroshige, 1853

MOUNT FUJI
The unpredictable nature of volcanoes has evoked feelings of fear and acts of worship in many countries. The numerous volcanoes of Japan figure in its religious beliefs, and shrines are often built on volcano slopes. Mount Fuji is said to be the most beautiful mountain in the world. It combines the symbolism of heaven, earth, and fire and thus inspires the feelings of awe, danger, and yet peace evoked by nature. It embodies the spirit of Japan, and is a place of pilgrimage.

CONFUCIUS
Confucius, who lived in the 6th century BC, remains for the Chinese the great teacher who propounded a doctrine based on loyalty and duty to parents, clan, and state. By stressing loyalty to clan, he underlined the importance of the ancestors and strengthened the ancestral cult, already popular in China. Images of Confucius can be found in many traditional household shrines, especially among the overseas Chinese, reflecting the respect accorded to him for classical Chinese values.

SACRED FIGURE FROM TIN HAU TEMPLE, HONG KONG

OCEAN MONARCH
The Chinese Monarch of the Sea personifies the spirit of the oceans. Offerings are made to him by sea-farers to ensure a safe voyage, as at this temple shrine in Hong Kong.

17TH-CENTURY PORTRAIT OF CONFUCIUS

CHINESE LANDSCAPE
The inner serenity of Taoist philosophy is expressed in landscape paintings. Such paintings portray not just the features of the land, but the very essence of nature. Often tiny human figures are placed within the landscape, to stress both the insignificance of man against nature and his place within the universe. Over centuries both Taoist philosophy and Confucianism have influenced Chinese thought: Taoism stresses the spiritual order within nature, and Confucianism stresses the moral order.

SEE ALSO
ABORIGINALS ☞
CRYSTAL 39; KANGAROO 63; HAWK 67

CHINESE LANDSCAPE ☞
THREE GREAT TRUTHS 22; BOW AND ARROW 91; SOUTH KOREA 115

MASKS ☞ MASKS 77

SHINTO ☞ BUDDHISM 22-23; CROW 65

MYTHICAL BEASTS

MANY FABULOUS CREATURES originated in the Mesopotamian valleys of the Tigris and the Euphrates, and from there moved both East and West. The phoenix and the many-headed serpent, for example, and the image of a great bird with a serpent in its talons are found in the iconography of many parts of the world. Those mythical beasts that are half-animal and half-human represent both animal instincts and human intellect. Monsters that are part-bird and part-land or sea creature take on the symbolic associations of both, representing perhaps the sun and the waters, in addition to their own innate symbolism.

DOUBLE-HEADED SERPENT
The double-headed serpent is a common image in the Americas, and is associated with life-giving rain. It was part of the rites of Tlaloc, Aztec god of the mountains, rain, and springs, to whom children were sacrificed in times of drought.

THE LION AND THE UNICORN, FRANCE, c.1500

The Virgin holds the mirror of truth

The horn can detect and counteract poison

The lion represents the male and the sun

The unicorn represents the feminine essence and the moon

UNICORN
The unicorn is pure and incorruptible. In China it represents gentleness, good will, wisdom, and longevity; in Christianity it represents Christ. According to medieval lore, a unicorn's horn was a powerful antidote to poison, but the animal was so wild that no hunter could capture it. Only a virgin could lure a unicorn to her side and tame it. Here a unicorn looks into the mirror of truth, representing the wisdom of self-knowledge.

KY-LIN
This fabulous beast from China generally has the head of a dragon, the mane of a lion, the body of a stag, and the tail of an ox. It is said to appear during the reign of virtuous monarchs and to herald the birth of great people. The Ky-lin often accompanies Chinese sages and immortals. It is gentle, and symbolizes good will and kindness, as well as fertility.

SLEIPNIR
The swiftest of all stallions was Sleipnir, eight-legged mount of Odin, the Teutonic magician-god of war. Sleipnir could overcome all obstacles and gallop across both land and sea. As the mount of Odin, he was associated with the power of that god and also symbolized the wind.

LOCH NESS MONSTER
First sighted in the Middle Ages, the Loch Ness Monster allegedly bit a swimmer to death in AD 565. Over the years there have been numerous sightings and countless investigations, and scientists have tried to make sense of these eyewitness accounts. Originally a symbol of danger, Nessie is now a benevolent monster.

SALAMANDER
A creature of fire, the salamander is usually depicted either breathing fire or surrounded by flames. It is so cold-blooded that it remains unharmed by the flames. As a symbol, it represents the righteous soul, which can emerge unscathed from the fires of temptation.

CENTAUR
With the torso and head of a man above the body of a horse, a centaur combines the instinctual nature of an animal with the judgement and virtue of a man. In Greek myth Chiron, a respected teacher, was a centaur. A centaur is also a Christian symbol of man torn between good and evil.

Seven visible heads

HYDRA
Linked to the many-headed naga of India, the hydra was a nine-headed serpent, sometimes depicted with a dog-like body. It was a formidable foe: if one head were cut off, two more sprang up in its place. In Greek myth it was killed by Hercules. It symbolizes the many problems that obstruct the path to truth.

The Athenian Theseus

The minotaur: half-man, half-bull

MINOTAUR
This creature, with the upper half of a bull, lived in the famous labyrinth of Crete. Every year it devoured seven youths and seven maidens chosen by lot to try to appease the monster. The hero Theseus decided to challenge the beast and end the reign of terror. The minotaur represents the baser instincts of man.

MAKARA

In India this sea creature is the mount of the sea god Varuna and also of Ganga, goddess of the river Ganges. It is part-fish and part-crocodile or elephant, and is symbolic of the waters of creation. It is often seen in conjunction with solar creatures, the two together representing fertility. The makara also represents the duality of good and evil.

NAGA

The naga is a many-headed serpent deity found widely in the art and legend of India and Southeast Asia. It may be depicted with human torso and serpent heads or as wholly animal. Nagas control the rains and are in constant conflict with Garuda, the bird of the sun. This enmity reflects in myth the real balance between sun and rain, which are both essential for the fertility of the soil.

BISHOP FISH

This curious creature, also known as the mitred bishop, has the shaven head of a monk and a large, fishlike body. One was allegedly captured in the Baltic in 1433 and presented to the King of Poland. Although the king wanted to keep it, he relented when the creature pleaded to be returned to the waters. On being released, the Bishop fish made the sign of the cross in gratitude.

HIPPOCAMP

In Greek legend the hippocamp is the mount of Poseidon, drawing his chariot across the oceans. It has the body of a fish and the forelegs of a horse, making it symbolic of both the waters and the earth. More familiarly known as a sea-horse, it is often used in heraldry to denote a laudable action at sea. In the arms of the City of Belfast it represents overseas trade.

MERMAIDS AND SIRENS

Mermaids and sirens appear in the mythology of many countries. The mermaid has the body of a beautiful woman and the tail of a fish. She is a creature of the waters, symbolic of fertility and the unconscious. Sometimes she carries a mirror, which represents truth and the soul. Male equivalents are rarer, although the Tritons of Greek myth – embodying wantonness – were mermen. Sirens may appear in two forms: half-woman, half-bird, or half-woman, half-fish. In their fish form they can be mistaken for mermaids. They represent temptation and seduction, the luring of man from his true purpose.

19TH-CENTURY JAPANESE FIGURINE

THE LURE OF DANGEROUS WOMEN

Ulysses is forewarned that he must beware the sirens of the waters, whose voices have the power to lure men to their deaths. He orders his crew to tie him firmly to the ship's mast and to stop their own ears with wax, so that he alone can hear their song in safety. The artist has represented two of the sirens in human form, but the third has the tail of a fish.

ULYSSES AND THE SIRENS, HERBERT DRAPER, 1905

TRITON JEWEL

Half-man and half-fish, Triton was the son of Neptune and may have been a god of seafarers. Late myths speak of a race of Tritons.

CARVED FIGUREHEAD

This mermaid graces the stern of a barge designed in 1732 for Prince Frederick, son of King George II.

SIREN FROM FRENCH ENGRAVING, c.1573

Protective mermaid

TRITON JEWEL, c.1590

Carved sea monster to ward off any danger

DRAGONS

Combining characteristics of the four elements, earth, air, fire, and water, the dragon symbolizes light and dark, the sun and moon, masculine and feminine, and the unity underlying these opposing forces. The dragon possesses the wings of a bird and the scales of a snake or fish. It breathes fire and often guards a hoard of treasure in its lair. In the East and in pre-Christian Europe, the dragon was seen as helpful and kind – indeed, the red dragon is the emblem of Wales. But Christianity, which saw the serpent as a symbol of evil, also viewed the dragon as a creature of ill-omen, representing destructiveness and inner chaos.

BASILISK

Usually depicted as a form of serpent, the basilisk can also have the legs and wings of a dragon. In medieval Europe its breath or gaze was believed to be fatal, and it is a symbol of death.

The five claws signify that this garment belonged to the Emperor

The pearl of immortality

Head with bared teeth

WINGED DRAGON

This stylized Anglo-Saxon dragon is from a shield. In its mouth it carries what looks like a pearl – perhaps the pearl of immortality.

VIKING DRAGON

In Norse myth the "dread biter" Nidhogg devoured corpses and gnawed ceaselessly at the roots of the ash tree Yggdrasil, the tree of life. Nidhogg symbolized evil.

Embroidered silk square, worn to denote rank

CHINESE DRAGON

A symbol of the Emperor, of male energy, and of fertility, the Chinese dragon is a benign animal and the fifth creature of the Chinese zodiac. It guards the East and represents sunrise, spring, and the rains. Indeed, torrential rain is known as "dragon rain". There are four types of dragon in Chinese legend – dragons of the air, the earth, the water, and the spirit. Dragon dances and dragon boat races are popular in China.

ST GEORGE AND THE DRAGON

Christians equate the dragon with the serpent, the tempter of Eve in the Garden of Eden. The dragon too was evil, an embodiment of man's lower nature. By slaying the dragon, the victor overcomes heresy and evil and also his own primitive desires. Saint George is patron saint of England and of all soldiers.

Moth markings on batlike wings, thought to be protective

The damsel symbolizes the anima or inner self

The spiralling cloud represents divine assistance

St George, symbol of the triumph of good over evil

Lance, symbol of masculinity

CLAWED FEET, AND JUST TWO LEGS, DENOTE THAT THE DRAGON REPRESENTS SATAN

ST GEORGE AND THE DRAGON, PAOLO UCCELLO, c.1460

Sun symbol

Flames

PHOENIX
The phoenix, sometimes known as the fire bird, sets itself alight every hundred years, dies from the flames, and then rises again from the ashes. It is a universal symbol of death by fire, resurrection, immortality, and the sun. It is also a symbol of gentleness as it lives only on dew, not harming any living creature. In China it represents the empress and, with the dragon, stands for inseparable fellowship. In Mexico the phoenix accompanied the great god Quetzalcoatl, and to early Christians it symbolized Christ.

GARUDA
The mount of Vishnu, Garuda is usually portrayed as part-man, part-eagle, and often has a golden body. It is a huge, noble creature that represents the sun and is a bird of life. The Garuda is often shown doing battle with his arch-enemies, the snakes.

KINNARA
Half-human and either half-bird or half-horse, this heavenly musician is part of the celestial chorus surrounding the principal deities in Indian belief. It is an auspicious symbol, sometimes found on temple doorways.

QITOU
This Chinese winged figure, half-human, half-beast, dates from the Tang dynasty. Qitou guarded the burial chamber of a person of high rank.

SPHINX
A popular symbol originating in Egypt and Babylon, the sphinx usually has the body of a lion and a human head. The Greek sphinx was a female monster that devoured passers-by who failed to answer her riddle. In different cultures the sphinx symbolizes the ruler, wisdom, and the enigmatic.

SIMURGH
This fabulous Persian creature, a mixture of peacock, lion, and griffin, also occurs in Russian and Caucasian mythology. It has magical, healing properties and symbolizes the union of heaven and earth.

Huge silver wings

Shakespeare described Pegasus as "pure air and fire"

PEGASUS
The great winged steed of Greek hero Bellerophon, Pegasus sprang from the blood of Medusa and carried Zeus' thunderbolt. As a symbol, Pegasus is associated with speed and with storms. A similar horse exists in medieval legend – hippogryph – symbol of innate power and the capacity to transform evil into good.

GRIFFIN
The griffin was a guardian creature with the head, wings, and talons of an eagle, and the body of a lion. It was said to be greater than eight lions and stronger than a hundred eagles. Sacred to Apollo and Athena, the griffin is a symbol of vigilance, vengeance, and wisdom.

HARPY
In Greek mythology the harpy symbolized the most negative, destructive aspects of the female. Harpies had the head and breasts of a woman and the wings and legs of a vulture. They could control the winds, causing storms and whirlpools, and were the agents of sudden death.

NATURE

*T*he natural world provides a vast and rich store of potential symbols. The sun, moon, and stars are widely seen as symbolic, affecting every aspect of our lives. Plants and flowers have diverse meanings, from flowers of love to fruits of fertility, and animals too have particular associations linked to their characteristics and cultural importance.

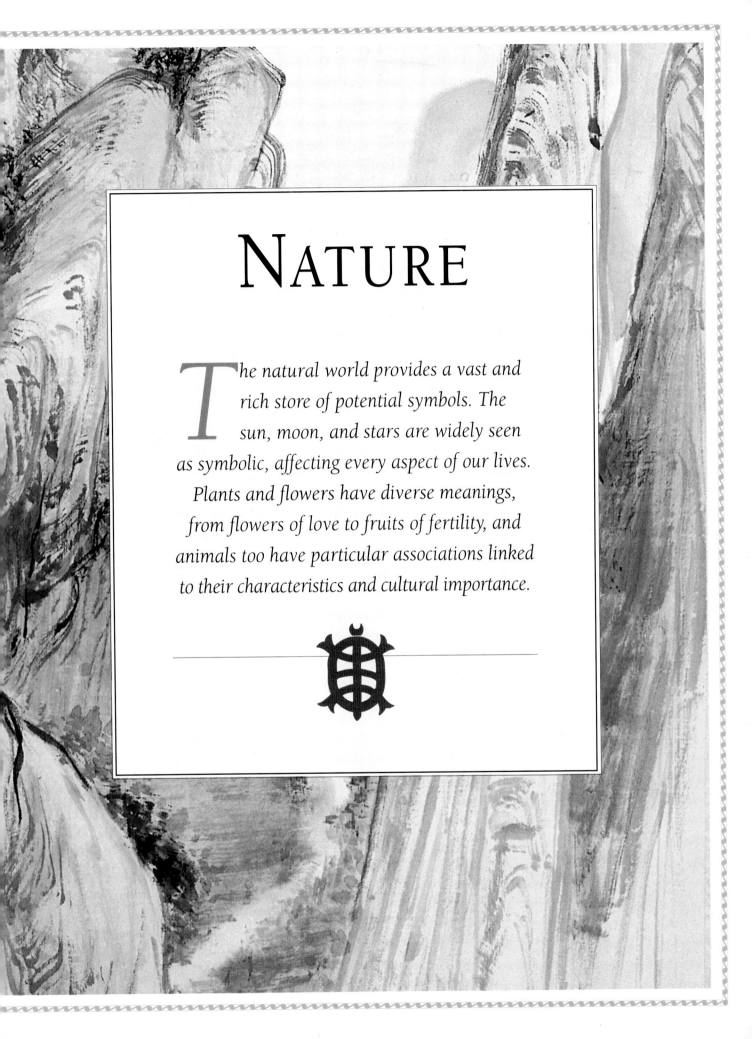

SUN & MOON

THE SUN AND MOON PLAY A POWERFUL ROLE in the imagery of mankind, shining impartially on all. For many cultures worldwide the sun is the embodiment of male energy, light, and warmth, and the moon, of female mystery and creation. Both are symbolic of death and rebirth: the sun because of its daily rising and setting, and the moon because of its monthly passage from new moon to full moon. The sun's powers warm the land and ripen the crops, while the moon has influence over the waters, controlling the flow of the tides.

Radiating power of the full moon

Diana, here as a crowned moon goddess

DIANA AND HER FOLLOWERS, 15TH-CENTURY MANUSCRIPT

CLOCK FACE
The moons on this 19th-century clock link time to the movement of the heavens.

MAN IN THE MOON
Although the moon is largely seen as feminine, in Europe people speak of the man in the moon. In popular myth, a man was nailed to the moon to atone for his sins.

BAYING AT THE MOON
The moon exerts its influence over creatures of the night. When wolves howl at a full moon they reflect the dark or sinister force of the moon.

ECLIPSE
An eclipse of the moon or the sun is regarded with fear by many who see it as a portent of evil. Hindu myth says that an eclipse is caused by the bodiless demon Rahu devouring the moon or sun, which passes through his neck and back into the sky.

MOONSTRUCK MADNESS
It has long been believed that the full moon brings on or aggravates the symptoms of madness. In this painting Diana the huntress and goddess of the moon is seated in the clouds above a group of lunatic followers. The very word lunatic comes from the Latin *luna*, meaning moon, and originally meant "moonstruck".

WATER

SUMMER EVENING, PETER SEVERIN KROYER, 1908

The oceans are governed by the moon, and, like the moon, water has associations with mystery and with the feminine creative principle. Water is central to many creation myths in which a "great flood" is a common theme. The sea represents the unconscious and infinity, the cosmic ocean from which all life has emerged and into which it must eventually dissolve.

White cloak of purity and moonlight

Symbol of the moon

PERSONIFICATION OF SUN AND MOON
In this illustration from a 16th-century alchemical treatise, the sun and moon are personified as king and queen. The moon (Diana) wears white, in contrast to the red of her twin brother the sun (Apollo). The flames beneath the sun's feet reflect alchemists' belief that the sun is the innate fire present in all matter. Diana's foot rests on the moon, of which she is both goddess and symbol.

Compasses and square, emblems of freemasonry

Sun-head, symbol of day

The key within the triangle represents the heart as keeper of secrets

FREEMASONRY
This sun-headed freemason is made up of the materials of his lodge, with symbols relating to his order.

FLAG OF JAPAN

FLAG OF URUGUAY

FLAGS
Many countries have adopted the sun as their national emblem. Japan, known as the "land of the rising sun", has a plain red disc while Uruguay has a more decorative sun face.

BLACK SUN
This sun adorns an 18th-century house in Prague known as the Black Sun. In alchemy, the black sun or *sol niger* is a symbol of Saturn and stands for the dark, destructive aspect of the sun.

SCARAB
The Egyptian sacred beetle is a form of the sun god Khepri, depicted here in winged form, clasping the solar ball and representing new life.

ART DECO MOTIF
Sunbursts were popular architectural motifs in the 1920s and 30s. In Britain, stained-glass versions brought a ray of sunshine to uniform mass housing.

APOLLO
Apollo, Greek god of the sun, is the slayer of darkness. In this mosaic from Corinth, his head, surrounded by flames, symbolizes his divine nature and the ultimate power of the sun.

FIRE

Torch blazes day and night as symbol of liberty lighting the world

Tablet bearing the date of the Declaration of Independence

Crown of sun beams, with 7 rays to represent the 7 seas and the 7 continents

Associated with the sun, fire is purifying, destructive, revealing. It is spiritual power and sacrifice, and plays a part in many rituals and religions throughout the world. The Statue of Liberty with her crown of sun's rays stands at the entrance to New York harbour. She holds aloft a burning torch which is a symbol of safety and assurance. The flame was literally a ray of hope to the thousands of homeless who sailed into the harbour.

The earth in flames beneath Apollo's feet

CALENDAR STONE
This Aztec stone calendar with its sun motif shows the year divided into 18 short months. The central position of the sun emphasizes its importance in the agricultural cycle.

SUN MASK
In this Native American spirit mask from northern British Columbia, the face represents the spirit of the sun. It is one of the sky spirits central to the tribe's beliefs.

Central face depicts spirit of the sun

SUN EMBLEM
This emblem on Siena's cathedral in Italy combines the crucifix within the flames of the sun. It was designed as a symbol of peace.

EARTH & SKY

THE RELATIONSHIP OF THE EARTH TO THE SKY is vital for the wellbeing of mankind, for it is the combination of sun, rain, wind, and soil that brings life, warmth, and nourishment. The sky is symbolic of transcendence, and the heavenly realms, and gods of the sky are linked to the masculine power and the creative aspect of the sun. The earth symbolism complements that of the sky and represents the Great Mother, receiving the fertilizing rain, producing crops, and nourishing humankind. Rivers and lakes represent the bountiful properties of the earth and share its feminine, nurturing qualities. Some rivers, such as the Ganges in India, are viewed as sacred.

SATELLITE PHOTOGRAPH

EARTH FROM SPACE
Far from demystifying our view of the heavens, man's exploration of space, has heightened our sense of wonderment at the vastness and magnificence of our world.

VOLCANO
Volcanoes, with their terrifying powers of destruction, have always been sacred and highly symbolic to the people who live in their shadow. An eruption may be interpreted as a sign of the fury of the gods. In parts of Southeast Asia a human sacrifice to a volcano used to be made in an attempt to avert its wrath.

RIVER
A river is both a symbol of fertility, since it irrigates land, and an image of the endless flow of time. Meandering slowly to the sea, the river can also symbolize a journey into death, its delta representing the merging of the soul with the Absolute. Journeys to the underworld often involve crossing a river, and the four rivers of Paradise are a source of power and spiritual nourishment.

RAINFOREST
The forest is a magical, heroic realm of danger and enchantment, and it can represent the unconscious mind. The forest is either the fearful haunt of spirits, wolves, and goblins, as in European folklore, or a place of seclusion where ascetics pursue spiritual contemplation, as in Indian culture. In the latter part of the 20th century the rainforest has come to represent the vulnerability of our planet, which is rapidly being destroyed by human encroachment.

THE ERUPTION OF VESUVIUS, JACQUES VOLAIRE, LATE 18TH CENTURY

DOME OF ST PETER'S, ROME

SKY
Probably because the sun, stars, and moon are seen above us in the sky, the sky has always been associated with creator gods and the forces of creation. The domes of cathedrals and mosques are often painted blue to resemble the sky, symbolically reminding the faithful of heaven above.

WATCHING A WATERFALL, ZHANG DAQIAN, 1935

WATERFALL
In Chinese symbolism a waterfall represents the feminine while a mountain or cliff is the masculine. Its downward motion is the harmonious counterpart to the upward-striving mountain. Here the tiny figures are deliberately insignificant against the mighty landscape.

WEATHER
The vagaries of the weather affect us all and in folktales personifications such as the North Wind and Jack Frost are blamed for miserable weather. Storms were traditionally attributed to the storm god in China and Japan, while Apollo caused the sun to shine on the Greeks.

SNOWFLAKE
Snow represents coldness and hardness in human nature, but the fragile beauty of a snowflake symbolizes truth and wisdom. The snowflake is also a symbol of individuality, since no two are alike.

THUNDER AND LIGHTNING
This Japanese god of thunder takes the form of a strong man beating his drum. The circle of balls around his head represent the reverberations of the thunder.

Balls of thunder

JAPANESE THUNDER GOD

Drumstick to beat out the rolling thunder

WIND CHERUB
This cherub blows the wind, probably to guide a boat on its course across the ocean. Such cherubs were a popular way of representing the winds in Western art.

CHINESE CLOUDS
Clouds symbolize the mystical and the sacred. The Chinese believed that they were formed from the union of female and male, yin and yang.

A LONDON FOG, F.D. BEDFORD, 1902

FOG
Fog, like cloud, is a symbol of the mystical and mysterious. It stands for the confusion from which the soul must emerge to attain enlightenment.

Dove of peace

NOAH'S ARK, GABRIEL LOIRE, 1975

Rainbow, sign of God's covenant

Noah's ark, symbol of the Christian Church

RAINBOW
In many cultures the rainbow bridges the earth and heaven and is often seen as a message of hope from the gods. In the Old Testament God sent a rainbow as a sign of his covenant after the Flood.

DESERT
A place of abandonment and desolation, the desert also represents peace and contemplation. In the Bible great events occurred in the desert. The children of Israel sojourned there for 40 years, and Christ was tempted in the desert.

SEE ALSO
GREAT MOTHER ☞
ANCIENT DEITIES *14*;
SACRED COW *21*; MAIZE *49*;
SPIDER *57*; PIG *61*; LIONS *62*;
QUEEN *88*

RIVER ☞ GANGES *21*;
FOUNTAINS *42*

SKY ☞
SKY GODDESS NUT *14*;
BLUE DOME *107*

VOLCANO ☞
MOUNT FUJI *27*

WATERFALL ☞
CHINESE LANDSCAPE *27*

PRECIOUS MATTER

THE WORLD'S MOUNTAINS, LAKES, AND WATERS are the repositories of hidden treasures – revealing the unexpected presence of pearls inside craggy oysters or substances such as metals and minerals which can be mined and transformed into objects of extraordinary beauty. In the past, the fascination with these materials stemmed from their colours or brilliance, but durability also played a part. Gold could last forever without tarnishing or corroding, and stones, cut and polished, seemed equally impervious to change. In a fragile, uncertain world, such beauty and permanence must have appeared to have magical, almost divine properties.

Mother-of-pearl

NATURAL PEARL IN OYSTER SHELL

CORAL

In the 16th century it was believed that the only way to cross rivers safely or to calm a raging tempest was to carry a piece of red or white coral. But the alleged powers of coral went far beyond this. Coral was thought to staunch the flow of blood from a wound, cure madness, imbue the wearer with wisdom, and offer protection against enchantments. Sprigs freshly gathered from the sea, such as the one hanging above the Madonna, are deemed the most powerful. Even to this day many Europeans give their children coral jewellery to protect them from harm.

This Italian child's bracelet with its carved hand clasp was designed to safeguard the wearer

CORAL BRACELET

Coral beads strung overhead afford further protection for the Madonna and child

Sprigs of coral, unworked and fresh from the sea, were thought to safeguard against evil

MADONNA OF VICTORY, ANDREA MANTEGNA, 1496

AN UNBROKEN BRANCH OF CORAL, ITS PROTECTIVE POWERS INTACT

PEARL

Prized in East and West alike, the pearl is a universal symbol of beauty and perfection. It is linked to the realm of the feminine – the moon, chastity, patience, and purity. Chinese dragons are usually portrayed clasping a pearl, symbol of wisdom, immortality, and light. Pearls were once thought to be the tears of the gods.

MOTHER-OF-PEARL

The shell's symbolism is clear from its name – it is the mother of the much-prized pearl, and as such represents fertility and birth. Its lustre and iridescence make it perfect for honouring the gods. Here, tiny casts have been placed into the shell of this pearl mussel to create images of the Buddha.

AMBER

With its bright golden sheen, amber was thought to be congealed sunlight; in ancient Greece it was sacred to the sun god Apollo. In Norse and Greek myth amber was thought to be tears – for the Vikings it was Freya's tears for Svipdag, and for the Greeks it was tears shed over the death of Phaeton by his three sisters.

JET

When in direct contact with the skin, jet was believed to become a part of a person's body and soul and to safeguard the wearer. It could protect against poisons, illnesses, and storms. In the 19th century jet became associated with death and mourning, and was worn as a symbol of love for a lost friend.

IVORY

Because it is white, ivory is a symbol of purity and so is associated with the Virgin; it was a favoured material for crucifixes. Ivory is also associated with moral strength. An ivory tower represents detachment from the world, possibly through arrogance or intellectual pursuits.

GOLD

Regarded as the most precious of metals, gold is a symbol of all that has the highest value or is the hardest to attain. The ultimate prize-winners are the gold medallists, perfect times are known as "golden eras", and treasured items are "worth their weight in gold". In most cultures gold is linked to the sun, giver of light, fire, and life. The sun god Apollo, symbol of all that is radiant and beautiful, rode his chariot of gold across the skies.

SILVER
Linked to the moon because of its colour, silver is bright but also tarnishes, symbolizing the corruptible side of human nature which needs cleansing. In China, silver is the lunar, feminine yin; in Christianity, it is purity, chastity, and eloquence.

COPPER
The power of copper to conduct has made it symbolic of connection. In alchemy it is in the sphere of Venus, and so is linked to warmth and femininity. Among North American tribes, copper denoted status.

OLYMPIC GOLD
Awarded for excellence in a given field, the gold medal is the most highly sought-after prize, symbol of exceptional achievement.

SUN KING
Louis XIV of France was known for his extravagant and opulent lifestyle. Nicknamed the Sun King after the sun god Apollo, he adopted the golden emblem of the sun to symbolize his power and his importance in the world.

EMBLEM OF LOUIS XIV, THE SUN KING

The sun's rays symbolize the extent of the King's power

GOLD FEVER
In the 1850s and 60s "gold fever" spread across the American continent as thousands of fortune hunters panned river-beds for gold. Gold's power to corrupt lends it a negative as well as positive symbolism, representing the sins of idolatry and greed – as in the legend of King Midas.

HUMAN-SIZED JAR
This Chinese ornamental jar, made of beaten gold, is as tall as a woman. The detailed scenes depicted on its surface took a team of goldsmiths over a year to complete.

GOLDEN OFFERING
In Thailand, worshippers honour Buddha by pressing fine leaves of pure gold onto his image. Over the years, the layers of gold render Buddha's form almost unrecognizable.

PILGRIM'S BADGE

LEAD
Lead's cheapness made it ideal for pilgrims' badges commemorating a journey to a saint's shrine. As the heaviest metal, lead symbolizes weight, as well as a heavy heart, or a person burdened by sin.

IRON
Iron denotes power, durability, and inflexibility; to rule with "a rod of iron" is to be harsh and unyielding. In Chinese, Egyptian, and Islamic belief, iron was darkness and the power of evil. In Mexican and Minoan cultures it stood for male strength.

ROCK
In the Bible a rock represents the strength and protection of God. It is the symbol of St Peter, the name Peter coming from the Greek *petros*, rock. In Greek myth, the wicked king of Corinth, Sisyphus, was punished by having to push a huge stone up a hill and watch it forever roll down again.

LODESTONE
Its magnetic properties imbued lodestone with quasi-sexual powers. In ancient Greece it was believed that a man could ensure his wife's faithfulness by placing a lodestone under her pillow while she slept. In Sanskrit the word for lodestone means "kisser", and in Chinese the word means "loving-stone".

CRYSTAL
Crystal symbolizes purity, clarity, and the mind. In Christianity, a crystal ball represents the world or the light of God. Crystals are widely believed to have magical powers: crystal balls hold secrets of the future, and wearing a crystal may promote health. To some Australian Aboriginals, crystals came from the creator spirit, the Rainbow Serpent.

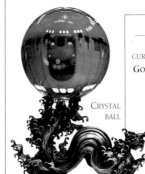

CRYSTAL BALL

SEE ALSO
CRYSTAL ☞ LIGHT CURE 79; CRYSTAL BALL 110
GOLD ☞ VIKING GOLD 93
JET ☞ MOURNING JEWELLERY 87; JET BLACK 106
PEARL ☞ WINGED DRAGON 30; 30TH ANNIVERSARY 87
SUN KING ☞ VERSAILLES 43

PRECIOUS STONES

DIAMOND, SYMBOL OF POWER AND WEALTH

FETISHES, AMULETS, AND TALISMANS played an important part in every culture, and continue to do so to this day. From the early Egyptians to civilizations of South America and cultures in the East, people have imbued stones with supernatural powers. There were stones to control the elements, calm the winds, and still rough seas; and others to work directly on the body, stimulating vital organs or creating a sense of wellbeing. There were stones for particular days of the week, and stones for the different months. Stones that capture and reflect light, such as moonstones and star sapphires, were deemed to bring good luck. Agates with central white rings carved into watchful "guardian eyes" could neutralize the power of the evil eye.

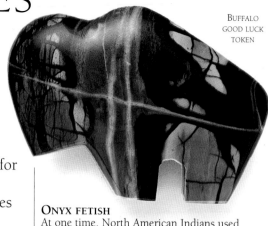

BUFFALO GOOD LUCK TOKEN

THE MEANING OF GEMSTONES

The symbolism of stones varies depending on their colour, their form, and the use to which they are put. For example, cut and faceted gemstones symbolize the soul set free from the base exterior of the human body.

ONYX FETISH
At one time, North American Indians used fetishes to help control the forces of nature and to tackle everyday problems. The fetish did not contain any innate power; its spirit force was given to it by its owner.

DIAMOND CADUCEUS BROOCH

Wings, symbols of transcendence

Twin snakes of good and evil

Mercury's winged staff, to bring harmony from strife

LAPIS LAZULI
In Mesopotamia, this blue stone symbolized the heavens and so was used to decorate the ceilings of temples. In Egypt, it was used to adorn statues of the gods, while in Europe it was viewed as a cure for melancholy and fever. In China, it symbolized vision and was used to cure diseases of the eye.

SAPPHIRE
Like lapis lazuli, sapphire symbolizes the blue of the heavens and also the heavenly attributes of truth, chastity and contemplation. The star sapphire is a powerful good luck charm. Its three shafts of light are thought to represent faith, hope, and destiny.

AMETHYST
This is the stone of humility, peace of mind, piety, and resignation. It was associated with Bacchus, god of wine, and was thought to cure drunkenness. It became a symbol of sobriety, possibly because water in an amethyst jug looked like wine but had no intoxicating effect.

RUBY
In India, this is the king of stones and is generally associated with royalty, dignity, zeal, and power. In Burma, rubies were thought to confer invulnerability, especially if they were embedded in the teeth or flesh so that they became a part of the body. They then allegedly prevented wounding by spears, swords, or guns. Worn as jewellery, rubies may ward off misfortune and illness.

DIAMOND BROOCH
The most prized as well as the hardest stone, the diamond is associated with incorruptibility and invincibility. Its transparency and purity make it also a symbol of constancy and sincerity. Here, diamond snakes entwine a staff of emeralds in this winged caduceus, symbol of medicine as the healing union of opposites.

EMERALD
Legend has it that emeralds are found in the nests of griffins. Revered and powerful stones, emeralds are thought to enhance the memory, sharpen the wits, and, when placed under the tongue, help in predicting the future. The emerald has been used as an antidote for poison; a cure for epilepsy; a treatment of eye disease, dysentery, and leprosy. Due to its colour, the emerald is the symbol of spring, of fertility, and of rain.

TOPAZ
This stone was also widely believed to cure poor vision. According to St Hildegard, the patient had to place a topaz in wine for a period of three days. Then on going to bed, he had to rub his eyes with the moistened stone to effect a cure. In the 15th century topaz was thought to heal plague sores. A Roman physician claimed many successes by touching open sores with a stone that had belonged to two popes.

QUETZALCOATL, GOD OF AIR AND EARTH

AZTEC TURQUOISE MASK
Turquoise was highly valued in Mesoamerica and was often used in representations of gods, or tied to weapons to ensure accuracy. The Aztecs called it the "stone of the gods". In ancient Egypt, turquoise was thought to be protective. The stone is symbolic of courage, fulfilment, and success.

BIRTHSTONES

CRYSTAL WITH ZODIAC SIGNS

Wearing one's birthstone is thought to be lucky. These are the most common birthstones:
January – Garnet
February – Amethyst
March – Aquamarine
April – Diamond
May – Emerald
June – Pearl
July – Ruby
August – Peridot
September – Sapphire
October – Opal
November – Topaz
December – Turquoise

OPAL
The opal is the national stone of Australia, as symbolized by this brooch. Shakespeare viewed the opal as a symbol of inconstancy, although its Christian associations are fidelity, prayer, and religious fervour. It is generally held to be unlucky (except for October's children), although this belief almost certainly comes from the fact that opal breaks very easily. Jewellers disliked working with it, and their misgivings turned into popular myth.

AGATE
Agate was thought to cure insomnia, to ensure pleasant dreams, to protect the wearer from danger, and to endow a person with a bold heart. Its popularity was widespread. In Sudan, agate amulets – black with a white circle to look like an eye – were carried as guardian spirits, to counter the effects of the evil eye. Black agate stands for courage, vigour, and prosperity; red for long life and spiritual love.

MAORI LUCKY CHARM
HEI TIKI AMULET WHICH KEEPS
EVIL SPIRITS AWAY

New Year dragons, emblems of good luck CHINESE DRAGONS

JADE
In China this is the most precious stone, symbolizing purity, perfection, and immortality. Bridegrooms give their fiancées jade butterflies to represent their eternal love. Jade is similarly valued by Mesoamerican Indians who adorn the masks of their gods with it, and the Spanish conquistadores believed it healed hip and kidney complaints.

RELIGION, SUPERSTITION, AND MAGIC

The rise of Christianity did little to dispel the belief in the magic properties of stones. Jewellers began to include pectoral crosses and rock crystal reliquaries in their range, and it was not uncommon in Spain and Italy to festoon children with protective jewellery. This Spanish child is armed with an all-powerful red sprig of coral, a protective fist, and a host of Christian symbols of salvation.

Patron saint
The child is safeguarded by her patron saint

Sprig of coral
Amulet with powers against magic spells

Malachite lozenge
Often given to children to help them sleep and keep evil spirits at bay

Clenched fist
The jet hand protects against the evil eye

Crucifix
Large and small crosses ensure God's embrace

Pomander
Containing spices to safeguard against infection

Tooth
Mounted animal tooth, for luck

LA INFANTA MARIA ANA CON SONAJEROS, JUAN PANTOJA DE LA CRUZ, 1602

CORNELIAN
Red stones were thought to be stimulating to the circulatory system and the cornelian was deemed particularly valuable to those timid in speech or weak of voice. In the West it is viewed as a stone of self-confidence, courage, and health. In the East it was thought to protect the wearer from other people's envy.

MOONSTONE
So named because it captures the sheen of the moon, this stone is sacred in India and is widely believed to bring good fortune. Legend has it that a person who places a moonstone in his mouth when the moon is full will be able to see into the future. It is symbolic of the moon, of tenderness, and of lovers.

BLOODSTONE
This stone was thought to contain the blood of Jesus and to be magical. It could allegedly cause thunder, lightning, and tempests. On a practical level, bloodstone was used to stem nosebleeds and haemorrhaging. When made into jewellery, it is symbolic of peace and understanding.

GARDENS

THE LITERATURE OF EUROPE, the Middle East, and Asia is full of the imagery of the garden: the garden represents paradise and the abode of the soul. Chinese and Vietnamese emperors had tombs built in exquisite, tranquil gardens, which they visited during their lives and where they were eventually buried. The biblical Garden of Eden symbolized the state of perfection from which Adam and Eve fell, while the walled garden with a narrow opening was a visual representation of the wall of purity that surrounded the Virgin Mary.

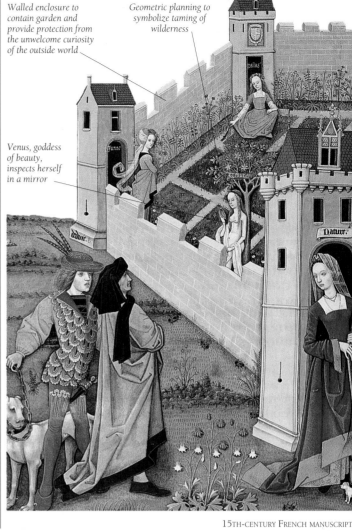

Walled enclosure to contain garden and provide protection from the unwelcome curiosity of the outside world

Geometric planning to symbolize taming of wilderness

Venus, goddess of beauty, inspects herself in a mirror

15TH-CENTURY FRENCH MANUSCRIPT

GARDEN OF EDEN

THE GARDEN OF EARTHLY DELIGHT (DETAIL), HIERONYMUS BOSCH, c.1510

This scene from the three-panelled painting by the Flemish painter Hieronymus Bosch depicts the biblical Garden of Eden, the pure state before the Fall. Here, the first humans, Adam and Eve, lived in harmony with the animals in a state of natural innocence until they were banished from Paradise. On the right is a detail showing the imperfect state of nature outside the garden.

DETAIL

WALLED GARDENS

The medieval walled garden was a symbol of the womb and the feminine, protective principle. It symbolized privacy, sometimes secrecy, as well as virginity. The walled garden had powerful religious symbolism, representing spiritual enlightenment. Chinese and Roman tomb gardens were the earthly counterparts of the gardens of heaven. In medieval literature, the "garden of delights" was an allegory for courtly love (as here), with symbols of love, beauty, and other pleasures.

FOUNTAIN GARDEN OF THE ALHAMBRA PALACE

FOUNTAINS

Four rivers are said to spring from beneath the Tree of Life at the centre of the world, the source of the elixir of immortality. This symbolism is echoed in formal European gardens in which four paths lead to a central fountain.

GARDENS OF SPAIN

For the Arab living in the desert, the garden was the earthly symbol of a luxuriant Paradise, described in the Koran as a place of "spreading shade", with "fountains of gushing water". The fountain was a symbol of everlasting life. The fourfold or courtyard garden, with a fountain in the centre, spread with the Moors to Southern Spain. Here, some of the loveliest examples can be seen in the grounds of the Alhambra at Granada.

UNDERGROUND GROTTO

GROTTO

Originally places where sacred rites were conducted in ancient Greece, grottoes were created in Greek and Roman gardens as artificial caves to reinforce the magical link between the garden and nature. In Renaissance times, the grotto was reintroduced as an essential element of classical garden design.

ENGLISH ARCHITECTURAL WATER FOLLY

Grand scale of design, including orangery, to reflect supreme status of the king

Formal layout of gardens signifies civilization through ordering of nature

KNOT GARDEN AT MOSELY OLD HALL, ENGLAND

THE ORANGERY AT VERSAILLES, FRANCE

LOVE KNOTS
Knot gardens are made up of interlaced bands of shrubbery, each with a central motif. They were popular in England in the 16th century, and reflected contemporary needlework designs. Knots, representing links and binding, are symbols of love and matrimony; they also symbolize fate and ward off evil.

SILVER BAY TREE

BAY TREE
The evergreen bay tree is a symbol of immortality and victory. Small bay trees are cultivated in pots as a symbol of honour and longevity.

VERSAILLES
The formal grandeur of Louis XIV's palace and gardens at Versailles, outside Paris, have an added political significance. Known as the Sun King, Louis wanted to show his supremacy by reworking the landscape so that his surroundings reflected his own status. The grand scale of Versailles was a conscious symbol of the power of absolute monarchy.

ABBOT'S GARDEN TO FUKUJI TEMPLE, KYOTO, JAPAN

WISHING WELL
A symbol of the feminine, life-giving principle, the well is often believed to have magical properties. A coin tossed into its depths can make a wish come true.

GARDEN GNOME

ORNAMENTS
As the garden can be seen as a symbol of the natural world, it is considered home to spirits of all kinds. Statuary can represent these spirits, from the classical gods of Greece and Rome to the humble gnome of Celtic origin.

MAZE AT HEVER CASTLE, KENT

MAZE
Though the maze is a classical device, it was used in gardens only from the Renaissance. It provided confusion and concealment for amorous pursuits. Mazes were thought to catch and hold evil spirits and often represent the journey from darkness into light, or secret wisdom discovered after overcoming trials.

LOVERS' ROSE BOWER

BOWER
The columns that enclosed the Roman *peristyle*, or courtyard, were echoed in the garden with trellises overhung with flowering plants to provide shade and fragrance. As an enclosed place of retreat, the bower reflects the safety of the womb; the rose, in this case, eternal love.

PURPLE MAPLE

BONSAI
The Japanese art of growing miniature trees, *bonsai*, symbolizes mastery over nature. As bonsai are often passed from generation to generation, they are also a symbol of immortality.

ZEN GARDEN
Beautiful, bare rock gardens are created in Zen Buddhist monasteries in Japan to represent the universe in microcosm. Some have raked sand; the Dry Landscape garden in Kyoto uses rocks and pebbles to create in miniature the impression of an ocean interrupted by islands. This illusion is intended to represent "ultimate truth", and as such is an aid to meditation.

TREES

THE TREE HAS SYMBOLIC significance in cultures throughout the world. It represents the Great Mother in her nourishing, sheltering form. Rooted in the earth, it draws water from the ground and reaches up to the heavens and eternity, acting as a world axis. It is closely linked to the symbolism of the pillar and the mountain. Individual trees, types of tree, and groups of trees all have particular associations. For example, evergreen trees symbolize immortality whereas fruit-bearing trees are often seen as trees of life, and forests or groves tend to be magical places where mysterious or momentous events occur.

OLIVE BRANCHES, SYMBOLS OF PEACE

TREE OF KNOWLEDGE   SPANISH SCHOOL, 12TH CENTURY

Symbol of temptation, the tree of knowledge grows in Paradise, and bears the fruit of good and evil. As Adam succumbs to Eve's enticements and takes a bite of the apple, he defies the will of God, signifying both his loss of innocence and his downfall – Adam falls from grace and mankind is doomed. In this Spanish painting, Eve blames the serpent, her tempter, and itself a symbol of evil.

WILLOW

In the West, the weeping willow is associated with death and mourning, and it is often depicted in funerary art. In China and Japan, however, it is a symbol of spring, of feminine beauty, and grace. In Taoism the willow, pliable in strong winds, represents strength.

PALM

As an important food source the palm was equated with the tree of life in the Near and Middle East. In Egypt, it was sacred to the sun god Re, and represented the fertility of the crops. In Judaism, it is an emblem of Judea; in Christianity, of Christ's entry into Jerusalem.

SYCAMORE

To ancient Egyptians, this was a celestial tree, a form of the sky goddess Nut. Its leaves provide shade which symbolized peace and rest in the afterlife. The fruit yields a milky substance, and so was associated with fertility and nourishment.

CHERRY

In China and Japan the cherry is a national emblem, and its blossom is a symbol of spring, femininity, and youth. In English lore, a cherry tree planted near the house brings luck, and the luckiest lovers are those who meet for the first time under a cherry tree.

LAUREL

Sacred to Apollo and a symbol of immortality and victory, the laurel was said by Greeks and Romans to be physically and spiritually cleansing, and to repel lightning. Worn as a wreath, it symbolized a poet, and excellence in the sciences and arts.

BEECH

Associated with death, the beech is sacred to Hades and Cybele, the mother of Zeus, and represents prosperity, divination, and immortality. Because of its leathery leaves and bark the beech symbolizes endurance, and the Freemason's hammer is made of beech wood. The beech tree is the emblem of Denmark.

PINE

As an evergreen the pine symbolizes immortality. In Japan, it has come to signify strength of character and vital energy due to its ability to withstand strong winds. In both East and West, the pine cone symbolizes life and fertility. It is an attribute of the Roman god Bacchus, and an emblem of Jupiter, Venus, and Diana.

YEW

The yew tree has poisonous seeds and needles and so represents death. It has become symbolic of mourning and is often found in English churchyards; however, as an evergreen it also symbolizes immortality and was grown in Celtic sacred groves. In the Middle Ages it was used as an antidote to enchantment.

THE CHRISTMAS TREE

Widespread throughout Europe and North America, the Christmas tree is a symbol of Christ as redeemer of original sin, the baubles on its branches representing the apples from the tree in the Garden of Eden. The custom of decorating an evergreen tree goes back to the pre-Christian period of "raw nights" (25 December – 6 January) when people would hang green branches in their houses, and light candles, to keep evil spirits at bay.

The candles are symbolic of Jesus, the "light of the world"

HOLLY

In Roman times holly was part of the Saturnalia festival celebrated in mid-December. In Christian lore it symbolizes both the crown of thorns, due to its spiked leaves and blood-red berries, and the joy of Christmas.

LIME OR LINDEN
In Europe, the lime or linden tree represents joy, beauty, and femininity. In Germany and Scandinavia, it was believed to repel lightning, and to cure disease if touched by someone who was sick.

MULBERRY
Its berries ripen in three stages: white represents youth; red the vigorous middle years; and black the ripeness of wisdom, age, and death. In China the mulberry symbolizes the sun and is a tree of life. In Greek myth it is a tree of misfortune.

CYPRESS
Associated with Pluto, Roman god of death, the evergreen cypress is nevertheless a symbol of immortality. It was thought to have the power to preserve bodies and so was, and still is, often grown in graveyards. In China it represents death but also the feminine realm.

ACACIA
With its red and white flowers, the acacia was sacred to the Egyptians, for whom it symbolized birth and death. Their gods were said to have been born beneath an acacia tree. The sacred wood of the Hebrew tabernacle was that of the *shittah*, or acacia tree. In Europe it symbolizes immortality.

PLUM
In China the plum is an emblem of winter. In Japan the tree represents the fleeting joy and innocence of youth; its beautiful blossom is a symbol of spring triumphing over winter, and virtue and courage triumphing over difficulties.

MYRTLE
Sacred to Venus and to the Egyptian goddess Hathor, myrtle brings luck to lovers, and was once the English bridal flower. Symbolic of immortality, good fortune, happiness, and peace in many cultures, it is also the flower of the gods. In dreams, it signifies prosperity, and a ripe old age.

SACRED TREES

A reverence for trees, and even tree worship, is widespread thoughout the world. Many traditions speak of a tree of life – a tree which is the central point and pivot of the world. This tree links heaven and earth since it is rooted in the underworld and its branches reach up to the heavens, symbolizing man's striving for perfection. The Scandinavians have the Yggdrasil, and Buddhists have the Bodhi tree. Christ is sometimes shown crucified on the Tree of Knowledge in the Garden of Eden, symbolizing a state of redemption. Muslims too kneel on carpets embroidered with trees of life when praying.

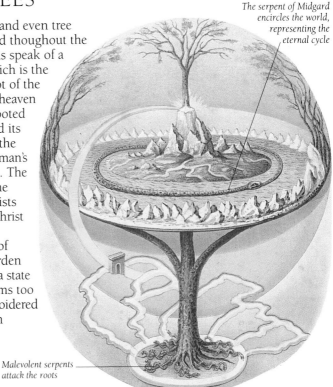

The serpent of Midgard encircles the world, representing the eternal cycle

Malevolent serpents attack the roots

YGGDRASIL
The Yggdrasil is the evergreen ash tree which in its mythological form represents the entire world. Its trunk represents the central axis of the universe, and from beneath its roots bubble the rivers – waters of wisdom.

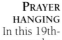

Flames of light, or enlightenment, encircle the Buddha's body

BUDDHA UNDER A BODHI TREE
The bodhi tree, a type of fig, is symbolic of the Buddha's Enlightenment, which he attained while meditating beneath its branches. Bodhi trees are often grown in monastery grounds as a reminder of this event.

PRAYER HANGING
In this 19th-century example, a stylized tree of life is intricately woven into the design. Muslim prayer rugs often depict this powerful symbol of ascent and salvation. The faithful kneel and say their prayers on a tree of life.

OAK
Often associated with the thunder gods, the oak is sacred to the earth mother, to Juno, Jupiter, and to the Celtic god Donar. In China it represents fragile strength since it does not bend in the wind and so breaks. To Christians it is a symbol of Christ's steadfastness, while in Judaism it is a symbol of the divine presence. In Europe the oak stands for heroism.

ACORN
As the seed of the "mighty oak", the acorn is a widespread symbol of life. In Scandinavia it is sacred to Thor, and is a symbol of fertility, life, and immortality.

SEE ALSO

BEECH ☞
FREEMASONRY *109*

OTHER TREES ☞
BAY *43*; BONSAI *43*

PALM ☞ SUKKOT *17*

SYCAMORE ☞
SKY GODDESS NUT *14*

YGGDRASIL ☞
VIKING DRAGON *30*;
NINE *103*

PLANTS

PLANTS ECHO THE CYCLE OF BIRTH, DEATH, AND REBIRTH. They were closely connected with the mother goddesses of many cultures and with fertility. Myths from around the world often feature a human or a god changing into a plant, or a plant sprouting from the dead body of a god. Wheat and herbs, for instance, grew from the body of the Egyptian god Osiris. Often the symbolism of plants is more direct, based on their shape, colour, smell, or habitat. The fact that ivy, for example, tends to grow on old university buildings has meant that the term "ivy-league" now symbolizes a respected and long-established place of learning, especially in North America.

ACANTHUS
This thistle-like plant has large, thorny leaves and takes its name from the Greek *ake*, meaning sharp point. The distinctive leaves, carved in stone or marble, are commonly seen on classical buildings, particularly on Corinthian capitals (shown above). Acanthus leaves signify the arts, or a love of the arts, while in Christianity, the thorns symbolize pain and punishment for sin.

REEDS
Rushes and reeds symbolize flexibility because they sway in the wind. Pan's pipes were made of reed.

BAMBOO
A symbol of pliability, grace, and strength because it bends in the wind but does not break, bamboo is central to the cultures of the Far East. As its shoots are always green, it symbolizes longevity. Bamboo's straight, jointed stem symbolizes the path and the steps towards enlightenment in Chinese philosophy, and it is often depicted in paintings.

DEADLY NIGHTSHADE
Also known as devil's berries, the fruits of this plant look edible, yet are highly poisonous. It is a symbol of deception and danger.

The plant's leaves form the "headdress" of the man

Mandrake's odd-shaped roots give the impression of a man's body

Symbolic of fertility and growth

ILLUSTRATION FROM 12TH-CENTURY MEDICAL TREATISE

The mandrake rides on a dog's back – a reference to the method of uprooting it

WHEAT
For the ancient Greeks, wheat was the symbol of the goddess Demeter, while the Egyptians associated it with the resurrection of the slain god Osiris. Ears of wheat motifs in Christian churches signify Christ's body and also his rebirth.

MANDRAKE
This plant, with its human-shaped roots, has been considered magical since the time of the ancient Egyptians. When uprooted, it was said to utter a shriek that killed anyone within earshot, so a dog was used to carry out the task. Mandrake is a symbol of enchantment, fertility, and prosperity.

SHAMROCK
Once an Arabian religious symbol, the shamrock or clover was also adopted by Christians. Its three leaves signify the Holy Trinity: Father, Son, and Holy Spirit. The plant is the emblem of Ireland and of its patron saint, St Patrick. A four-leaved clover is thought to bring the finder luck.

IVY
Like most evergreens, ivy is associated with immortality, but it is also a plant of death, drawing vital moisture from trees. Sacred to Dionysus, the Greek god of wine (shown above with trailing ivy), it was thought to cure drunkenness when worn as a garland.

FENNEL
In old herbals, fennel seed was thought to improve eyesight, and to cause snakes to shed their skin. It was thus a symbol of clarity, and of renewal and revival.

GOURD
The gourd with its abundance of seeds is a widespread symbol of fertility. In China it is associated with long life, while in Africa, the gourd represents the womb.

MISTLETOE
In Europe mistletoe, once considered magical, is now linked to Christmas. To stand beneath the mistletoe is to invite a kiss. The custom may stem from the idea that mistletoe's power frees people from restrictions.

THISTLE
The national emblem of Scotland, this prickly plant causes pain but also repels enemies, and so symbolizes both evil and protection. It also represents Christ's suffering and may appear in paintings at the foot of the cross.

HYSSOP
This scented herb was used as a purgative and so represents purification and regained innocence. As Hyssop grows on poor, stony ground, it is a plant of humility.

THE LANGUAGE OF HERBS

Although to many people herbs are simply plants to use in cooking, they have long been an indispensable source of medicine. Their effects can be powerfully healing or harmful, so many acquired magical or sacred powers, while others became associated with evil and suffering. Shapes and scents can be important factors in determining a plant's symbolic meaning.

GINGER
According to Chinese superstition, eating this finger-like root while pregnant was harmful and could produce a six-fingered child.

BETEL NUT
In Southeast Asia, the betel nut is associated with love and marriage. Betel shavings are traditionally chewed with lime, cloves, and other spices as a mild sedative.

SAGE
This popular garden herb was so highly prized for its healing powers that regular use was reputed to bestow immortality. In medieval Christian paintings, sage is a symbol of the Virgin Mary.

FUNGUS
In the Far East, the fungus is an important symbol of longevity, and in the Taoist religion, fungus is the food of the immortals. It is therefore a sacred plant and carved fungus decoration can be seen on precious objects such as the antique Japanese boxwood sceptre shown above.

ROSEMARY
Sprigs of this herb, which symbolizes fidelity, were once included in bridal bouquets, and tapping your lover with it would ensure constancy. Rosemary signifies remembrance and is often planted on graves.

PARSLEY
This herb is so slow to germinate that people once imagined its roots went down to the devil. Parsley was a symbol of death for the ancient Greeks who used sprigs in wreaths.

GINSENG
Ginseng's forked root, like the mandrake's, symbolizes the human body, and for this reason it is considered a life-giving herb. Ginseng's Chinese name means man-root, and it is a masculine, or yang, herb, reputed to increase virility.

GARLIC
To the ancient Greeks, garlic, with its pungent smell, provided protection against evil spirits. Offerings of garlic were left at crossroads for the feared Hecate, goddess of the underworld. In Central European myth the cloves were reputed to ward off vampires. In China, garlic is considered a lucky plant that will bless parents-to-be with many children.

SEE ALSO

GINSENG ☞ TWO *102*;
I CHING *111*
HERBS ☞
PASSOVER PLATE *17*
IVY ☞ BACCHUS *15*;
GRAPES *48*
OTHER PLANTS ☞
HENNAED HANDS *83*;
VULVA *74*;
COLOUR OF LIFE *107*
PLANTS ☞
FLOWERS *50-53*
REEDS ☞ PAN PIPES *81*
SHAMROCK ☞
FOUR-LEAF CLOVER *79*

NATURE'S FOODS

FOOD GIVES US LIFE and thus unity with all other living things. It grows through the interaction of earth, sun, and water. Foods that must be harvested, like corn and rice, are linked to the gods of abundance and fertility. Water is symbolic of life and purity, and milk represents the nourishment of mother earth. Food is part of life's cycle: all that lives must die and return to earth, fertilizing it for new growth.

PORCELAIN DISH, QING DYNASTY

FIG
The fruit of the fig tree with its many seeds represents the feminine realm, fertility, and prosperity. A basket of figs symbolizes woman as goddess or mother. The fruit has erotic symbolism and was sacred to Bacchus, god of wine and vegetation. Adam and Eve covered their nakedness with leaves from the fig tree.

APPLE
The apple, especially if red, symbolizes love and fertility and is an emblem of Venus as love and desire. Its round shape indicates eternity and also the earth. In the Old Testament the apple represents temptation, although as an attribute of the Virgin Mary it means redemption.

ORANGE
Sometimes shown in the hand of the infant Christ, the orange represents good fortune and fertility. Like the apple, its shape symbolizes eternity and immortality, and due to its distinctive colour it is associated with the sun.

LEMON
A symbol of purity and faithfulness, the lemon was traditionally thought to have protective properties which could counter magic spells and poison. In Judaism the lemon represents the human heart.

PEACH
The peach is a symbol of immortality. In China it brings joy and protects against evil. In the hand of the infant Christ it represents salvation.

CHERRY
In Japan the cherry is associated with self-sacrifice, particularly in relation to Samurai warriors, the red flesh of the fruit symbolizing their blood. In Christianity, cherries are a fruit of paradise and are sometimes depicted in the hands of the infant Christ.

POMEGRANATE
Because of its colour, the pomegranate symbolizes the sun, life, and blood, while its many seeds make it a symbol of fertility. In ancient Rome newly married women wore pomegranate wreaths, and pomegranate juice was used as a remedy for infertility.

GRAPES

SWEET ITALIAN GRAPES

Many types of grapes produce wine, symbol of revelry and immortality but also of blood and sacrifice. Grapes brought back from the Promised Land symbolized the promise of a new life to the Israelites. In Islam wine is the drink of the chosen in Paradise, and to Christians it is the blood of Christ.

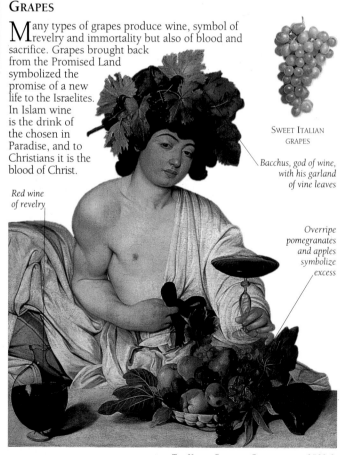

Red wine of revelry

Bacchus, god of wine, with his garland of vine leaves

Overripe pomegranates and apples symbolize excess

THE YOUNG BACCHUS, CARAVAGGIO, c.1591-3

PLUM
In the Far East the plum is a symbol of ripening female sexuality, and may be viewed in the same way when it appears in dreams. In Christianity, the plum represents fidelity.

DATE
In the desert regions of North Africa, clusters of dates traditionally represent life and fruitfulness. Because of their shape and abundance, dates are seen as a symbol of male fertility.

PINEAPPLE
The pineapple is a life-giving fruit and a symbol of fertility. In parts of America, pineapples were a sign of hospitality and sailors would place a pineapple on the gatepost to tell neighbours that they were home from sea. In the late 1800s Lord Dunmore echoed this custom by building a fruit-shaped summer house to announce his return to Scotland from America.

THE PINEAPPLE, DUNMORE, STIRLINGSHIRE

EGG
The egg as origin of the universe is found in myths throughout the world. The egg contains the potential for life and so represents the womb, birth, and the universe. It is also a symbol of hope and of immortality, and in Christianity can represent Virgin Birth.

SALT
Because of its purity, salt represents immortality. Named after Salus, Roman goddess of health, salt was once used in ceremonies in her honour. A grain dissolving in the ocean symbolizes the union of the human soul with the infinite. In Christianity salt has come to represent suffering.

BREAD
Bread symbolizes spiritual nourishment. It is the food of the body and of the soul. Bread is particularly important in Christian symbolism, where Christ is seen as the "bread of life". Bread at the communion service represents the body of Christ and its consumption represents oneness with Christ. The ceremonial "breaking of bread" may symbolize the death of the sacrificial victim.

FOOD OF THE GODS
The people of Israel are seen below gathering **manna**, food sent by God from Heaven to sustain the Jews in the wilderness during their long journey from Egypt. In the Old Testament it is described as white, like coriander seed, and tasting of wafers made with honey. Manna is also mentioned in the Koran, and is a symbol of God's love.

Nectar was the name used by Homer for the beverage of the Greek gods which conferred immortality and beauty.

Amritsa is the elixir of immortality, which emerged during the churning of the milky ocean and was consumed by the gods in Indian mythology.

Ambrosia was the food of the gods in Greek myth.

GATHERING OF THE MANNA, DIERIC BOUTS, c.1464-8

The leek, symbol of Wales

The Queen's crown

LEEK
The leek represents victory and was thought to protect against wounds. It appears on the British pound coin as the emblem of Wales, and is also an attribute of St David, patron saint of Wales.

HONEY
Honey is the food of the gods and represents immortality, rebirth, and fertility. It is associated with the moon and the feminine. To ancient Greeks it represented wisdom and to Christians it symbolized Christ's gentleness and compassion. Paradise was known as "the land of milk and honey".

RICE
Rice is an essential food and represents immortality and nourishment, both spiritual and literal. In many parts of Asia it is thought to possess a soul. The spirit of rice is revered and every stage of cultivation is accompanied by ritual to ensure a good crop. In the West, rice is traditionally thrown over brides at weddings to ensure the happiness and fertility of their union.

Aztec corncob vessel

MAIZE
In the Americas maize is a symbol of life, especially when it is intact as "corn on the cob", and it is used as a motif in pottery. In ancient Mexico a maize plant depicted with a humming bird symbolized the Sun Hero and new growth. In Europe and the Mediterranean maize represents peace, plenty, and the fecundity of the mother goddess.

MILK
The first and most nutritious food, milk symbolizes spiritual nourishment and immortality. It is often associated with the moon due to its colour, and is seen as the food of the gods. In Hindu legend, Vishnu reclines on the cosmic milky ocean from which wonders of creation were churned at the dawn of time. In the Bible its symbolism is linked to that of honey.

ONION
The many-layered onion represents unity. It also symbolizes revelation, as one peels off the layers to reveal the centre. Its round shape symbolizes the cosmos and immortality and because of its strong smell it is used to ward off evil. It is said to be particularly effective against the dangerous influences of the moon.

OLIVES
An attribute of Athena and Apollo, the olive is a symbol of immortality and fruitfulness. A crown of wild olives, representing Zeus, was worn by the victor at the Olympic games. In the Old Testament the dove returned to the ark bearing an olive twig. This was a sign that the Flood sent by God was receding, and so the olive represents peace and reconciliation.

OLIVE OIL
The oil from the olive has its own symbolism. In Judaism, it is considered holy and is used as fuel for the sabbath lamp and for the menorah in the festival of Hanukkah.

SEE ALSO
CHERRY ☞ CHERRY 44; SAMURAI SWORD 91;
FIG ☞ TREE OF KNOWLEDGE 44; FIG LEAF 84;
FOOD OF THE GODS ☞ FUNGUS 47;
NATURE'S FOODS ☞ PASSOVER PLATE 17; COMMUNION 19; WEDDING CAKE, CHOCOLATE 83; FOOD OFFERINGS 93;
PINEAPPLE ☞ PINEAPPLE QUILT 70;
RICE ☞ BLESSINGS 83

FLOWERS

FROM EARLIEST TIMES and in every culture flowers have held a special place in people's hearts and lives. In ancient times certain flowers were viewed as earthly forms of the gods. People treasured them, used them in worship, and imbued them with magical powers. A flower in bud is symbolic of new life and potential, but flowers also accompany the dead to the grave. Flower motifs adorn churches and temples, are incorporated into jewellery, and have been used to decorate everything from fabric to furniture. Flowers have also wound their way into our language – we view the world through "rose-tinted glasses" or see life as "no bed of roses". Many flowers have taken on particular meanings, but what a certain flower means can differ from one culture to another.

ANEMONE
From the Greek *anemos*, wind, this flower denotes the transitory nature of life. In Greek myth, anemones sprang from the blood of Adonis and so they represent death. In Christianity they are the blood of the saints.

POPPY
An opiate, the poppy symbolizes the ultimate sleep of death. Popular lore has it that the red poppies which sprang up after the battle of Waterloo grew from the blood of the dead.

IRIS
Named after the Greek goddess of the rainbow who transported women's souls to the underworld, irises were placed on graves. Louis VII adopted the iris as his emblem during the Crusades and it evolved from the *fleur-de-Louis* to the *fleur-de-lis*, the three leaves symbolizing faith, wisdom, and valour.

FORGET-ME-NOT
European legend has it that a youth drowned in a river after picking this flower for his beloved. His last words were "Forget me not!" as the current pulled him under. Thus it is a symbol of desperate love.

VIOLET
In Greek myth a nymph was spared Apollo's lust by being turned into a violet. In Christianity: humility.

CYCLAMEN
Dedicated to the Virgin Mary, the spot at its centre symbolizes her bleeding heart. Once used in love potions, it is now associated with voluptuousness.

PASSION FLOWER
Often used in stained-glass windows, this flower is a Christian symbol. The Spanish believed it grew around the cross, others saw in its form the wounds of Jesus, and some viewed its flowering as God calling for converts.

PEONY
In ancient times, this flower was thought to have magical properties. The Greeks used it to keep evil spirits at bay. The Japanese linked it to masculinity, riches, and good fortune. In China, as a symbol of love and spring, it was related to marriage and fertility and much used as a motif on temple walls.

CARNATION
In Renaissance portraits, this is a symbol of betrothal, particularly when held in the sitter's hand. In China the carnation is a common symbol of marriage.

PANSY
The word stems from the French *pensées* (thoughts), and the flower is poetically linked to thoughts, thoughtfulness, and remembrance, as well as love. Placed over the eyes of someone asleep, the pansy can impel the dreamer to fall in love with the first person to appear. It is said to be sacred to St Valentine, and is a Christian emblem of the Trinity.

HYACINTH
The Greek god Apollo created this flower from the blood of his beloved friend, Hyacinthus, who was murdered while throwing the discus with him. It is a Christian symbol of prudence.

ORCHID
In China the orchid is a symbol of perfection. In England purple spots on an orchid's petals are said to represent Christ's blood.

PRE-RAPHAELITE FLOWER IMAGERY: SHAKESPEARE'S OPHELIA

OPHELIA, JOHN EVERETT MILLAIS, 1852

Driven to madness by her beloved Hamlet's murder of her father, Ophelia drowns herself in a stream. The garlands in her hair and the flowers which surround her are all charged with symbolic meaning. The willow represents forsaken love; the nettle growing in its branches represents pain; and the daisies near Ophelia's hand are symbolic of innocence. The chain of violets around her neck is associated with faithfulness, chastity, and untimely death. The poppy is also a symbol of death; other flowers floating in the water are linked to sorrow; and the forget-me-nots on the bank are an entreaty not to forget Ophelia.

THE LANGUAGE OF THE ROSE

More than any other flower, the rose and its symbolism have entered the human consciousness. In different cultures it has come to represent youth, purity, perfection, earthly love, and rebirth. It is the flower of courtship, of marriage, and even of death. Its essence has been distilled into love potions, perfumes, cosmetics, teas, and medicinal remedies. In the West there was a custom that a rose suspended over the dinner table meant that all confidences were to be held sacred, hence the central ceiling rose of Victorian architecture, and the white rose as symbol of secrecy. The rose is also intricately linked to Catholicism – the rosary was originally made of rose hips strung together.

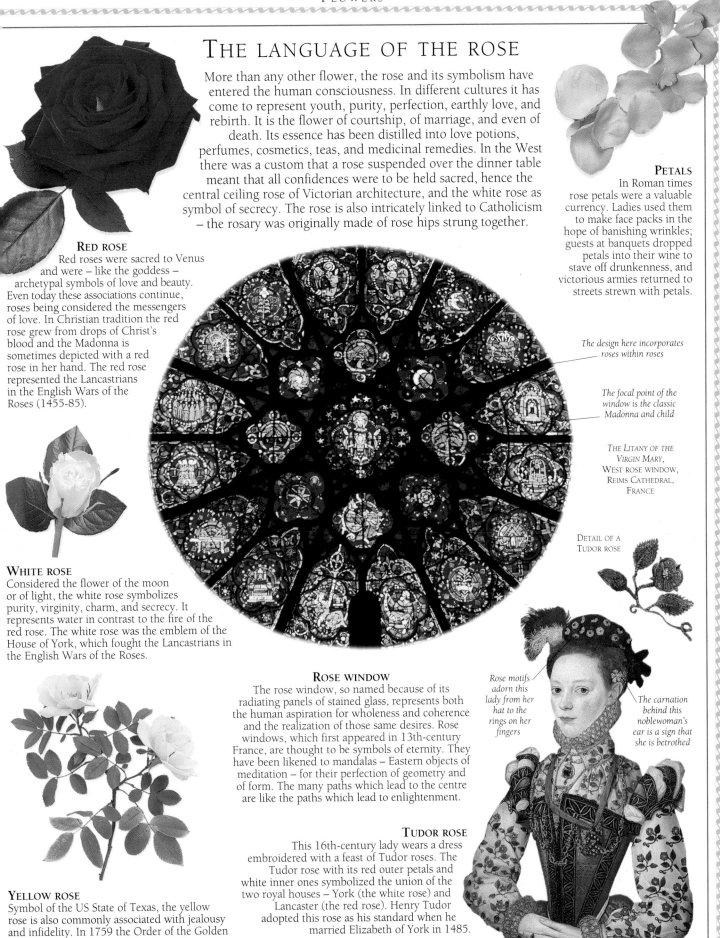

RED ROSE
Red roses were sacred to Venus and were – like the goddess – archetypal symbols of love and beauty. Even today these associations continue, roses being considered the messengers of love. In Christian tradition the red rose grew from drops of Christ's blood and the Madonna is sometimes depicted with a red rose in her hand. The red rose represented the Lancastrians in the English Wars of the Roses (1455-85).

PETALS
In Roman times rose petals were a valuable currency. Ladies used them to make face packs in the hope of banishing wrinkles; guests at banquets dropped petals into their wine to stave off drunkenness, and victorious armies returned to streets strewn with petals.

The design here incorporates roses within roses

The focal point of the window is the classic Madonna and child

THE LITANY OF THE VIRGIN MARY, WEST ROSE WINDOW, REIMS CATHEDRAL, FRANCE

DETAIL OF A TUDOR ROSE

WHITE ROSE
Considered the flower of the moon or of light, the white rose symbolizes purity, virginity, charm, and secrecy. It represents water in contrast to the fire of the red rose. The white rose was the emblem of the House of York, which fought the Lancastrians in the English Wars of the Roses.

ROSE WINDOW
The rose window, so named because of its radiating panels of stained glass, represents both the human aspiration for wholeness and coherence and the realization of those same desires. Rose windows, which first appeared in 13th-century France, are thought to be symbols of eternity. They have been likened to mandalas – Eastern objects of meditation – for their perfection of geometry and of form. The many paths which lead to the centre are like the paths which lead to enlightenment.

Rose motifs adorn this lady from her hat to the rings on her fingers

The carnation behind this noblewoman's ear is a sign that she is betrothed

TUDOR ROSE
This 16th-century lady wears a dress embroidered with a feast of Tudor roses. The Tudor rose with its red outer petals and white inner ones symbolized the union of the two royal houses – York (the white rose) and Lancaster (the red rose). Henry Tudor adopted this rose as his standard when he married Elizabeth of York in 1485.

PORTRAIT OF A LADY, BRITISH SCHOOL, 1569

YELLOW ROSE
Symbol of the US State of Texas, the yellow rose is also commonly associated with jealousy and infidelity. In 1759 the Order of the Golden Rose was created by papal decree, an honour reserved mainly for female Catholic sovereigns.

THE LOTUS

One of the most ancient symbols to appear in Asian art, the lotus symbolizes both creation and purity. Its long stem is the umbilical cord which holds man to his origins while its perfect flower represents enlightenment, and the purity to which the human soul aspires. The thousand-petalled lotus represents the sun emerging from the cosmic ocean, the sun and the waters being vital to growth. The lotus symbolizes divine birth, since the god Brahma emerges from Vishnu's navel seated on a lotus, and then creates the universe. It also symbolizes the sun and the round of birth and rebirth, since its petals open at dawn and close at sunset.

FLOWER OF PERFECTION
The lotus emerges unsullied from swamps and lakes. For this reason, and because its petals open and close with the passing of the day, it is highly symbolic in the East.

FERTILITY SYMBOL
This 3rd-century Indian figurine represents the mother goddess, shown here squatting in childbirth. She has a lotus – a symbol of fertility – for a head.

CHRYSANTHEMUM
In China and Japan, the chrysanthemum is an emblem of autumn and long life, of scholarship and contentment. It was thought to hold the key to eternal life. The Japanese have adopted it as a national emblem and as the badge of the Imperial family.

Floral inlays and moulds

FIRST FLOWER OF EGYPT
Often appearing in decoration, the lotus embodied royal power. It was associated with the god Nefertem and the sun god Re who was sometimes depicted as a child lying on a lotus. Capitals of Egyptian columns were often carved to resemble lotuses, either in bud or full flower.

The gods are standing on beds of lotuses

MARIGOLD
In Chinese belief, the marigold is the emblem of long life – "the flower of ten thousand years". The Mexicans claim the flower's colour is tainted by the blood of the Aztecs who were massacred by the Spaniards in their quest for gold.

HE-HE GODS
In China, the lotus represents purity, perfection, and spiritual grace combined with fertility and the ripeness of summer. Here, both of the He-he, twin gods of prosperity, carry a lotus in a jar. The garment worn by the god on the left is also decorated with a lotus. The He-he themselves symbolize concord and harmony between married couples.

Protective lotus flowers surround the Buddha's halo

In this typically Tibetan example the Buddha is richly ornamented with jewels

BUDDHIST JEWEL IN THE LOTUS
In Buddhist cosmology the lotus symbolizes both purity and the primordial waters from which all life is created. Because the beautiful flower grows out of mud and water, it is associated with human aspiration and potential. The Buddha is often represented as the jewel in the lotus, seated on a lotus throne, the pinnacle of perfection.

The thousand-petalled lotus supports the Buddha, the two together being a potent symbol of enlightenment

A TIBETAN *THANG-KA*, SACRED TEMPLE BANNER

SUNFLOWER
In Greek myth, Clytie is turned into this sun-worshipping flower as a consequence of her blind love for the sun god Apollo, hence the flower's association with blind infatuation. Some environmentalists have adopted the sunflower as their symbol because it absorbs air pollutants.

NARCISSUS IN GREEK MYTH

ECHO AND NARCISSUS (DETAIL),
J.W. WATERHOUSE, 1903

In Greek mythology, the youth Narcissus spurned the love of the beautiful nymph Echo who could only repeat the last words spoken to her. Echo wasted away until only her voice remained. The gods decreed that Narcissus' punishment would be to fall in love with his own image. When he saw his reflection in a pool he was unable to tear himself away and died. He was changed into the narcissus flower, which grows at the water's edge.

LILY
A white lily is the most widely accepted symbol of purity and perfection in the West. It is also a symbol of peace, divinity, and innocence. In Graeco-Roman mythology the lily was believed to have come from the milk of the goddess Hera/Juno. To the Jews, it is the emblem of the tribe of Judah.

LILY OF THE VALLEY
This is the flower of Ostara, Norse goddess of springtime. Throughout Europe it represents spring and new life, and so also symbolizes the advent of Christ. In France, it is the workers' flower, traditionally given to employees on Labour Day, 1st May.

MAGNOLIA
This flower is a Chinese symbol of feminine beauty and gentleness. In ancient China, the plant was the exclusive property of the emperor. A gift of a magnolia plant to a subject was therefore a sign of special favour. Historically, it is also associated with a celebrated heroine who shares her Chinese name, *Mu-lan*, with that of the flower. Mu-lan disguised herself as a man in order to battle on behalf of her father.

NARCISSUS
The sweet, intoxicating scent of the narcissus was once believed to cause madness. Narcissism means vanity and the flower symbolizes the dangers of vanity. To Christians, the flower is a symbol of divine love. In China, its flowering at New Year signals good fortune.

CROCUS
People once believed that wearing garlands of crocuses would ward off drunkenness. The species saffron was highly prized in medieval times when its pigment dyed garments a brilliant yellow, a symbol of light and nobility.

HONEYSUCKLE
Given by the French to their loved ones to symbolize their union, the honeysuckle represents more broadly generous love. It was once used medicinally to charm away boils.

THE ANNUNCIATION, SIMONE MARTINI AND LIPPO MEMMI, 1333

The angel Gabriel holds a lily – a symbol of Mary's chastity

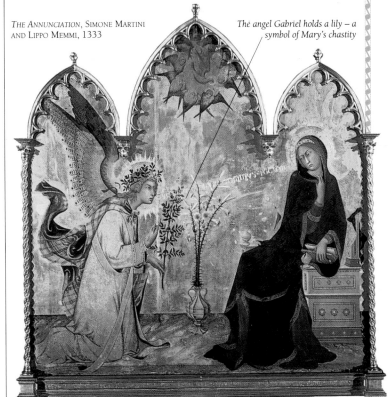

THE LILY AND CHRISTIANITY

The lily is associated with the Virgin Mary – its whiteness representing her purity, untainted by sin. It is often depicted in paintings of the Annunciation, either held by the angel Gabriel or in a vase. It is the flower of Easter and is sometimes seen with a sword at the Last Judgement, the two together symbolizing innocence and guilt. The lily is associated with chastity and is the emblem of a number of saints, for example Catherine of Siena, Francis of Assisi, Francis Xavier, and Thomas Aquinas. In the New Testament the lilies of the field are referred to by Christ as a symbol of simplicity and purity.

PRIMROSE
The primrose heralds the spring and an end to winter gloom, and is associated with purity and youth. In Germanic folklore he who wears a primrose will find hidden treasure.

JASMINE
This perfumed flower is prized in India. It is a love symbol and so it is carried in Hindu bridal garlands. In China jasmine is an emblem of beauty; in Christianity, a symbol of heavenly happiness.

DAISY
Originally the "day's eye", the daisy represents innocence and is sometimes an attribute of the Virgin. It is an emblem of the Germanic mother goddess Freya.

SEE ALSO

CHRYSANTHEMUM ☞ IMPERIAL FLOWER *115*

IRIS ☞ FLEUR-DE-LIS *105*
LILY ☞ LILY WHITE *106*; LILY *93*

LOTUS ☞ BODHISATTVA *23*

PEONY, ROSE ☞ TRANSITORY NATURE OF LIFE *57*

ROSE WINDOW ☞ YANTRA OR MANDALA *104*; KNOT *105*

SEA CREATURES

ONE OF THE MOST IMPORTANT SYMBOLS in world myth, the fish represents fertility, life, and death, and is generally auspicious. It is associated with the mother goddess, the moon, and the primeval waters from which all life grew. It is one of the earliest symbols in Christianity, signifying both Christ and the faithful, swimming in the sea of life. Jonah was swallowed by a great fish, and similar stories abound in other cultures. In Hinduism the god Vishnu's first incarnation was in the form of a great fish that saved mankind from the Flood.

Grapevines, attributes of Dionysus, god of wine

Pirates turned into dolphins

CONTEMPORARY CHINESE CARP

Symbol of courage and good fortune

CARP
This is an important symbol in the Far East. In China it represents perseverance and success owing to its ability to leap formidable rapids. In general, the carp symbolizes patience, determination, and long life. Its armourlike scales are linked to valour; in Japan it is a symbol of the Samurai and of courage.

SEA HORSE
The delicate sea horse is the mount of Poseidon/Neptune, the Graeco-Roman god of the sea. It also appears in heraldry, often to signify courage at sea, and as a civic emblem to show overseas trade.

A phallic-shaped sexual symbol

EEL
The eel plays a part in Polynesian flood myths and also has erotic associations. In Tahiti it is an ancestor figure. In China it is a symbol of carnal love, while in Britain the term "slippery as an eel" signifies a person who wriggles out of trouble.

DOLPHIN
In Graeco-Roman myth this noble fish conducts souls to the world beyond, saves the shipwrecked, and symbolizes safety and speed. It is associated with the sun god, Apollo, and is linked to Dionysus, god of wine. The dolphin is a widespread symbol of virtue.

INUIT IVORY CARVING

WHALE
In the Old Testament, Jonah was swallowed by a great fish, probably a whale, and disgorged alive onto dry land three days later. A similar legend exists among the Inuits. The whale has thus come to signify death and rebirth, and darkness before the light. In Arctic, Slav, and Russian myth the earth rests on the back of a great whale. When the whale moves, there is an earthquake.

SALMON
Like the carp, the salmon swims determinedly upstream in search of its birthplace and so symbolizes perseverance and courage. It is associated with the moon, and is a symbol of death and rebirth.

SHARK
One of the most potent symbols of terror, the shark is revered as an ancestor figure in the Pacific regions of Polynesia, Melanesia, and the Solomon Islands. In Hawaii, as in parts of West Africa, sharks are also held sacred.

SWORDFISH
In the Sepik region of New Guinea the swordfish is a totem figure, and swordfish-shaped masks are worn during sacred dances. The Ainu of Japan worship a sea divinity that takes the form of a swordfish.

The octopus was a familiar sight in Aegean life, and art

MYCENAEAN JAR, C.1400 BC

OCTOPUS
Because of its spiralling tentacles, the octopus is related to the symbolism of the spiral – air, waters, and rolling thunder and lightning. It is also a symbol of fickleness and changeability since it alters colour when under threat.

THE LANGUAGE OF SHELLS

Shells share water's symbolic associations and are linked to the moon and to the feminine, yin principle. Venus, goddess of love, was born in the waters and transported to land on a scallop shell. In China shells symbolize a successful journey and good fortune, and in Christianity they represent the baptismal waters, perhaps because shells were sometimes used to carry water. Those shells that consist of two halves fused together are symbolic of secrecy or sexual passion, and shellfish such as oysters are thought to be aphrodisiacs.

SIENESE SYMBOL

SCALLOP SHELL
The scallop shell is an emblem of Venus, and also represents the female sexual organ. In Christianity it often signifies pilgrimage, particularly to the shrine of St James in the Spanish city of Santiago de Compostela, where pilgrims wore the scallop on their clothing. The shell was also adopted as an emblem in Siena.

OYSTER
Possibly because the oyster nurtures the pearl, it represents the feminine realm – the womb, the fertility of the waters, and the moon. With its tightly sealed shell, it is also a symbol of secrecy.

CEREMONIAL CONCH
The conch shares the symbolism of the spiral owing to its convoluted shape. In Mayan culture it represents the waters. It is the emblem of Neptune, as well as of the god Vishnu as Lord of the Waters.

CEREMONIAL BUDDHIST CONCH

EGYPTIAN LUCKY GIRDLE
The Egyptians believed that the cowrie shell had protective powers because it resembled the female sexual organ. For this reason it was deemed particularly effective as a fertility charm, or to safeguard a pregnancy, when worn low down on a woman's body.

SECTION OF EGYPTIAN GIRDLE WITH COWRIE SHELLS

Heh, god of "millions of years", symbolizes long life

Beards or sidelocks of youth

Fish amulets, to prevent drowning

Cowrie shell

To sell

Treasure

CHINESE CALLIGRAPHIC SYMBOLS

COWRIE SHELLS
These small shells were used as a form of currency in a number of ancient cultures. In China the graphic design of the shell became the symbol of money in the writing system. The pictogram was then incorporated with other written symbols to represent concepts related to money.

CRAB
Because of its protective shell, the crab is associated with the womb and with motherhood. It is the symbol of Cancer, fourth sign of the zodiac, which is ruled by the moon. Due to its habit of walking sideways, the crab also has associations of evasiveness and deceit. In Buddhism it is linked to the periods of cosmic night between the ages of Brahma, or the sleep of death between one incarnation and the next. In Africa the crab is considered a symbol of evil.

LOBSTER
In the East, the lobster is viewed as a good omen and is often portrayed without claws. In ancient Greece it was similarly valued and was considered sacred. In Chinese art it is sometimes seen at the feet of the Bodhisattva Kuan Yin, and it symbolizes wealth and marital harmony. In Japan it appears on many New Year presents as a token of congratulation and, because of its curved, brittle form, as an emblem of long life.

STARFISH
Seen in Europe as a symbol of the undying power of love, the starfish in Christianity represents Mary guiding the faithful through the storms of love.

SEA URCHIN
In Celtic lore the sea urchin is known as the serpent's egg, and in its petrified form it is viewed as a symbol of the world. It is thought to be able to foretell the approach of a storm when it attaches itself to a rock, using it as an anchor. Blind and largely defenceless, it is also a symbol of all weak creatures in God's care.

INSECTS & OTHERS

INSECTS, SNAILS, AND SPIDERS differ biologically but are commonly referred to as "creepy-crawlies" – lowly animals to be shunned and that are often feared. In ancient times, however, they were the focus of much interest. The Egyptians singled out the beetle as a creature to be revered, incorporating it in the form of a scarab in their art and their jewellery, as well as in funerary offerings. For other cultures the spider is particularly important, due in part to its remarkable weaving abilities, and the bee has ambivalent associations because of its poisonous sting but also its life-giving honey.

FLY
In many cultures the fly is seen as evil and corrupt, and sometimes represents weakness or insignificance. But in parts of Africa there is a fly god, and among the Navaho of America the Big Fly is a heroic figure. The ancient Egyptians wore fly amulets to keep real flies away.

DRAGONFLY
Probably so-named because of its long, sinuous body, this beautiful insect shares the symbolism of the butterfly, representing immortality and regeneration. It is the national emblem of Japan, which is known as the "Island of the Dragonfly", but it also represents unreliability and instability, perhaps due to its hovering and darting movements. In China the dragonfly is symbolic of summer but also of weakness. To Native Americans the dragonfly symbolizes change and illusion, and also speed, the whirlwind, and activity.

WINGED SCARAB

LADYBIRD
Named the Bird of Our Lady because of its good works in ridding plants of pests, the ladybird is a symbol of luck. Its red colouring adds to its popularity.

EGYPTIAN SCARAB
The scarab, which takes its form from the humble dung beetle, was the most popular good luck charm in ancient Egypt. The beetle was deemed sacred because it mimicked the passage of the sun across the heavens in its own heroic struggle to roll balls of dung containing its eggs over long distances. The young hatched from these balls, representing new life emerging from the earth. Scarab amulets were commonly buried with the dead as symbols of regeneration.

DUNG BEETLE

THE SIGNIFICANCE OF BEES
Bees evoke feelings both of fear and of admiration. The bee is widely seen as a symbol of immortality and rebirth, as well as of diligence and social organization. It is an emblem of several Graeco-Roman and Indian gods including Cupid and Kama, both gods of love. Kama is sometimes depicted with a line of bees following him, representing the sweet pain of love.

HONEY BEE

BEES IN CHRISTIANITY
In Christian allegory the Queen bee sometimes represents the Virgin Mary, the Queen bee's production of honey likened to Mary giving birth to Jesus. The hive is then a symbol of the Church.

"Busy bees" in a "hive of activity"

Butterfly of joy

BUTTERFLY AND CICADA ON CHINESE 19TH-CENTURY PURSE

POPE URBAN VIII'S ARMS
The coat of arms of Pope Urban VIII features the keys to the kingdom of heaven, plus the Barberini bees, symbols of his family. These same bees grace a 17th-century fountain in Rome, *Fontana delle Api*, designed by Bernini to honour the Pope.

The Barberini bees   COAT OF ARMS

BUTTERFLY
Because of its metamorphosis from a caterpillar, the butterfly is seen as a symbol of rebirth and resurrection. As it emerges from its chrysalis it represents the soul leaving the body. To ancient Greeks the butterfly represents the soul, and to the Chinese and Japanese it is both immortality and joy. In Chinese art, butterflies combined with plum blossom symbolize long life, and two butterflies together stand for a happy marriage.

JAPANESE-STYLE "SIGNATURE OF THE ARTIST WHISTLER

THE TRANSITORY NATURE OF LIFE

VASE OF FLOWERS, JACOB VAN WALSCAPELLE, C.1670

The insects in Dutch flower paintings often enhance the symbolism of the flowers. Here, overblown roses, peonies, tulips, and a variety of other blooms illustrate the transitory nature of worldly joys: youthful beauty soon languishes and fades; love loses its innocence; riches cannot be taken to the grave. The short-lived fly crawling over the white rose in the centre is a symbol of transience; the centipede and bugs amid the rose's petals hint at corruption and decay. Butterflies, however – common symbols of everlasting joy – offer signs of hope and renewal.

FLY AND CENTIPEDE

SNAIL
Since it constantly emerges from and withdraws into its shell, the snail is associated with the waxing and waning moon, and symbolizes birth and rebirth. It is generally viewed as lucky, and folklore has it that if a girl places a snail on a piece of slate it will "write" the name of her husband-to-be.

WORMS
Historically, the worm was associated with the devil, and it continues to have quite sinister connotations. In the Bible it denotes degradation and humiliation. More generally, this legless creature symbolizes the earth or lowly life emerging from the earth, but also darkness.

SPIDER
Spider myths occur in many cultures. In China a spider sliding down a thread symbolizes good fortune descending from heaven. In general, the spider represents the Great Mother as weaver of destiny, or the sun: the spider creates a radiating web just as the sun generates rays from its fiery centre. Spider-woman, creator-daughter of the sun, appears in the myths of Native Americans, and in Japan a similar spider woman can ensnare unwary travellers.

ASANTE SCORPION TOE GUARD

MOTH
As the moth is irresistibly attracted to the light, so the soul is drawn to the divine truth. The moth is thus a symbol of the soul's quest for truth. Because of its delicate structure and brief lifespan, it also represents fragility and impermanence, frequently dying in its pursuit of light.

ANT
Like the bee, the ant is widely seen as a symbol of thrift, hard work, and diligence, and also of community life. It is respected in most cultures. To the Chinese the ant represents patriotism, virtue, and orderliness. To Hindus, it is more like the moth, symbolizing the transitory nature of life.

WASP
Wasps represent order within the community. However ancient Egyptians and Persian Zoroastrians linked the wasp with evil, as did the Greeks and Romans. According to Polish legend, bees were created by God, but when the Devil tried to create bees, they turned into wasps.

LOCUST
Because of its voracious eating habits and capacity to strip large areas of vegetation, the locust is widely associated with calamity and destruction, as well as with greed. In the Old Testament the locust is an instrument of punishment, sent as a plague by God.

SCORPION
Widely associated with evil, destruction, and death, the scorpion also symbolizes envy and hatred, and represents darkness since it lives below the earth. Ancient Egyptians worshipped the goddess Selket in the form of a scorpion. The Asante wore scorpion rings as charms against scorpion bites.

REPTILES & AMPHIBIANS

AMPHIBIOUS CREATURES, animals that live both on land and in the water, take on the symbolic associations of the waters, the source of all life. Reptiles are mostly associated with the earth and therefore assume the fertility symbolism of the earth, although their appearance often inspires fear and disgust. Reptiles that hold a special place in the popular imagination are dinosaurs, ancient inhabitants of the earth. Their symbolism is mixed – they are both giant monsters, terrifying to behold, and among the most fascinating of all the creatures known to us.

ASANTE CROCODILE FIGURE

TYRANNOSAURUS REX
A formidable 15m (47ft) high, T. rex is certainly the best known and most feared of the dinosaurs. It has been popularized in films, fiction, and children's cartoons, and although a symbol of extinction, is far from extinct in people's minds.

CROCODILE
The crocodile has long been feared and revered. Living both on land and in water it carries the symbolism of each and is thus very powerful. "Crocodile tears" are false tears from the belief that crocodiles weep while devouring their victims.

NEWT
The newt is generally thought of as an evil, harmful creature. Such was its reputation that in *Macbeth*, Shakespeare listed "eye of newt" as one of the ingredients in the witches' brew, designed to conjure up evil spirits that would reveal the future.

JAPANESE SYMBOL OF LONG LIFE

FROGS AND TOADS

Frogs and toads are both associated with the waters and the moon, and therefore with fertility and the feminine realm. Both undergo the process of metamorphosis from a tadpole and so are symbolic of resurrection. The frog was an emblem of Aphrodite, and Heket, Egyptian goddess of birth, took the form of a frog. The toad, however, became associated with witchcraft and with a more sinister symbolism.

Frog motif on Zuni bowl

FROG BOWL
The frogs modelled around this Southwestern bowl indicate the high regard given to frogs in the Americas. They were esteemed as harbingers of rain and for their cleansing and purifying powers.

ANASAZI FROG
The widespread association of the frog with fertility was particularly strong among Native American peoples. The ancient Anasazi people who lived on the border of Arizona and New Mexico used jet and much-prized turquoise in the making of this ornament, reflecting the importance of the frog in their culture.

QING FROG
In China the frog represents the lunar, yin principle and the frog spirit is revered as a healer and bringer of prosperity.

Inlaid turquoise eyes

CHAMELEON
The chameleon's changing colour symbolizes inconstancy and changing fortunes. Its eyes, which can see in different directions, see into both past and future. In parts of Africa it is seen as magical and brings rain.

TORTOISE OR TURTLE
Linked to the moon and the waters, the tortoise and turtle also symbolize fertility and long life. Various world myths speak of a tortoise supporting the world, and in Hinduism a man-tortoise was the ancestor of mankind. In Aesop's *Fables* the tortoise represents steady determination.

LIZARD CHARM

LIZARD
The lizard's sun-seeking habit symbolizes the soul's search for awareness. The Romans believed that the lizard hibernated, and for them it represented death and resurrection. To Native Americans, lizards contained magic.

SEE ALSO
FROGS AND TOADS ☞ WITCH'S FAMILIAR 79

ROD OF AESCULAPIUS ☞ DIAMOND BROOCH 40; CADUCEUS 108

SNAKES ☞ DOUBLE-HEADED SERPENT, HYDRA 28

THE FALL ☞ TREE OF KNOWLEDGE 44; FIG 48

SNAKES

The snake or serpent is probably the most widely revered of all creatures because it embodies so many forces. Its underground lair allies it to the underworld and it is associated with the primal waters from which all life was created. The serpent symbol was widespread in agricultural societies, where it was used to represent the fertility of the soil.

PUEBLO
SNAKE STICK

19TH-CENTURY
SRI LANKAN MASK

SNAKE STICK
Among the Pueblo peoples of America, the snake is associated with thunder and lightning. Snake sticks such as this were used in annual rituals to call down the rain that ensured a good harvest. The snake sticks were themselves symbols of lightning.

Sacred snakes which banish evil spirits

SNAKES & LADDERS
This childhood game represents life's journey. Ladders are positive symbols of success and achievement, whereas snakes represent the slippery slopes of misfortune.

EGYPT
In Egypt the serpent was feared and worshipped. Several deities are depicted in the form of a snake and in this tomb painting a worshipper is seen kneeling before the serpent goddess Meretseger, the guardian of the Valley of the Kings.

SNAKE DEMON MASK
This Sri Lankan mask of Naga Rassa, or snake demon, is worn in dances to chase away evil spirits causing sickness. *Nagas*, or sacred snakes, have the power to be both protective and destructive.

EGYPTIAN
TOMB
PAINTING

THE FALL
The fall from grace of Adam and Eve is inextricably linked with the serpent. It was a serpent, here in female form, that tempted Eve to taste the forbidden fruit of the tree. The serpent is therefore viewed as a symbol of smooth-tongued evil and deceitfulness, and as the embodiment of temptation and sin.

ROD OF AESCULAPIUS
A serpent coiled around a rod is both the emblem and symbol of Aesculapius, the Roman god of medicine. This association with healing comes from the snake's shedding of its skin, making it a symbol of renewal and regeneration. In alchemy, a serpent around a pole represents the harnessing of the metal quicksilver (mercury).

SHIP'S
EMBLEM

MEDUSA
With hair of writhing serpents, Medusa's appearance was so hideous that all who looked at her turned to stone. In addition to being a symbol of terror, she embodied enchantment and cunning.

*THE TEMPTATION OF ADAM AND EVE,
TOMMASO MASOLINO, c.1427*

MAMMALS

WITH THEIR COMPLEX AND OFTEN INTIMATE relationships with humans, animals have always played a prominent part in our imagination and in mythology. Many animals, especially the predatory species, were worshipped and were credited with protective powers; people even claimed descent from them, and names of animals were given to the constellations. Certain animals are traditionally paired in conflict – the lion and the unicorn, which are associated with the sun and the moon, for instance. This perhaps represented the balance between opposing forces in nature that result in the earth's fertility.

EGYPTIAN CAT
In ancient Egypt cats were revered, and the male cat was an emblem of the sun god. Cats were also sacred to the goddess Bastet who had the head of a cat and who represented the power of the sun to ripen crops.
So valued were cats that thousands were mummified after they died and buried in special graveyards in honour of Bastet.

BLACK CAT
Being largely nocturnal the cat is associated with the moon. It is also credited with supernatural powers, both good and evil, and is the companion of witches. In Norse legend, if a black cat crossed your path it was a sign that Satan was thinking about you. In America, a black cat crossing your path brings bad luck, but in England and Japan this is a good omen.

HARE
A nocturnal animal, the hare is widely associated with the moon, and also with lust and fertility. To Native Americans the Great Hare represents opposing characters: part-clown, part-god, creator and transformer of our animal nature. In China it is the yin, symbol of the feminine principle. The hare's association with fertility probably accounts for the Easter Bunny, representing spring and the growth of new life.

HARE, MEDIEVAL PSALTER

MOUSE
In Western mythology, the mouse is associated with the powers of darkness. The Bible considers it unclean and devilish. Elsewhere, however, the mouse is considered orderly and methodical.

Intricate pattern of bandaging

MUMMIFIED
EGYPTIAN CAT

THE OLD SHEPHERD'S CHIEF MOURNER, SIR EDWIN LANDSEER, c.1837

DOG, PROTECTOR AND LOYAL FRIEND
In Greek mythology Cerberus was the three-headed dog who guarded the gates of the realm of the dead and acted as a spirit guide. In Judaic and Islamic traditions the dog is considered unclean, while in Zoroastrianism it is regarded highly. Everywhere, however, the dog is a symbol of faithfulness and protectiveness, of blind love and obedience. The dog is the eleventh sign of the Chinese zodiac.

ASS OR DONKEY
A beast of burden, the ass or donkey is a symbol of poverty, of stupidity, and also of fertility. Greek writers used the ass to represent foolishness, and we still use the term "silly ass". For the Egyptians, the wild ass of the desert symbolized loneliness and isolation. In Christianity, the humble ass is blessed: it bore Mary to Bethlehem and Jesus into Jerusalem.

"The most ill-starred of quadrupeds, pitiful and miserable."
Roman writer

BRAYING ASS

FOX
The fox universally represents cunning and deception. In some traditions, it has the power to transform its shape in order to deceive. In the East, the fox can become a beautiful maiden who creates trouble. Also, like the wolf in *Little Red Riding Hood*, a fox sometimes dresses in the clothes of a trustworthy person in order to catch unwary prey. Some North American Indians have fox tribes and clans.

HEDGEHOG

In antiquity the hedgehog was reputed to collect grapes by rolling over them and carrying them home on its spikes for storage. In Christianity it was associated with the devil and with evil, as this practice was likened to stealing people's souls. The hedgehog sometimes symbolizes witchcraft, as witches were thought to assume the form of hedgehogs to drink milk from cows.

RAM

The ram embodies virility, the masculine force, and creative energy. It is associated with many gods, and is a common sacrificial animal, its blood symbolically returning fertility to the soil. The Hebrew ritual horn, *shofar*, is made from a ram's horn.

Spiral-shaped horns, used by Jews to call people to worship

Goat's-head wine cup, symbol of Bacchus and drunken revelry

GREEK DRINKING CUP

GOAT

Because of its agility and urge to climb, the goat is a symbol of the far-seeking quest for truth. However, the goat also stands for lawlessness, demonic powers, lust, and fertility. Satyrs were half-human, half-goat and the devil is often depicted with the horns and hooves of a goat.

ROMAN CLAY PIG

PIG

The boar is a symbol of courage (its head was eaten as protection against danger), and the sow was associated in many cultures with fertility and the mother goddess. In Judaism and Islam the pig is viewed as the most unclean of all animals, and in Christianity it is linked to Satan and symbolizes gluttony.

HORSES

The horse represents speed, grace, and nobility. It is both a solar and lunar symbol: the heavenly chariots of Apollo and the Indian sun god Surya were drawn by fiery or white horses, as was Neptune's ocean chariot.

BUCKING BRONCO

In parts of the United States men compete at riding untrained horses, the aim being to complete a round without being thrown. This challenge emphasizes the horse's reputation as a wild and noble creature.

20TH-CENTURY WATERCOLOUR

Hands kept free to draw bow while riding

MONGOLIAN HORSEMAN

In Mongolia herdsmen had expert cavalry skills: they raced without harness and reins. This custom probably originated when their warlike ancestors rode horses into battle and had to keep their hands free to fight.

MONGOL WARRIOR

OX

The symbolism of the ox has much in common with that of the bull and the buffalo. While clearly symbolizing male power and strength, all three animals, because of their crescent-shaped horns, also have lunar, hence feminine, attributes. The bull is the mount of Shiva in Hinduism, and in Taoism the sage Lao Tzu is shown riding an ox to represent the taming of the ego.

Crescent-shaped horns associated with the moon

Rope, symbol of man's attempt at controlling beast

HUMPED OX, FROM 18TH-CENTURY INDIAN MINIATURE

LION, KING OF BEASTS

The lion is the king of the beasts in most parts of the world. Its golden colour, fiery mane, and great strength make it a natural contender for association with the sun, although the lioness may also be linked with the moon and with the great mother goddesses. Lions are often carved into gateposts and thrones to act as guardians.

LION FAMILY, 13TH-CENTURY ARAB MANUSCRIPT

ORIENTAL LIONS
In antiquity lions were found not just in Africa but also in the Middle East and India. They were kept by kings as a symbol of royal power and were used in the hunt. The lion is also a Buddhist symbol.

CHINESE TIGER, 13TH CENTURY

LION GARGOYLE

Spout for draining water

HERALDIC LION
The lion is the most important animal in heraldic art, probably because the nobility wished to be associated with its valour and strength. It is shown "rampant", standing on its hind legs, or "sejant", seated.

CHURCHILL FAMILY EMBLEM

Lion in the "sejant" position, seated with one paw raised

GUARDIAN LION
The lion's image was often placed on buildings, perhaps to add protection. As a gargoyle it carried water away from the roof, its solar nature combining with water as a symbol of fertility.

TIGER
Like the lion, the tiger symbolizes royalty, courage, and strength. It is particularly important in the Far East where it replaces the lion as king of beasts. In China, where it is the emblem of the West, if a tiger devours a man, that man's soul becomes the tiger's slave and preys upon other men.

EGYPTIAN JACKAL-HEADED URN

JACKAL
The head of the Egyptian god Anubis is that of a jackal. Jackals were thought to haunt graveyards and were reputed to see both by day and night. Clear-sighted Anubis was a pathfinder or "psychopomp", guiding spirits to the next world. Canopic jars, which contained embalmed organs, had Anubis-shaped stoppers.

ST JEROME AND THE LION
There are several stories of a fierce lion helped by a devout man whom it then befriends. Like Androcles in Aesop's *Fables*, St Jerome is said to have extracted a thorn from a lion's paw. In return the lion renounced its fierce nature and lived peaceably with him. This symbolizes man's mastery of his own animal nature.

St Jerome removing thorn from lion's paw

ST JEROME AND THE LION, NICCOLO COLANTONIO, 1450

GOLD WEST-AFRICAN MASK, 16TH CENTURY

LEOPARD
Symbol of courage, cruelty, and untamed instincts, the leopard is greatly revered in Africa, where it also represents the light of the morning sun. Leopard skins denote royalty and are worn to ward off danger. Because its markings resemble eyes, the leopard is sometimes known as the Great Watcher.

HERALDIC STAG

ISLAMIC PLATE

STAG
Associated with the hunt, the stag is a solar animal and an enemy of the serpent. The shape of its antlers recalls the Tree of Life, and because the antlers are renewed each year, the stag is a symbol of regeneration. In European and Asian mythology, stag hunts often lead to a supernatural encounter.

GAZELLE
The swift running gazelle is a symbol of beauty and of the soul, particularly in Arabic literature. It can also be used as a metaphor for the beloved. In Christianity, when the gazelle is shown fleeing from an animal of prey such as a panther or lion, it represents the soul fleeing from earthly passions.

AUSTRALIAN BARK PAINTING

KANGAROO
Among some Australian Aboriginals the kangaroo is an ancestor-spirit that protects and guides them and plays a major part in their myths. Each Aboriginal group has a different animal ancestor and feels a kinship with that species. The kangaroo ancestor left many traces of its journey at the time of creation, seen today in features of the landscape.

CANADIAN HEADDRESS

BEAVER
According to Native American myth, the beaver brought mud from the ocean-bed to create the earth. There are many beaver clans and the beaver is seen as an ancestor figure. In Europe it is a symbol of energy and industry.

CHINESE BATS OF HAPPINESS

BATS
In the West, the bat is generally seen as unclean and associated with darkness and death. It was seen as a form of the devil, and vampires such as Dracula could become bats. But to the Chinese, bats stand for happiness and good luck.

CHINESE ENAMELLED ELEPHANT, 18TH CENTURY

Ornate enamelling, befitting an imperial elephant

ELEPHANT
Because of its bulk and strength, the elephant is generally a symbol of power. It also signifies patience, wisdom, and chastity – probably because, according to Aristotle, a bull elephant remained celibate during the two-year long gestation period of his mate. The Hindu god Ganesha has an elephant's head and with his huge belly represents prosperity and benevolence. The white elephant is a symbol of royalty and is associated with the Buddha.

Water plant denoting water habitat

EGYPTIAN HIPPOPOTAMUS MODEL

HIPPOPOTAMUS
Owing to its natural affinity with water as well as earth, the hippopotamus is associated with fertility. It was known to the Greeks and the Romans as the "beast of the Nile" and it played a particularly important role in Egyptian mythology – the fertility goddess Taueret was depicted with the head of a hippopotamus.

THREE MONKEYS, JAPAN

MONKEY
The monkey is sacred to some West African tribes for whom it is an ancestor figure. Generally it represents mischief and inquisitiveness, but the monkey-god Hanuman is highly regarded in Hinduism, and from Japan comes the common motif of the three Mystic Monkeys that see no evil, hear no evil, and speak no evil.

NATIVE AMERICAN FEAST DISH

BEAR
In northern countries the bear replaces the lion as king of the beasts. It was an ancestor of the Lapps, who called it grandfather. Because it hibernates and wakes in the spring, it symbolizes resurrection. The bear also represents power, and to the Celts, warfare. It is the national emblem of Russia.

CLAY CAMEL, ALGERIA

CAMEL
The "ship of the desert" is highly valued in Middle Eastern cultures. In Arabia it is regarded as ennobled by God – the prophet Mohammed took an oath on one, and where his camel is said to have knelt on the flight to Mecca, now stands the holiest spot in Islam. As a pack animal, the camel represents stamina, obedience, and temperance. Because it kneels, it is also a symbol of humility.

SEE ALSO
BEAR ☞ BEAR 114
DOG ☞ MANDRAKE 46; WAR DANCE 76; DOG 113, 114
ELEPHANT ☞ GANESHA 20
HORSES ☞ SLEIPNIR 28; PEGASUS 31; HORSE 113
JACKAL ☞ ANUBIS 14
LION ☞ UNICORN 28; GRIFFIN, SPHINX 31; LEO 112; LION 114
MONKEY ☞ HANUMAN 20
OTHER ANIMALS ☞ SACRED COW 21; RAT, RABBIT 113
OX ☞ OX 113
RAM ☞ SHOFAR 16
TIGER ☞ TIGER 113

BIRDS

THERE IS A WIDESPREAD AND ANCIENT BELIEF that after death the soul leaves the body in the form of a bird, and the bird consequently is a symbol of the spirit. Birds can be mediators between gods and men, and can act as vehicles for the gods. Many religions have heavenly beings or spirits with wings: angels, cherubs, and seraphim for example. Birds are seen in the Tree of Life, and are sometimes depicted fighting with or carrying a serpent, symbolizing the uneasy balance between the sun (as bird) and the waters (as serpent). In Christian art this symbolizes the struggle between good and evil.

FALCON PECTORAL

CUCKOO
Because of its habit of laying its eggs in other birds' nests, the cuckoo is sometimes regarded as evil. It is a symbol of unfaithfulness in marriage and, in Japan, of unrequited love. But it also has positive associations, linked to fertility and rain. The song of the first cuckoo heralds the spring and the sowing of crops. If it is heard too early, it is taken as a sign of frosts and a poor harvest.

SPARROW
In the Old Testament the sparrow is viewed as a symbol of loneliness, while in the New Testament it represents lowliness and insignificance. However it is also associated with lust and fertility, and in Greek myth with Aphrodite, goddess of love. In Japan the sparrow is traditionally a symbol of loyalty, perhaps because of the bird's sociable nature.

SWALLOW
Returning north from its summer habitat only with the arrival of warmer weather, the swallow symbolizes spring, renewed life, and fertility. Because the swallow is almost always airborne, in parts of Africa it is seen as a symbol of purity, as it does not soil its feathers by walking on the earth. In China two swallows flying together represent marital happiness.

PELICAN
An early Christian legend is unclear about whether the female pelican killed her young or whether the chicks were killed by a serpent. Nevertheless the female was reported to mourn them for three days. After this, she stabbed her own chest and resuscitated them with her blood. The pelican thus symbolizes self-sacrifice and devotion, and to Christians it represents Christ, who shed his blood for mankind and was raised from the dead after three days. The bird is often carved on church lecterns.

FALCON
In general, the falcon is a symbol of the sun and the masculine powers in nature. It is particularly important in Egyptian mythology where it was sacred to Re, god of the sun. It was also a popular form of the god Horus. Like the eagle, the falcon, with its strength and high flight, represents freedom of the spirit, which perhaps explains its popularity as a sporting bird in Renaissance Europe. In China the falcon has both the healing power of the sun and the destructive power of war.

COCKS AND HENS
Cocks and hens have long been used in ritual. In the past they were thought to have talismanic powers and were used to avert danger. In some parts of the world cocks are still sacrificed so that their blood returns fertility to the soil, and seers foretell the future from the entrails of the hen.

COCK
The cock is associated with courage and battle, with masculinity and the sun. Its crow heralds the dawn and symbolizes the victory of light over darkness. It is equated with fertility, and cock-sacrifice forms part of many harvest rites. In Christianity the cock is a symbol of resurrection, and the all-seeing weathercock represents vigilance.

ROMAN MOSAIC, 1ST CENTURY BC

HEN
The hen is widely seen as a symbol of maternal care and protectiveness. In Christianity the hen with its chicks represents Christ and his believers.

NORTHWEST AMERINDIAN TOTEM

RAVEN
Although often seen as an evil omen and a sign of war, illness, or death, the raven was viewed in China, Japan, and Persia as a messenger of the gods and as a symbol of the sun. In Norse legend the god Odin is accompanied by two ravens, and according to Native American myth the earth was created by a raven that dropped pebbles to make islands in the sea.

CRANE
In China, as elsewhere, the crane is seen as a good omen, a messenger of the gods and a bearer of maternal love and happiness. It brings high status, longevity, and immortality, and symbolizes spiritual enlightenment. In parts of Africa and North America the crane was associated with wisdom.

Talon holds the "shenu", symbol of eternity

CROW

The black crow is widely regarded as a bird of ill omen and to many Native Americans, a crow's black feather spells death to an enemy. To the Chinese the black crow paired with the white heron represents the yin/yang, male/female principle, and in Japanese Shintoism the crow is a messenger of the gods.

DOVES OF LOVE AND PEACE

The dove is a symbol of the soul and of peace, innocence, gentleness, and purity. Two doves together are considered a sign of marital love and fidelity. Doves are held sacred in many countries. In Greek legend the dove was linked to Aphrodite, the infant Zeus, the Fates, and the Furies.

SEVEN GIFTS OF THE SPIRIT

In Christianity the white dove is a symbol of the Holy Spirit and sometimes of martyrdom. Seven doves encircling a cross represent the seven gifts of the Holy Spirit: wisdom, understanding, counsel, fortitude, knowledge, piety, and fear of the Lord.

GREENPEACE DOVE

Greenpeace, the international movement for protecting the environment, has adopted a dove bearing an olive branch as its emblem. It is symbolic of peace and also of hope.

KIWI

According to legend the kiwi, which is flightless and without a tail, was created from a gourd by Tane, a Polynesian ancestor god. It is the emblem of New Zealand.

PARROT

The parrot symbolizes spring and fertility, as well as imitation and mockery due to its gift of mimicry. It is held sacred by the Hopi peoples of North America. In Hinduism the bird is associated with Kama, god of love, and also with prophecy and rain-making.

KINGFISHER

In the East the kingfisher denotes married bliss and its feathers are prized for their colour and are thought to be magical. According to legend, after the Flood the kingfisher flew too close to the sun and scorched its breast red whilst its back took on the colour of the sky.

CONDOR

To the Incas condors were revered and were thought to be the embodiment of the gods of the air. Condor feathers were prized and used in religious ornaments.

MAGPIE

The magpie is a bird of ill omen in the West where its chattering foretells trouble between husband and wife. But in the East, particularly China, it is a bringer of joy, and its call heralds the arrival of welcome guests. Two magpies together symbolize marital bliss.

PEACOCK

This royal bird with its fan-shaped tail is a symbol of the sun; its circular tail represents the vault of heaven and the "eyes" the stars. In Buddhism the many eyes symbolize watchfulness, although the feathers are often thought to be unlucky, a form of the evil eye. In Hinduism, the peacock is the mount of Karttikeya, god of war. The male peacock courts its mate with such pride that it has become synonymous with vanity.

GOOSE

The goose is a bird of the sun. It was associated with many Greek and Roman gods and was kept to guard temples. Thus it came to symbolize watchfulness and love. In Hinduism the goose is the mount of the god Brahma and in China and Japan it is associated with the autumn moon and is a bearer of good news.

SWAN

In Greek myth Zeus took on the form of a swan to seduce the beautiful Leda. The swan is also associated with Venus/Aphrodite: her chariot is sometimes borne through the air by swans. In Native American lore, the swan is a symbol of trust and submission. The song of the dying swan is said to be one of joy at the prospect of entering the afterlife.

DUCK

In North American myth the duck acts as mediator between the sky and water and it was one of the creatures that helped to renew the earth after the Flood. According to Hebrew tradition the duck symbolizes immortality, while in China and Japan it represents contentment, marital bliss, and fidelity.

STORK

In ancient Egypt and Greece young storks were believed to treat their elders with kindness and so they symbolized filial duty. In Europe the stork is associated with the spring and with birth, and babies are said to have been "brought by the stork".

EAGLES

State symbols of power and strength

ASANTE THRONE DECORATION

Universally viewed as the king of birds, the eagle is a symbol of the sun, royalty, and the gods, especially sky gods. It represents authority, strength, victory, and pride, and in China the male yang principle, keen vision, and fearlessness. The eagle is often identified as the mythical Indian Garuda seen in deadly combat with the serpent. Like the hawk the eagle is reputed to gaze straight at the sun as it flies upwards and so in medieval Europe it came to be associated with prayer ascending to god, and with the ascension of Christ. In Australian lore the sea eagle carries the souls of the dead back to the Dreaming.

NAPOLEONIC EAGLE
Perhaps inspired by the Roman practice, every French regiment in Napoleon's army carried a bronze standard in the form of an eagle. The example shown here was the emblem of the 105th regiment, and was captured by the British at Waterloo. In its right talon the eagle holds Jupiter's emblem of a thunderbolt.

NAPOLEONIC EAGLE

US BALD EAGLE
In 1782 the United States adopted the bald eagle as a national emblem. It appears both on their coins and their paper money, and is symbolic of power and strength. Its outstretched wings demonstrate its strength, and it rests above an olive branch of peace.

Jupiter's thunderbolt

Eagle feathers representing success in hunting and war

LIP ORNAMENT
To the Aztecs the eagle symbolized the rising sun and celestial power. It was associated with the warrior clans, and this eagle head was worn as protective jewellery.

EAGLE FEATHERS
To the Sioux the spotted eagle represents the essence of all life. The eagle's feathers are regarded as rays of the sun, and the eagle-feathered headdress is a symbol of Thunderbird, the Universal Spirit. By putting the headdress on before battle the warrior identified himself with the power and strength of the eagle god.

JAY
Although often viewed as a chatterer and a sign of bad luck, to Native Americans the jay is a Creator bird which helped to recreate the world after the Flood. It is the guardian spirit of some tribes, and warns of the approach of the enemy.

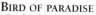

GOLDFINCH
Essentially a Christian symbol, the goldfinch represents both the soul and the Passion of Christ. Goldfinches like to eat thistles and thorns and so the bird has become associated with Christ's suffering on the cross. The red spot on its throat is said to represent the drop of blood that fell as the goldfinch drew a thorn from Christ's brow.

BIRD OF PARADISE
The feathers of these magnificent birds, found in New Guinea, are so beautiful that it was thought in Europe that the birds came from paradise. The birds achieved mythical status, people believing that they lived on dew drops and would moan in pain if captured. Their feathers were prized and were once worn as a fashion item.

HUMMINGBIRD
The hummingbird is seen as a symbol of joy, giving pleasure through its loveliness. In Native American myth it is a truthful bird that represents beauty, harmony, and enjoyment. The Aztec war god Huitzilopochtli and Quetzalcoatl, the Mayan god, both wore its feathers, which are widely thought to have magical properties.

IBIS
In ancient Egypt the ibis was a symbol of the soul. It was sacred to the lunar deities Isis and Thoth, and represented the moon (with the hawk as the sun). However the ibis also had a solar significance when seen in battle with serpents, emblems of the water. In Christian art the ibis symbolizes devotion and perseverance.

OWLS

In ancient Greece the owl was sacred to Athena, goddess of wisdom and night, and came to symbolize the city named after her, as well as wisdom. The owl was then incorporated into the design of Greek coins, and was so popular that countries such as Italy, Egypt, and Turkey issued similar coins.

BIRD OF THE NIGHT
Because of its association with the night, the owl is widely seen as a bird of ill omen with a cry that heralds death and misfortune. To the Celts the owl was a "night hag" linked to corpses. In parts of Africa it was associated with magic and its head was used in preparing spells.

BLACKBIRD
The much-loved blackbird was sacred to the Greeks for its sweet song, but as this song is so alluring the bird is also a symbol of the temptations of the flesh. In some Christian writings the black plumage makes the blackbird a symbol of evil.

NIGHTINGALE
The song of the nightingale, both sweet and plaintive, was particularly meaningful in Persia where it was seen as a symbol of love, longing, and pain. Because its song heralds the dawn, it is said by Christians to represent the soul's yearning for Christ.

DODO
The dodo, hunted to extinction in the 17th century, has become a symbol for something obsolete, hence the phrase "dead as a dodo".

ROBIN
The robin is a symbol of compassion. Its red breast is said to be the result of scorching when it carried water to the parched souls in hell. Alternatively, the robin was pricked when trying to remove nails from Christ's cross.

WREN
Although killing a wren is considered unlucky, it was not always so. In England and France it was once a part of Christmas rites to hunt and kill wrens, burying them in the churchyard as a symbol of the ending of the old year.

HAWK
This predatory bird is one of the great solar birds, with similar associations to the eagle and the falcon. In ancient Egypt it was the bird of Re the sun god and represented the soul. To Greeks and Romans it was the messenger of Apollo. In Native American myth the hawk helped to fire the sun and recreate the world after the Flood. Australia's eagle hawk is a totem for some Aboriginals.

ALBATROSS
Because of its ability to fly great distances over water, the albatross is a symbol of the sea and long ocean journeys. When it circles a ship it is thought to herald the advent of a storm and is symbolic of rough weather. In the West there is an ancient belief that the albatross embodied the soul of a dead sailor and so it was considered extremely unlucky to kill one, as reflected in Coleridge's *Rime of the Ancient Mariner*.

WOODPECKER
The woodpecker was widely believed to have magical powers and to bring good luck. It was sacred to Mars, Roman god of war, and was seen as a symbol of lightning and fire by Germanic peoples. The Ainu of Japan viewed it as evil but also believed that the woodpecker was sent by God to show them how to hollow out tree trunks to make boats.

OSTRICH
In medieval times the ostrich was reputed to leave its eggs to hatch in the heat of the sun. In some cultures this was seen as a sign of cruelty to its young; in others as a symbol of belief in the power of the heavens. The ostrich also represents those who hide from the truth, owing to its reputation for burying its head in the sand. An ostrich egg is a symbol of rebirth.

HOOPOE
The hoopoe has conflicting symbolism. In Egypt it was known as the "doctor bird" and in Arab literature it is described as a messenger of love. However, it also has negative associations. It is said to betray secrets, and in Europe it is a symbol of the devil and of witchcraft.

QUAIL
In Russian lore the quail symbolizes the sun, with the hare as the moon. The quail was also a symbol of the tzars. To the Chinese, as to the Romans, it was a symbol of courage and victory in battle although when caged it symbolized the soul imprisoned in the body. Elsewhere it is associated with good luck and the spring, and because it is thought to have an extremely amorous nature it has sexual associations.

HERON
The heron, like the stork and the crane, represents both the sun and the waters, and is thought to predict changes in the weather. In ancient Egypt the heron was associated with renewal and the annual return of flood waters to the Nile, but in Greece it was a symbol of treachery, as its wading in shallow waters revealed a fordable path to enemies.

VULTURE
Closely associated with several Egyptian deities, the vulture is seen as feminine and represents maternal instinct, as vultures were supposed to feed their young with their own blood if necessary. Zoroastrians view them as "compassionate purifiers" since they eat the flesh of corpses in Parsee Towers of Silence. However, vultures are also feared because of their carnivorous appetite.

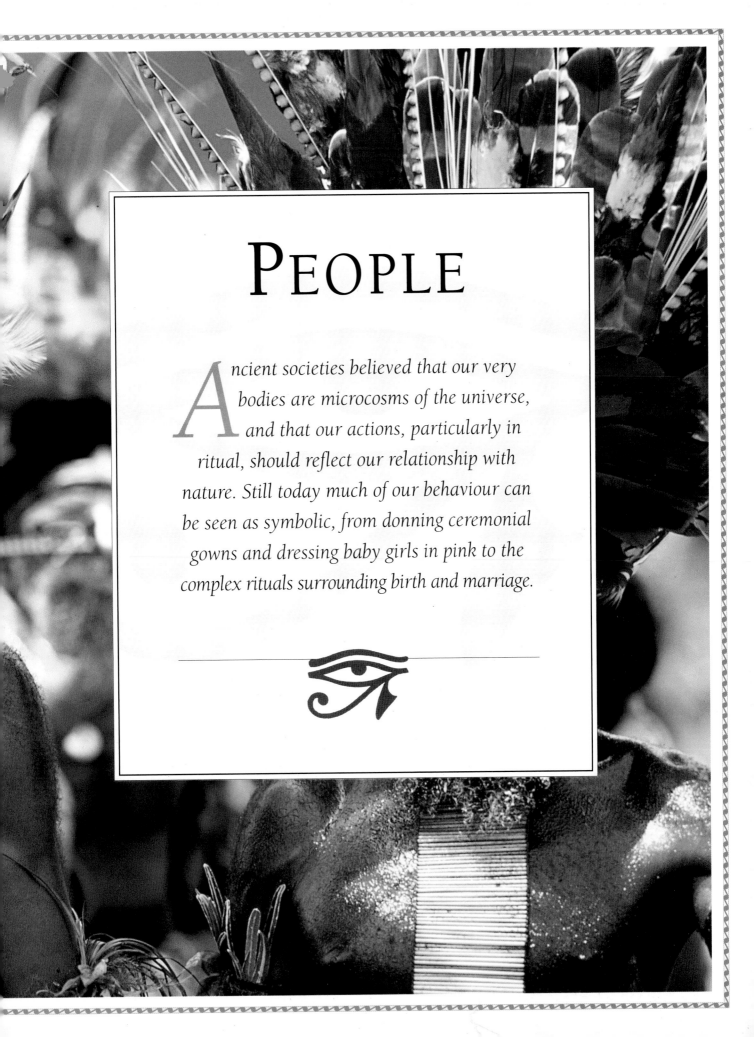

PEOPLE

Ancient societies believed that our very bodies are microcosms of the universe, and that our actions, particularly in ritual, should reflect our relationship with nature. Still today much of our behaviour can be seen as symbolic, from donning ceremonial gowns and dressing baby girls in pink to the complex rituals surrounding birth and marriage.

SEX & FERTILITY

FOR MANY PEOPLE NOWADAYS, especially city-dwellers, the fertility of the soil is a rather remote concept. But for thousands of years this, along with human fertility – and thus the continuation of the species, has been the greatest preoccupation of humankind. For this reason all societies have had fertility gods and goddesses to ensure the continued wellbeing of the community. There are countless images which have for us a sexual symbolism and are thus essentially to do with fertility. Many are straightforward sex symbols and relate to the union of man and woman; others are to do with the earth's bounty.

Pomegranate of fruitfulness

BRAZILIAN WAIST ORNAMENT

Fish of fertility

Key to womanhood

SILVER CHARMS
This richly decorated waist ornament includes many items connected with fertility and may have been a gift to a young bride. Hanging from its garland of flowers are silver keys, a fish, pomegranates, grapes, and a festive tambourine.

Three stripes of Shiva worship

Shiva's face protected by two cobras

LINGA AND YONI
The linga is the most commonly worshipped form of Shiva, its phallus-shaped pillar representing the god as the male creative principle. Here it is set into the yoni, the vulva-shaped feminine element. Together they represent fertility and creation.

FERTILITY DOLLS
Dolls such as these were worn by women and young girls in Angola to enhance their fertility. They are made variously of corn cobs or forked sticks and beeswax – the corn cob being itself a symbol of fertility.

PINEAPPLE QUILT
This American bridal quilt is ornamented with pineapples, symbols of life and fertility, and also with meadow lilies and tulips, which symbolize love. Quilts are traditionally made as part of a bride's trousseau when she marries, and are often designed to promote "fruitfulness".

SEX SYMBOLS
The symbolism of sex varies greatly from culture to culture, according to lifestyle, social etiquette, and taboos. In the West, classic sex symbols tend to be young and glamorous, and are often film stars or musicians. Objects that symbolize male sexuality tend to be associated with a phallic shape and with power, whereas female sexuality is related to round shapes, symbolizing receptivity and abundance.

ELVIS
Known as "Elvis the pelvis", the king of rock 'n' roll was revered as much for his girating hips and simmering good looks as his voice.

MARILYN
Idolized by millions, Marilyn Monroe was the classic Hollywood sex symbol, doomed to die young.

STILETTO SHOE
The high-heeled shoe operates on two levels: it elongates the leg, thereby accentuating a Western symbol of femininity; and its spiky heel suggests domination.

ROCKET
The rocket is a classic phallic shape and an object of great power and thrust. In addition, it is symbolic of what is essentially a male urge to conquer: man-the-hunter sets out to penetrate the ultimate new frontier – space.

Sprouting leaves of plenty

CARVING, NORWICH CATHEDRAL CLOISTERS

GREEN MAN
The foliate head has continued as a symbol of life and fertility from a pre-Christian era well into this century. In church architecture it stands for the regenerative force of Christ himself. More recently it has been adopted as an ecological symbol for preserving and protecting nature.

PINE CONE
This vast bronze pine cone is part of an ancient Roman fountain. As the fruit of the pine tree it is a powerful symbol of life and fertility. The Romans associated it with Venus, goddess of love, and it is one of her emblems.

WHEAT SHEAF
The sheaf of wheat or corn is a well-known symbol of the fertility of the earth, and of growth and abundance. It represents the fruitful union of the sun and the soil.

CORNUCOPIA
The cornucopia is the horn of plenty, spilling over with fruit. It is a symbol of fertility and an attribute of gods of vegetation. Hollow and horn-shaped, it is both female and male.

BIRTH
Giving birth is the ultimate symbol of creation, and as such is mythologized throughout the world. In the West, babies often appear as if by miracle, snatched by storks from the cosmic waters. In other parts of the world the process is more direct – resulting from the blessed union of man and woman.

BIRTH PLATE
In this commemorative plate, a stork delivers a baby to its crib. In folklore, storks became associated with birth because of their renowned devotion to their young.

Woman giving birth, helped by two women

PERUVIAN CHILDBIRTH
A single act of creation mirroring the whole of creation, childbirth is seen as a moment of spiritual vulnerability and is surrounded by rituals. The umbilical cord is treated with respect as a link between worlds and often, as in Peru, would have been preserved by the family.

GODDESS OF FERTILITY
This gold figure represents Astarte, the Canaanite goddess of fertility, and dates from the 16th century BC. Although highly stylized, with a pubic triangle set within a larger one, the sexual organs are clearly defined.

The breasts are a prominent feature

Stylized pubic triangle

LOVERS
This Japanese print is an illustration from an 18th-century "pillow poem". It is one of thousands of erotic paintings depicting the union of male and female. The union can be seen as purely a sexual act or as the male and female principle combined in a symbolic act of creation. Illustrated stories about men taking their pleasure with courtesans were highly popular at the time.

THE POEM OF THE PILLOW, UTAMARO, 1788

SEE ALSO

BIRTH ☞ STORK 65; BREASTS 74

FERTILITY SYMBOLS ☞ EMERALD 40; ACORN 45; APPLE, DATE, FIG, ORANGE, PINEAPPLE, POMEGRANATE 48; EEL 54; VULVA 74; ELECTRIC GUITAR 80; BASKET 96

PHALLIC SYMBOLS ☞ SCEPTRE 89; PLOUGH 90; GUN, SPEAR 91; SKYSCRAPER 94

HUMAN BODY

THE HUMAN BODY is seen by many people as a microcosm of the universe. In some parts of the world buildings are laid out with this symbolism in mind. A Southeast Asian house, for example, has sections that correspond to the human head, body, and feet, the head area being the most sacred. In other parts of the world the body is referred to as the "temple of the soul". Composed metaphorically of the four elements, it can be seen as representing life, and linking gods and humans. Gods, in fact, frequently appear in human form, and the Bible tells us that "God made man in his own image".

HAMLET AT THE GRAVE

EYES

The eye symbolizes the sun, the all-seeing eye of God, and eternal watchfulness, as well as the power of evil. It is the window of the soul and the light of the body. The eyes on Buddhist shrines symbolize wisdom and omniscience, whereas the widespread belief in an "evil eye" – and the consequent need for a "lucky eye" – reflects the fear that curses can be transmitted with a single glance.

Watchful eyes of Buddha

ALL-SEEING SHRINE
Four pairs of eyes mark this Buddhist stupa in Nepal. These represent the eyes of the all-seeing Buddha, gazing out in all directions. The question-marklike nose is a symbol of unity, and slightly above each pair of eyes is a third eye representing the Buddha's clairvoyant powers.

Eye of sea monster wards off evil

PROW OF BOAT
The prow of this Portuguese fishing boat is painted with *oculi*, or great eyes. They see the dangers that lie ahead and also ward off evil. The eyes cause the boat to look like a great sea monster, thus deceiving the dangerous spirits of the ocean into keeping away.

LUNAR EYE
In ancient Egypt the right eye of Horus, the sky god, was his solar eye, and the left eye his "wadjet eye" or eye of the moon. This wadjet eye symbolizes the power of light and was one of the most sacred and powerful protective amulets in Egyptian magic.

EYE OF WISDOM
This 15th-century eye is an Islamic illustration based on an almond-shaped mandala. It represents the spiritual gateway that leads to the soul and to ultimate truth and wisdom. Within the soul's outer circle is a smaller, inner one which stands for a person's true spiritual centre.

EYE IDOL
This alabaster figure with oversized eyes (3500–3000 BC) is one of thousands of similar idols found at the Eye Temple at Tell Brak in present-day Syria. The temple derived its name from its cache of visionary figures.

SKULL
In this famous scene from Shakespeare's play, the prince holds the skull of Yorick, a former servant. The scene stresses the impermanence of life and the pointless vanity of worldly matters, both symbolized by the skull.

SKULL-AND-CROSSBONES
In the 1600s, a variation of the skull-and-crossbones emblem was adopted by pirates as a sinister warning of their evil intentions. It filled sailors with dread, signalling death to all who saw it.

TONGUE
The tongue is likened to a flame because of its colour and quick movements. It can be a fertility symbol and also represents the voice of the deity. In some churches, devotees speak "in tongues". Here the Indian goddess Kali's protuding tongue is a symbol of her creative and destructive energy.

Golden head of god-king

TROPHY HEAD, ASANTE

EARS
In the East, large earrings were once worn by kings and princes. The Buddha is usually shown with long ears, perhaps stretched by such earrings during his youth as a prince. Long ear lobes thus signify both royalty and spiritual authority.

NOSE
The nose may signify arrogance if it is raised or wrinkled. In literature it is often linked to the phallus – its size used as a veiled reference to male prowess. In the story *Pinocchio*, however, a big nose symbolizes dishonesty, since the puppet's nose grew whenever he lied.

TEETH
In many parts of the world teeth are ritually filed at puberty as a sign of beauty. In the animal world, baring the teeth is a sign of defence or threat, but in the well-known story of *Dracula* the fangs of the vampire draw blood from his innocent victims.

BRAIN
The brain is equated with the intellect. Its location in the skull gives the head its association, in Western cultures, as the seat of intelligence.

GROTTO ENTRANCE

HEAD
The head is widely seen as the seat of the life force within us and so is the most sacred part of the body. Head hunters sought to capture this life force, which was equated with fertility and power, and in Japan heads are bowed in greeting as a sign of respect. People in authority are known as the head of an organization. This golden head is that of a West African Asante king killed in battle.

MOUTH
The mouth gives judgement and so symbolizes the word. It can represent the all-devouring earth or a door into the realm of the unconscious. The demon, above, from a Baroque Italian garden, invites passers-by into his cavernous mouth.

HAIR

SAMSON & DELILAH (DETAIL), MANTEGNA, c.1500

Hair is often seen as holding the strength and energy of the body as it grows from the head, seat of spiritual power. In popular stories, hair worn loose denotes a free spirit, even wantonness, although in Christianity it represents penitence or the virgin saints. Often, when hair is covered, it is a sign of respect for God. Christian nuns cut their hair short to symbolize their renunciation of worldly vanity.

SAMSON AND DELILAH
In the Old Testament, Samson performs feats of extraordinary strength. Delilah discovers that his power lies in his long hair and betrays him to his enemies by cutting it off while he sleeps. Thus she renders him as weak and vulnerable as any other man.

DREADLOCKS
Dreadlocks are worn partly to show membership of the Rastafarian community, who, though mostly West Indian, look back to the ancient culture of Ethiopia. Wearing hair long and matted challenges the norms of everyday fashion.

SHAVEN HEADS
In many Buddhist sects, monks and nuns shave their heads as a sign of humility. By doing this they imitate the Buddha, who cut off his long hair when he embraced a life of asceticism.

THE HEART

To Christians the heart is the source of love, joy, sorrow, and compassion. Many Christian saints hold a heart as an attribute, sometimes pierced by arrows or crowned with thorns. In ancient Greece, the heart was the centre of thought, feeling, and will, while in Islam, it is the spiritual centre.

SACRED HEART
This French greetings card depicts the sacred heart of Jesus within a stylized crucifix. It combines a flaming heart surrounded by a crown of thorns with other Christian imagery.

LOVE
This is the classic symbol of love: Cupid's arrow pierces a heart and his victim is struck by the unexpected pleasure and pain of desire.

PLAYING CARDS
Hearts are one of the four suits in a standard pack of playing cards. They represent warmth and the heart of the world. The queen of hearts stands for love. The king is more powerful than her, but the ace is generally even more so, and to be "ace" is thus to be best.

HUMAN SACRIFICE
In Central America, human sacrifice was ritually practised as a form of communion with the gods; these deities were periodically fed to maintain cosmic order. For the Aztecs the heart was the centre of the life force, and it was this which had to be offered to the gods to ensure the fertility and the renewal of crops.

SPLEEN
In European and Arab countries the spleen is the seat of the humours: laughter, anger, ill-humour, and melancholy. To be "splenetic" is to be melancholy.

LIVER
In China the liver is linked to courage and filial duty. Elsewhere, to be "lily-livered" is to be cowardly.

INTESTINES
The twisting nature of the intestines gives them their symbolic relationship with the labyrinth of life. The Bible refers to the bowels of Christ, meaning compassion.

SKELETON
The personification of Death, the skeleton is often shown carrying a scythe or an hourglass as a reminder of the speedy passing of time.

RIBS
In the Old Testament, after God created Adam, he decided that Adam needed a companion. He therefore caused him to fall into a deep sleep and, according to Genesis, took out one of Adam's ribs and fashioned it into a woman – Eve. The rib is thus a symbol of woman, born from the body of man.

EARLY CHALK MAN, ENGLAND

PHALLUS
As symbol of fertility the male sexual organ represents the generative forces of nature and the Creator. An erect phallus is depicted in the art of many countries as a powerful symbol of regeneration and renewal. This English chalk figure from Cerne Abbas is 55m (180ft) high.

COCO-DE-MER, SOUTH INDIA

VULVA
This strange palm nut, known as a double coconut or coco-de-mer, is seen as a symbol of the female genitalia and so of fertility and creation. In India it was worshipped as a manifestation of the vulva of the earth goddess, and thus of all creative energy.

NAVEL
The ancient Greeks placed this huge stone carving in the sacred city of Delphi to mark the centre of the world. They believed that two birds flying from opposite ends of the earth would meet here, and so erected the *omphalos*, or navel, to physically represent the centre of the world, from which all creation originated. Its rounded top was a symbol of the point of connection between the realms of the gods, of humans, and of the dead.

BREASTS
Nowadays breasts are often seen as simply erotic. However in the past, and still in many cultures, they have symbolized motherhood, nourishment, and abundance. Fertility goddesses thousands of years old are depicted as large-breasted women, sometimes in the act of giving birth, making the link with maternity clear.

STONE-AGE VENUS, AUSTRIA

HANDS

Hands, by their gestures, can signify blessing, protection, justice, and authority. Healers often work through the "laying on of hands", and we speak of giving a "helping hand" when we assist someone. Two people holding hands is a sign of love and affection.

HAND OF THE FUTURE
This Roman hand was used in divination. It bears symbols such as a cockerel's head and a pinecone. These were linked to the cult of Bacchus and the visions of the future that arose out of drunken revelry.

HANDPRINTS OF THE STARS
In Hollywood, film stars leave their handprints in wet cement as a lasting testament to their fame. Thousands of fans try out the impressions to see how they match up to their idols.

JOINED HANDS
In 1973 a special fifty-pence piece was minted to commemorate Britain joining the European Economic Community. It features a series of hands clasped in a continuous circle of friendship.

HAND OF GOD
This Jewish symbol of strength and power is worn as a good-luck charm.

LEGS
The three-legged symbol has various meanings. It represents the swift-footed sun as it rises, sets, and ebbs each day. It is a symbol of good luck, like the swastika, symbolizing fertility and regeneration with its continuous cycle of footsteps, and it is also the chosen emblem of Sicily and the Isle of Man. The motto of the Isle of Man is *Quocunque Jeceris Stabit* – "whichever way it is thrown, it will stand".

ARMS
If raised, the arms may signify supplication or prayer. They may be raised in battle (bearing weapons) or in surrender (open-palmed). Generally, the arm symbolizes action. The arm of justice is a common metaphor, as is the "strong arm of the law". In Eastern religious iconography, arms represent power. Thus a many-armed deity represents the many-powered nature of the god.

SPINE
This Egyptian djed-pillar represents the backbone of Osiris and symbolizes stability – both the stability of the pharaoh's rule and that of the heavens, which the pillar supported. The spinal column as the central support of the body is a symbol of the world axis.

VIETNAMESE NOBLE, C.1880

FEET
In the West, bare feet are a sign of humility and poverty, thus pilgrims often went barefoot. The foot is the most lowly part of the body and in parts of Asia it is rude to sit with one's feet pointing at another person. In the footprint of Vishnu, above, the symbols on the sole relate to his nature or incarnation. Buddha's footprints bear auspicious symbols of the universe to demonstrate how far above wordly considerations he has risen.

FINGERNAILS
In the 19th century, long nails were evidence of wealth in eastern Asia, since they implied exemption from manual work, which was left to others. Some African cultures share the belief, although often restricting it to the little finger.

SEE ALSO
EYES ☞ MAGIC EYE 79; WINDOW 94; LUCKY EYE 100; TRACING BOARD, SIGN LANGUAGE 109
FEET ☞ FOOTPRINT 22
HANDS ☞ HAND OF GOD 24; CORAL 38; LOVE RING, MOURNING JEWELLERY 87
LEGS ☞ TRISKELE 105
TEETH ☞ TOOTH FAIRY 79

DANCE & THEATRE

DANCING IS MOVEMENT, ENERGY, EXCITEMENT. It is a part of everyday life as a symbol of pleasure and as a ritual of courtship. In different cultures it is associated with initiation ceremonies, fertility rites, rain, war, and death. It is used in harvest festivals to improve the crop and in war rituals to induce a state of frenzy. Many of today's dances have developed from earlier rituals: Britain's maypole dance, for example, has its roots in Greek and Roman rites of spring. Drama, with its more controlled actions and gestures, provides us with a symbolic representation of the world we live in.

WAR DANCE
Native American tribes of the plains, such as the Hidatsa, were formed into military "Dog Societies". The Dog dancer, Pehriska-Ruhpa (Two Ravens) enacts a war dance to enlist the aid of spirits and to prepare the warrriors for battle.

WHIRLING DERVISHES
In their ecstatic dances the whirling dervishes (holy men) of Turkey pace out the turning of the earth on its axis as it orbits the sun. Through the dance, the dervish symbolically brings the spiralling of the universe into being.

LORD OF THE DANCE
Encircled by a ring of fire and on the back of the dwarf of ignorance, the Hindu god Shiva dances out the end of one age and the start of another. He enacts death and rebirth in one frenzied dance. With his drum, Shiva beats out the pulse of the universe and the pounding of the heart.

The river Ganges borne in the hair of Shiva

Shiva's hand drum

PUPPETS
Puppets are scaled-down versions of men and women, or the gods they believe in, and their performances often concern human behaviour. The puppets' appearance, their clothing, and their actions are often symbolic.

JAVANESE SHADOW PUPPET

MARIONETTES
In Burma, string puppets are used to act out epic stories involving princes and deeds of valour. These moral fables serve to inspire noble deeds in others.

SWORD DANCE
Dances involving swords occur all over the world. They were probably used to ward off evil spirits and to strengthen the power of the sword in battle. Some sword dances end with a motion symbolizing the cutting off of a head, suggesting a link with ancient rites of sacrifice.

The ribbons form a pattern around the pole

SHADOW PUPPET
The famous shadow puppets of Java and Bali enact the great epics of Hinduism. The flickering shadows projected onto a white screen create a world of mystery in which the stories of the gods and heroes are filled with symbolic meaning.

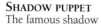

MAYPOLE DANCE
The dance around the maypole has been performed since Greek and Roman times to celebrate spring. In Britain it is often associated with May Day celebrations. The maypole represents the earth's axis and also acts as a phallic symbol, representing male fertility.

GREEK TRAGEDY

In ancient Greece, drama presented a powerfully symbolic portrayal of human behaviour and emotions. By resolving huge issues such as jealousy, love, and incest, such performances enabled the audience to identify with the characters and overcome anxieties in the process. Thus drama often had a healing effect.

MIME

Mime is a symbolic form of drama that is enacted without words. It uses only expressions and gestures to convey meaning, and so can be "read" universally.

Flames in ring of fire symbolize purification and destruction of illusion

THAI DANCERS

The costumes of Thai dancers make them look like heavenly creatures. Their stylized dance movements reinforce this impression.

CLASSICAL INDIAN DANCE GESTURES

Hand gestures used in classical Indian dance are also used in modified form in Southeast Asia. They represent moods, actions, and objects or creatures. Every movement of the dancer is symbolic and has meaning.

HEAR

SPEAK

BEAUTIFUL

SORROWFUL

Dwarf of ignorance under Shiva's feet

BIRDS

FLOWER

MASKS

GREEK COMEDY MASK

Because they present other faces and other realities, masks are used everywhere in dance and drama. In many sacred rituals they are worn to represent the gods or ancestors. In Japanese Noh theatre the actors are masked, and they "dance" the moments of greatest intensity.

GREEK TRAGEDY MASK

CHANGING FACES

Native American Kwakiutl dancers can take on more than one identity with a "transformation mask". When the dancer pulls levers and strings, the outer mask opens up to reveal another.

Strings pull back to form beaked eagle head

KWAKIUTL TRANSFORMATION MASK

NOH MASK

The Japanese Noh theatre is distinctive for its use of painted wooden masks. The masks represent five general groups – male, female, the aged, deities, and monsters – as well as certain emotions.

HUSK MASK

Native American Iroquois dancers wear masks of plaited maize husk for their midwinter ceremonies, when they call on spirits for a good harvest.

"THE DYING SWAN"

BALLET

Like other dance forms, ballet uses costume and gestures to convey meaning. A ballerina fluttering in white tulle, for example, can convincingly suggest the death throes of a swan.

MAGIC & CHARMS

THROUGH FAIRY TALES WE BECOME AWARE OF the world of magic and ritual at an early age. As adults, many things in life remain mysterious to us so what we cannot explain by rational means we try to explain by magic; and similarly, when we find ourselves powerless to control the forces that affect us, we look to magic. Many people still use spells to cure illness, to harm enemies, or to ensnare a lover. Even the sceptical among us may wear lucky charms, avoid walking under ladders, and consult fortune tellers. Magic and ritual, though disparaged by some as superstition, are still practised by many people throughout the world.

FENG SHUI COMPASS
Feng Shui is an ancient Chinese art based on living in harmony with one's surroundings. Using this compass Feng Shui diviners locate the right combinations of elements, such as time, wind, and water, to determine the best site for homes, temples, or burial grounds.

WITCH
According to folklore, witches could fly on broomsticks and cast spells. In the past, they were thought to be in league with the devil and thus were symbols of evil. In Europe many women healers were unjustly branded as witches and by 1700 over 200,000 had been put to death.

FIVE-POINTED STAR
The five-pointed star, upside-down, was a symbol of evil. Pointing up, as here, it symbolized light and spirituality, and was painted on houses to ward off witches.

MIRROR OF TRUTH

MIRROR
The mirror symbolizes divine truth and the wisdom of the universe. This "vision" is shattered if a mirror is broken, and it is a popular superstition that seven years' bad luck will follow.

LOVE POTION

THE LOVE POTION, EVELYN DE MORGAN, 1903

W̲hen all else failed, unsuccessful lovers often resorted to magic to beguile the object of their desires. This could take the form of love potions, usually made from phallic-shaped ingredients such as the mandrake root, ginseng, or ginger, plus an appropriate spell. Many foods are reputed to be aphrodisiacs or love enhancers, and are used in much the same way as the age-old love potion.

LOVE-STRUCK PAIR

EGYPTIAN MAGIC KNIFE

Serpent armed with knife

CHINESE COIN SWORD

Coins strung together to cover sword shape

MONEY CURES
Money is a symbol of power, and so by extension it has come to be imbued with spiritual, as well as practical, properties. In China, a sword made of coins was hung over the bed of a sick person to dispel the demons or evil spirits that might be causing the illness.

EGYPTIAN KNIFE
This curved knife of animal bone was used in Ancient Egypt to strengthen the weak parts of a house. It would have been drawn against the relevant area to create a magical protective barrier. The various animals and patterns depicted on it endow the knife with their collective power.

NATIVE AMERICAN LOVE CHARMS

LOVE DOLLS
These male (right) and female (left) dolls were used by Native American witch doctors as medicine. In the Menominee tribe, the dolls were given the names of a couple and tied facing each other, to make sure they remained faithful to one other. In the Potawatomi tribe, they were used as love charms to draw two people together.

FOUR-LEAF CLOVER
Finding a clover with four rather than three leaves is so rare that a four-leaf clover has become a widespread symbol of good luck. The four leaves are supposed to represent fame, wealth, a faithful lover, and good health – all important components of happiness.

HORSESHOE
The horseshoe is made of iron which has power over the Evil Eye. It brings luck if it is hung on a door with the open end uppermost, as it will then catch good luck and hold it safely. If it is hung upside down, it is considered unlucky as the luck will run out.

DICE
Dice represent chance – the random pairing of numbers symbolizing life's unpredictability. Thus the phrase "the die is cast" means that one's fate has been decided. Dice are also a Christian symbol: after Christ was crucified, Roman soldiers threw dice for his cloak.

MAGIC EYE
A belief in the Evil Eye is widespread in the Mediterranean and the Near East. Charms that look like eyes are thought to turn away the Evil Eye or deflect the look of anyone with evil intentions. Such charms are often made of glass to make them seem lifelike.

MAGIC CARPET
Riding on a magic carpet is the stuff of many dreams. Flying symbolizes release of the spirit and overcoming all physical limitations. King Solomon had a flying carpet, which carried him, his throne, and both his armies wherever he wished. In *The 1001 Nights*, Aladdin flew on a carpet.

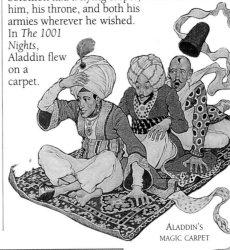

ALADDIN'S MAGIC CARPET

POWER TO PROTECT
Many people wear charms about their bodies to protect them from illness and danger. These charms vary from amulets worn by babies to those worn by soldiers in battle. Certain objects and images are also used in healing the sick and are thought to actually absorb the illness, thus ridding the sick person of disease.

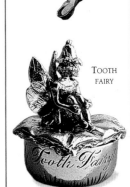

LIGHT CURE
A crystal will refract light in many directions. It is thought that when the crystal is placed on the body, its energy will be absorbed and have a healing effect.

HEALING CRYSTAL

TOOTH FAIRY

TOOTH FAIRY
Fairies people children's stories, as well as their imaginations. They have magical powers and are generally symbols of goodness – fairy godmothers can right the wrongs of the world. Here a tooth fairy guards a lost tooth, and collects money for it.

ROMAN VOTIVE LEG

VOTIVE LEG
Gifts are often promised to gods in return for a favour, such as curing an illness. This bronze votive leg, dedicated by a Roman called Caledus, was probably a symbol of his gratitude for having been cured of a leg injury or infection.

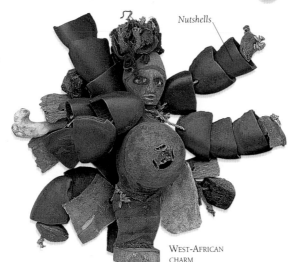

Nutshells

WEST-AFRICAN CHARM

FOR GOOD HEALTH
The Nte'va people of the Upper Congo in West Africa use little figures, such as this one made up of rags, bone, leather, nuts, and wood, to "watch over one's body", so protecting them from illness.

THE SPIRIT OF SMALLPOX

AMULETIC SHIRT
This Burmese undershirt is covered with charms, spells, and horoscope details. It was made to protect its wearer, probably in battle. In the past, many Burmese men had tattoos with similar markings.

WITCH'S FAMILIAR
Because toads eat spiders, they are thought to be able to repel evil and poisonous things. Parts of the toad were often included in magic potions.

AFRICAN CURE
This Nigerian figure, covered in spots that represent the smallpox rash, symbolizes the disease itself. When treated with spells and incantations by witch doctors, the figure can cure the illness – or cause it.

SEE ALSO
CLOVER ☞ SHAMROCK 46
POWER TO PROTECT ☞ CORAL 38; AZTEC TURQUOISE MASK, RUBY 40; AGATE, CORNELIAN, JADE, JET HAND 41; RELIGION, SUPERSTITION, & MAGIC 41; FLY 56; PACIFIC CHARM 86
STAR ☞ STAR OF DAVID 16, 115; STAR & CRESCENT 24; ISRAEL 115; EUROPEAN FLAG 116
WITCH ☞ BLACK CAT 60; WITCH'S FAMILIAR 79

MUSICAL INSTRUMENTS

MUSICAL INSTRUMENTS SYMBOLIZE harmony and oneness with nature, the beat being the pulse of life. They bring pleasure but may spell danger, pipes in particular having the power to lure listeners to their doom. Stringed instruments represent the sounds of the heavens while percussion instruments are associated with divine truth, revelation, and ecstasy.

BURMESE GONG CIRCLE

Dragons symbolize celestial power

ELECTRIC GUITAR
Since the 1950s the electric guitar has come to symbolize youth and rebellion, with groups vying with each other to create the loudest sounds. The guitar itself has male associations, with certain musicians using it in performance as an exaggerated phallic symbol.

DRUMS

The drum symbolizes the first sounds, divine truth, and speech. It is associated with the symbolism of thunder and lightning, and to Native Americans the drum represents the heart of the universe. Drums are traditionally used to accompany dance throughout the world and are a vital component of ecstatic dance.

The motto "Celer et audax" means "speed and courage"

MILITARY DRUM
Once used to accompany soldiers into battle, the rousing, regular beat of the drum became associated with warfare. Nowadays this military rhythm is an integral part of the brass or marching band.

AFRICAN DRUM
In Africa the drum is highly symbolic and forms an essential part of ritual dance. It represents the beat of the human heart and is played to summon up magic powers.

GONG
The gong is traditionally used in Buddhist temples to mark the stages of the service and to ward off evil spirits. It is a valued religious object in the East and is often highly ornate, as in this example found in Borneo. In secular use, sounding the gong signals a call to dinner, particularly in a formal setting.

CYMBALS
These ancient percussion instruments date back to 3000 BC and are still widely used today. In worship they symbolize contact with the heavens, and in Tibetan temples they are sounded in the worship of Buddhist deities.

MU-YU
Mu-yu means wooden fish in Chinese. These instruments are played in temples and are symbolic of ceaseless prayer because, like fish, they never seem to sleep.

INDIAN TABLAS
The drum is an attribute of the Indian god Shiva, who beats out the pulse of the universe on it as he dances his great dance of birth, death, and purification.

TIBETAN BELL
The bell symbolizes contact between heaven and earth. It rings out the voice of the divine and the harmony of the cosmos. In the West the church bell is a call to prayer, but can also be sounded as a warning. The sanctus bell at the altar announces the coming of Christ. In Buddhist countries it is rung or struck after devotions, while small bells sounding in the wind represent the gentle sounds of heaven.

Headdress of Buddhist monk

CHINESE ZITHER
A Chinese scholar should be accomplished in the four arts – literature, painting, chess, and music – and the zither, or *qin*, was the symbol of music. According to Chinese lore, a zither played by a sage had the power to reveal to him the essential truth. The mother-of-pearl discs mark finger positions.

ORPHEUS' LYRE
Orpheus, musician to the gods, enchanted all animals through his playing of the lyre and even succeeded in calming a storm-tossed ocean. In his hands the music of the lyre calmed all beings, causing them to be aware only of him. The lyre's seven strings corresponded to the seven known planets, and its sides to the relationship between heaven and earth.

LUTE
Popular in Europe from the mid-15th century, the lute is an attribute of music. It is also a symbol of purity and faithfulness. In Western art, when shown with a broken string it signifies discord.

TRUMPETS
The trumpet or bugle was blown as a call to arms in Roman times and has been associated with battle or fame ever since. Traditionally, a trumpet fanfare heralds the arrival of royalty or important persons, and the post horn announced the arrival of the mail coach.

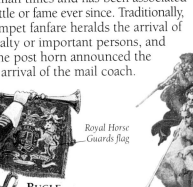

Royal Horse Guards flag

BUGLE
The bugle heralds the morning and evening in military camps. On Remembrance Day a two-minute silence is followed by the call to Reveille, to symbolize both mourning and a fanfare for the resurrected souls.

THE LAST JUDGEMENT
Both the Bible and the Koran state that the trumpet will be sounded on the Last Day, when the dead shall be raised.

THE LAST JUDGEMENT (DETAIL), MICHELANGELO, 1536-41

CEREMONIAL TRUMPET
The trumpet, with its masculine and authoritative associations, is used at ceremonies and grand occasions in many countries.

Moroccan ceremonial trumpet

Gold Irish shamrocks on national green

IRISH HARP

HARP
An attribute of King David in the Old Testament, the harp symbolizes sacred music in both Judaism and Christianity, and angels are frequently depicted playing harps. St Augustine explains the ten commandments in terms of the ten strings in David's harp. In Celtic lore, the harp is an attribute of the fire god Dagda, and the harp is a symbol of both Ireland and Wales.

SHENG
The Chinese mouth organ originated 3,000 years ago and is made up of 17 individual bamboo pipes bound together and held within a mouthpiece. It is a very ancient symbol of the phoenix which it is said to resemble. The sheng is played at weddings and funerals.

Krishna's flute

FLUTE
The shape of the flute gives it a phallic, masculine dimension while its tone is gentle and feminine. In Hinduism, Krishna's flute is said to be the voice of eternity calling all living beings to himself. More generally, the flute is sometimes associated with anguish and extremes of emotion. In Christianity it symbolizes the soul's longing for God.

ORGAN
A church instrument, the organ has come to symbolize the praise of God. St Cecilia, patron saint of music, is said to have invented it and dedicated it to the service of the Lord.

PAN PIPES
Played nowadays in the Andean region of South America, pan pipes represent the harmony of nature. In Greek legend they were carried by the god Pan and by satyrs, and had the power to entrance all who heard them.

SEE ALSO
BELL ☞ PIECE OF CAKE 83
BUGLE ☞ WREATH OF RED 93
DRUMS ☞ LORD OF THE DANCE 76
GONG ☞ BUDDHISM 22-23
KRISHNA ☞ KRISHNA 20; KRISHNA'S LOVE 82; BLUE-SKINNED GOD 107

LOVE & MARRIAGE

A POPULAR VIEW IS THAT LOVE MAKES THE WORLD GO ROUND. Love is central to life – the force which has inspired poets, writers, and artists from time immemorial the world over. Love binds man to woman, mother to child. It can be sexual, the powerful attraction of opposing and complementary forces found in nature, or platonic, the deep, binding emotion that forms the fabric of our society. In a more spiritual context, love reflects the longing of the soul for God or ultimate truth. The sexual act is then an expression of the soul's urge to merge with the cosmos.

LIPS
Lips pursed into a kiss are a classic symbol of love or sexual attraction and the red lipstick kiss ends many a passionate love letter. Lipstick on the collar, instead, signals infidelity.

Lovers transformed into doves

The willow, which shed its leaves as they made their escape

CHINESE WILLOW-PATTERN PLATE

THE TWO SIDES OF LOVE

VENUS AND CUPID, LUCAS CRANACH THE ELDER, 1545

This painting shows Cupid at his mother's side, in tears because he has been stung by bees. Venus, in response, reproves Cupid for inflicting more painful wounds on others than bee stings. Both Venus and Cupid are gods of love and here represent the two sides of love – the pleasure and the pain. The fact that Cupid is covered in bees is symbolic of love's sting in the tail.

HONEYCOMB OF PURITY AND SWEETNESS

WILLOW-PATTERN
This plate reflects the story of Koong-see and her lover Chang. The girl's father forbids their marriage but the lovers flee just as the willow tree sheds its leaves. When soldiers pursue them and kill Chang, Koong-see, heart-broken, sets fire to herself. The lovers are then transformed into doves, emblems of their constancy.

Winged Cupid

Twin hearts aflame

Red roses, symbols of passionate love

Valentine's card speeding to its destination

White turtle dove of love and fidelity

Forget-me-nots, symbols of yearning

VICTORIAN VALENTINE CARD

KRISHNA AND RADHA, KANGRA MINIATURE, c.1785

KRISHNA'S LOVE
In this scene Krishna sits in a forest glade with Radha, his favourite *gopi*, or milkmaid. All the *gopis* love Krishna, the embodiment of heavenly love, but Radha is the one who captures his heart. The love of the *gopis* for Krishna represents the longing of the soul to merge with God.

VALENTINE CARD
The valentine card first appeared in the 16th century, with its imagery reaching the height of sentimentality in Victorian times. Exchanged on St Valentine's day, February 14, these cards often depict love symbols such as hearts, doves, and cupids. Valentine's day was originally known as the "birds' wedding day" from an old belief that birds selected their mates on that day. People then followed suit and made it a day for declarations of love.

MARRIAGE

The ritual of marriage is conducted in some form in every society and is traditionally a contract uniting two families. In some cases a man may marry more than one wife while occasionally, as in Nepal and Tibet, a woman marries several brothers. Whatever form the marriage takes, it is a celebration that symbolizes the union of god and goddess, heaven and earth, man and woman, and the uniting of opposites to form the complete whole.

Bright clothes symbolize luck and fertility

CHINESE WEDDING
Chinese legend recounts how the man in the moon ties invisible threads around the legs of newborn boys and girls to link their destinies. When they grow up they are irresistibly drawn to each other, and marriage is inevitable.

WEDDING BANDS
The custom of giving engagement rings goes back to Roman times although the traditional diamond ring – symbol of faithfulness – dates from the 15th century. The plain gold band of the wedding ring symbolizes eternity and the cycle of life.

ENGAGEMENT AND WEDDING RINGS

PIECE OF CAKE
The wedding cake has been part of wedding celebrations since Roman times. Bride and groom must cut the first slice together to symbolize lifelong harmony, and their eating of the cake is associated with sexuality. Sharing the cake among the guests represents the union of the two families.

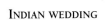

Bride and groom, united on the cake, united in life

Silver bells to ward off evil spirits

A chimney sweep wishing a bride happiness is a particularly good omen

Horseshoe of good luck

Red roses of love and passion

INDIAN WEDDING
An Indian bride's red sari stands for fertility. Here the bridal couple is literally bedecked with good wishes. The fragrant garlands of roses and tuberoses represent beauty and happiness, while the bank notes are symbolic of prosperity.

Decorative lace-like tracery is considered auspicious

HENNAED HANDS
In the Middle East and India, brides' hands are intricately painted in red for good luck. The red colouring comes from the dye of the henna plant. A bride's appearance would be incomplete without it.

CONFETTI

RICE

BLESSINGS
The practice of showering newly married couples with confetti comes from an older, Eastern tradition in which rice, a symbol of fertility, was thrown so that the couple might be blessed with many children. In Saxon times red and white rose petals were thrown to represent the union of passion and purity.

Symbol of good luck, particularly when tied to back of newlyweds' car

---

LOCKET

SILVER LOCKET
The heart is the classic symbol of love, although it also represents sincerity and compassion. Heart-shaped lockets, with either a photograph of a loved one or perhaps a lock of their hair, are common gifts of friendship.

WINGED HEART INSIGNIA

WINGED HEART
This symbol combines the emblem of the heart, representing love, with the characteristic wings of Cupid or Eros, god of love. A doubly powerful image, it represents the capacity of love to penetrate the heart of anyone.

I ❤ NY
BUMPER STICKER

HEART AS WORD
In the "I love New York" logo the heart is universally recognized as a symbol of love, making the use of the word itself unnecessary. This is one of the most modern and familiar versions of the pictogram.

CHOCOLATE

CHOCOLATE HEART
With aphrodisiac as well as romantic connotations, chocolate has long been the food of love, given at times of celebration or as a token of affection. This heart-shaped chocolate is probably a Valentine's day gift.

BROKEN HEART

HEART-BROKEN
The phrase "to be broken-hearted" has wound its way into our language and imagery. The heart splits in two, representing the ultimate pain of grief or loss. Spurned lovers have broken hearts as do those separated from the ones they love.

CLOTHING

CLOTHING IS AN EMOTIVE ISSUE, reflecting the ways in which society regards individuals in terms of sex and status, and also how individuals regard themselves. What you wear says a great deal about who you are, or who you wish to be. More powerful members of society tend to wear more elaborate clothing in public, for instance, and it is often of finer, more expensive, cloth. Clothes can be sensible or seductive, businesslike or frivolous. Youth characteristically dons clothing to denote rebellion, although youth fashions often develop into mainstream fashions.

MATERIALS

The materials we choose to wear are highly significant. Slinky synthetics, for example, show a pride in one's body and flirtatiousness. Cotton, by contrast, is functional and economic; Gandhi spun his own as a symbol of India's independence and would wear nothing else.

SILK
Spun by silkworms fed on mulberry leaves, silk has always represented luxury.

LACE
Lace was a symbol of privilege. It was made by working women for the upper classes.

COTTON
Traditionally worn by working people, homespun cotton is a symbol of simplicity.

TARTAN
The chequered patterns of tartans are like heraldic devices, each denoting a Scottish clan.

FUR
In some cultures fur is functional, in others it is a luxury or a symbol of cruel death.

LEATHER
Leather is functional and readily available. Today it is often associated with youth culture.

FIG LEAF
The fig leaf, as the very first item of clothing, symbolizes a loss of innocence, modesty, and shame. Adam and Eve donned fig leaves when they first noticed their nakedness.

RUSSIAN NAVY SAILOR'S SHIRT

SAILOR'S TOP
The traditional sailor-suit, or matelot shirt, is woven with horizontal blue and white stripes. The blue of the stripes is called navy blue, or just navy, as it is thought to represent the colour of the sea.

17TH-CENTURY BUCKLE

ORNATE SILVER BUCKLE

BELT BUCKLES
For western men, buckles are a way of showing individuality. The lower one belonged to a South-American gaucho.

BLUE JEANS
Originating in the 1850s as hard-wearing clothes for cowboys, jeans have become one of the most popular items of clothing worldwide.

KENYAN TRIBESMAN
This East African warrior wears simple clothing and distinctive jewellery. This suits his active hunting lifestyle – and he would feel undressed without his staff or spear. In this and many similar societies, individuality is expressed more through jewellery than through clothing.

FASHIONS IN FOOTWEAR

Shoe styles reflect social and cultural attitudes and tell us something about a person. To remove shoes on entering a temple or home is symbolic of leaving earthly matters outside the door as a mark of respect.

DOC MARTEN
Doc Marten first made protective working boots in 1967, and they were the runaway success story of the '80s and '90s, symbolizing working class credibility.

GLASS SLIPPER
In the tale of *Cinderella*, the glass slipper represents truth and transformation. When Cinderella's foot fits into the shoe she left at the ball, the prince recognizes her, and she is transformed from pauper to princess.

PLATFORM SHOE
Platform shoes have been in and out of fashion for centuries. These date from the 1970s. They are the literal embodiment of the human desire to "walk tall".

14TH-CENTURY SHOE
These shoes, worn by noblemen, reached an amazing 46cm (18in). A status symbol to some, the clergy viewed them as the work of the devil.

JAPANESE CLOG
These Japanese shoes are for outdoor use. Their deep wooden soles – some 10cm (4in) high – add stature to the wearer and induce a delicate gait.

CHINESE SHOE
Until early this century, it was common in China to bind women's feet. Symbolically tiny feet reinforced the image of women as delicate and helpless, as well as preventing them from straying.

TRAINER
Sports shoes have become the status symbols of our time, with accompanying high prices. They are worn as walking shoes by both men and women, and create the image of a fit and healthy lifestyle.

HEADGEAR

In most cultures, the covering or uncovering of the head is redolent with meaning. Depending on the religion, places of worship require covered heads or uncovered ones. Hats are a sign of respect as well as an immediate indication of status and occupation.

KITCHEN ORDERLY

SOUS CHEF

MASTER CHEF

CHEF'S ORDER
The relationship between height and status is evident in the range of chef's hats, from lowly dish-washer to respected master chef.

TOP HAT
Immortalized by the dancer Fred Astaire, the top hat came into fashion in the 1820s, and remains the ultimate symbol of male elegance. Worn less often nowadays, it complements the tailcoat at weddings and other formal occasions.

BERET
The circular beret is associated both with peace and war. In navy blue, it is the classic symbol of the French working man; in other colours, notably red and green, it is a symbol of military courage and excellence.

18TH-CENTURY WIG
Wigs were worn by both sexes in the 18th century. They were a sign of affluence and high status.

FEZ
This was part of Turkish national dress until the country became a republic in 1923, and the hat was outlawed.

CHADAR WITH VEIL
In orthodox Muslim countries, women are veiled outside the home so as not to draw male desire.

MORTAR-BOARD
Derived from a cap worn by the Roman Catholic clergy, the mortar-board is now a symbol of erudition.

EXTRAVAGANZA
At Ladies Day at the Ascot race course in England, women traditionally wear outrageous hats.

TURBAN
Made of bright material, this West African turban is worn on important occasions and confers status.

CLASSIC S-SHAPED CORSET

CORSET
Corsets of the early 1900s were reinforced with whalebone and were designed to exaggerate the natural curves of a woman's body. A tiny waist was the ideal, and corsets have come to symbolize the way in which women willingly subject themselves to pain in the pursuit of fashion.

KID GLOVES

GLOVES
Originally gloves were a symbol of power and gentility, and were presented as part of investiture ceremonies. Until recently, a lady or a gentleman was expected to always wear gloves in public. In everyday speech, to handle "with kid gloves" is to treat someone or something with the utmost care, and to "throw down the gauntlet" represents a challenge.

HEDGEHOG PRESERVATION   "ART" TIE

TIES
Given the fairly rigid code of dress that men are expected to conform to, ties are one of the few areas of self-expression open to them. A man may choose to wear a club tie or military tie to signify his affiliation to that organization, or he can strike out in any number of more individual ways.

EDWARDIAN DRESS
This fashionable figure shows how Edwardian dresses distorted the body. The bust was pushed forwards and the hips back in what was known as the S-shape. It was not unusual for women to faint from the pressure on their lungs.

The high lace neck suggests modesty

Diminutive waist – fashion fights nature

Gloves as symbols of gentility

JEWELLERY

TRADITIONALLY, JEWELLERY IS BOUGHT AS A GIFT and tends to mark the important stages or events in a person's life – from christening to 21st birthday, wedding, and anniversary presents, as well as more familiar tokens of love or friendship. Its symbolism lies not so much in its form as in what the item represents; whether it is the plain gold ring which binds a man and woman together or a locket with a loved one's photograph. Much of our jewellery has ancient origins: a child's charm bracelet is essentially a modern version of amuletic jewellery – the charms protect the wearer from harm.

SERPENT NECKLACE, c.1870

THAI EARRINGS
A love of intricacy and delicacy is visible in these 18th-century earrings. Made from gold-painted animal skin, they represent mythical creatures.

EGYPTIAN COINS
Although jewellery often symbolizes wealth, in many cultures the relationship is more direct – jewellery actually is wealth. On marrying, girls are given coin necklaces, headbands, and belts as part of their dowry. The wealthier the family, the greater the value of the coins.

ROPES OF BEADS WORN AS NECKLACES AND WAISTBANDS

White beads indicate love
Pink beads usually indicate "bride price"

AFRICAN BEADS
In Africa, beads are a form of communication as well as decoration. They have particular meanings according to the colour of the beads and the order in which they are strung. Young girls will make "love letter" necklets for their boyfriends to wear. After marriage, girls are allowed to adorn themselves with more and more strings to show their heightened status.

BEAR CLAWS
This necklace, made from the claws of several bears, was the prize possession of a Native American chief. Like other pieces made from nails, teeth, or tusks, it denoted both status, because of the prowess involved in killing the bear, and the bear's power.

FRUITFULNESS

Symbols of fertility abound in the jewellery of different cultures, from Egyptian cowrie-shell amulets to the Spanish *higa* or clenched fist. The concern with fertility may be less marked now, but it is still around, as in the decorative examples of fruit shown here.

VICTORIAN VINE BROOCH

AMETHYST GRAPES
This cluster of grapes may well have been a wedding present from groom to bride – grapes are an ancient symbol of fertility. Grapes were associated with all the pleasures – and excesses – of wine.

LEG ORNAMENT
In parts of Africa, jewellery denotes the wealth of a woman, just as the number of goats or sheep signified that of a man. Leg ornaments are prized both for their craftsmanship and their bulk, some weighing as much as 15kg (33lb). This leg ornament shows Islamic influences, as Muslims prefer silver, signifying purity, to gold.

PACIFIC CHARM
This 17th-century necklet from the Cook Islands conferred power and protection on its wearer. Although jewellery made from wild beasts was quite common in many cultures, this piece is unusual. The bones and teeth are carved into talismanic shapes rather than being worn in their natural state.

ANCIENT GREEK PENDANT

POMEGRANATE
This pendant was made by a Mycenean craftsman c.1300 BC and would almost certainly have been worn by a young bride. The many-seeded pomegranate has widespread associations with fertility.

VINE LEAVES
Dating from around 1850, this gold pendant is covered in grape vines, symbols of Bacchus, Roman god of wine and revelry.

SIGNET RING
Examples of swivelling signet rings date back to the 15th century BC. They were both functional and a mark of status since only a person of considerable wealth could have his image carved onto a stone. By pressing the ring onto damp clay the owner was able to seal and identify his goods.

MOURNING JEWELLERY
The death of a loved one is marked by stages of ritual and symbolic behaviour. People adopt different colours of dress and shed their everyday jewellery in favour of more sombre forms of adornment to demonstrate that they are in mourning. In the West, black is the traditional colour of mourning, and jet the classic stone.

RING
In the 17th century, finger rings such as the one above would have been handed out to relatives at a funeral.

LOCK OF HAIR
The brooch below swivels so that it can be viewed from both sides. The back holds a lock of hair, symbol of an absent friend.

This dove bears the heart of a loved one

GLOVED HAND
This jet brooch is of a gloved hand holding a funeral wreath.

UNDYING LOVE
Jet became popular during Queen Victoria's reign when mourning jewellery was at its most fashionable.

CHARM BRACELET
Silver charm bracelets were thought to protect the wearer – often a child – from harm. This one has a lucky horseshoe, a wishing well, and a wise monkey, plus a fish and a frog for fertility. The fashion of wearing charm bracelets is relatively recent – a specifically western, 20th-century form of amuletic jewellery.

CHINESE PADLOCK
In China this lock is traditionally given by a father to his child in order to lock in the child's spirit and stop evil forces from stealing it. One hundred families contribute towards the purchase of the lock. They become the child's guardians, bound to protect the child throughout his or her life.

30TH ANNIVERSARY
A symbol of beauty and perfection, the pearl has long been the jewel of love. If the diamond is the "king of jewels", the pearl is the queen. Pearls are the birthstones of those born in June and are the gems used to mark the 30th wedding anniversary.

ENGAGEMENT RING
The custom of giving engagement rings goes back to Roman times. The rings were often plain iron circles, the shape symbolizing the cycle of life and eternity. In the 15th century diamonds – emblems of fidelity – were added to these simple bands. In addition to fidelity, diamonds were thought to protect against all the forces of evil.

FORGET-ME-NOT
Flower jewellery takes on the symbolism of the particular flower involved. In giving this brooch, an admirer was probably hoping that he would not be forgotten.

VICTORIAN BUCKLE BRACELET
Jewellery with buckles was popular in the 1800s, both as rings and as bracelets. What they represented, however subtly, was an era of male dominance. The man gave the piece to a loved one and in doing up the buckle she, willingly or unwittingly, accepted the symbol of his ownership.

LOVE RING
Love rings became fashionable in the 18th century. Made of interconnecting hoops, they had hands which clasped together to enclose a central heart. Part of their romantic symbolism lies in the fact that the rings can never, ultimately, be separated.

LUCKY AT THE HUNT
During the heyday of hunting, jewel-studded foxes, hounds, and riders were very much in vogue. The items were worn for luck, as well as being symbols of the landed gentry.

SYMBOL OF LOVE
This 18th-century choker with its clasped hands is a classic emblem of love. Hands are often represented in jewellery and take on different meanings depending on the position of the fingers. A single hand with thumb and forefinger touching, for example, is a talisman against evil; a fist, instead, is a symbol of fertility.

FAMILY MEMENTO
Before the era of the camera, those who could afford it commissioned miniature enamelled portraits of their loved ones. Fashionable ladies could then keep their children close to their heart at all times.

SEE ALSO
AFRICAN BEADS ☞ ROSARY 18; PRAYER BEADS 25; CORAL 38

CHARM BRACELET ☞ EGYPTIAN LUCKY GIRDLE 55

ENGAGEMENT RING, LOVE RING ☞ WEDDING BANDS 83

FRUITFULNESS ☞ POMEGRANATE, GRAPES 48

LEG ORNAMENT ☞ LEGS 75; VOTIVE LEG 79

MOURNING JEWELLERY ☞ JET 38; HEARSE 92; BLACK 106

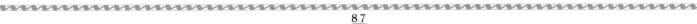

ROYALTY

THE INSTITUTION OF ROYALTY is highly symbolic. Many Asian courts were laid out as microcosms of the universe, with the throne, at the centre of the palace, representing the sacred mountain at the axis of the world. A king had four chief queens and four chief ministers, symbolizing North, South, East, and West. On his health the health of the nation and the land depended, and in parts of Africa and southern India the king was ritually sacrificed while still strong and virile, so that the shedding of his blood might renew the fertility of the soil and thus ensure the wellbeing of his people. The king was widely believed to rule by divine right, and in some cultures to be semi-divine.

Crown
The crown is a symbol of sovereignty and honour

Sceptre
Originally a magical symbol, the sceptre signifies the king's responsibility for his people's prosperity

Ermine
The winter coat of the weasel, ermine is a royal fur. It symbolizes purity and incorruptibility

Mantle
The mantle denotes protection, as well as mystery and transformation

QUEEN
As the feminine counterpart of the king, the queen is associated with the mother goddess or Queen of Heaven. Together the king and queen represent the perfect union of opposites, two halves of the whole, the sun and moon, and day and night.

KING
The king is the ultimate symbol of power. Traditionally the monarch was surrounded by courtiers, who had the same function as the heavenly beings surrounding God. He was thus seen by his subjects as an earthly counterpart of God and a symbolic link between heavenly and earthly power. The king is also a symbol of consciousness, the ruler over our unconscious urges.

Orb
The king symbolically holds the whole world in his hand

Throne
The throne is the seat of authority. It marks the spiritual centre of the kingdom and the metaphorical centre of the world. Its ornate appearance denotes the rank of the ruler. The Virgin Mary, who was crowned in heaven, is often depicted enthroned.

POWER GAMES

Many games are based on the balance of power and involve kings, queens, courtiers, and armies. The object of the game can be to defeat the other players by conquering their court and army, or to build up a royal power base with which to trump one's opponents.

CARDS
Playing cards are divided into four suits, each of which is headed by its own king, queen, and jack (or prince). Packs of cards also include two jokers or jesters, more powerful than their lowly title suggests. In many games the aim is to build up cards to complete the suits, symbolically placing the king in his personal court.

CHESS
The ancient game of chess is a symbolic playing out of the conflict between opposing forces. The black and white squares represent negative and positive, male and female principles. The king, his court, and his army carry the symbolism of their roles, although in chess the queen is more powerful than the king. Each game is an epoch, and each move a possible choice in life.

CHINESE CHESS PIECES

KNIGHT   BISHOP   QUEEN   KING   CASTLE   PAWN

PHARAOH
The famous mask found on the mummy of the boy king Tutankhamun reflects the glory of the pharaoh. For the ancient Egyptians the pharaoh was more than a monarch, he was a god. He was the centre of all existence, son of Re, the sun god, and an intermediary between heaven and earth.

EMPEROR

In China and Japan the emperor is the Son of Heaven, symbol of the moral order and responsible for maintaining harmony between heaven and earth. The Moghul emperors of India took on a similar role. Here the first Moghul emperor, Babur, receives envoys.

PRINCE & PRINCESS

The prince is usually seen in legends as a hero, an embodiment of courage and moral action, while the princess is a symbol of the highest good and beauty. The prince endures hardship to bring about change or rescue a captive princess. His quest represents the way truth can be obtained only after a spiritual struggle.

KNIGHT

When seated on a horse, which represents speed, the knight denotes a superior human. He maintains order in the kingdom, and symbolizes moral courage, devotion to duty, and nobility. Clad in shining armour, he represents invincibility.

FOOL OR JESTER

As a simpleton the fool was exempt from court etiquette. But often he was the wisest member of the court and the only one able to speak his mind to the king. The fool represents innocence in a world of human experience.

UMBRELLA

The umbrella, or more properly the parasol, represents the canopy of heaven and, with its ray-like spokes, the sun itself. It is a symbol of royalty in parts of Asia.

SEAL

All documents of state or letters written by the king would be sealed with the monarch's own seal, representing authority and power. The seal is also a mark of ownership and can be a symbol of belonging to God.

FLY WHISK

Possibly originating from the flail, an instrument of submission, the fly whisk is a symbol of royalty in Eastern and African cultures.

CROWN JEWELS

The crown jewels, the essential accoutrements of royal office, have assumed almost mystical significance for a ruling monarch. Without them, he or she would lose all authority. The crown jewels, orb, and sceptre are essential to the coronation ceremony when they are worn or carried by the newly crowned monarch.

18TH-CENTURY RUSSIAN IMPERIAL CROWN

CROWN

Made of precious metal and jewels, a crown symbolizes sovereignty. It adorns the noblest part of a person, the head, or intellect. Jesus was crowned with an ironic crown of thorns. A crown also denotes supreme accomplishment, as in "crowning glory".

ORB

The orb is composed of a globe, representing the world, with a cross on top, which symbolizes the king's spiritual authority over his subjects, mirroring that of God over mankind.

SCEPTRE

The sceptre was once believed to have magical properties, rather like a magic wand, and is a phallic symbol. The orb and sceptre together symbolize completeness and the creative power of male and female.

PRUSSIAN SCEPTRE

GERMAN ORB

CORONATION CEREMONY

Queen Elizabeth II was crowned in Westminster Abbey in 1953 in a solemn and highly symbolic ceremony. She was invested with the state regalia, which symbolize her role as head of state and of the Anglican church.

AMPULLA & SPOON

The new monarch is anointed with holy oil, poured into the anointing spoon from the ampulla, here in the shape of an eagle.

PALACE

As the residence of royalty, a palace can symbolize heaven or the heart of the realm. A palace figures in many legends and fairy tales. Of its many chambers, some are secret, holding treasures, and represent the unconscious with its spiritual truths.

SEE ALSO

CROWN ☞ TORAH 17; CROWN OF THORNS 18; FOOTPRINT 22; FIRE 35; LEEK 49; SACRED HEART 74; STATUS SYMBOLS 114

KING ☞ PERSONIFICATION OF SUN 34; SUN KING 39; HUMAN SACRIFICE 74

KNIGHT ☞ KNIGHTING 91

QUEEN ☞ PERSONIFICATION OF MOON 34

TOOLS & WEAPONS

ALTHOUGH THEY ARE PRACTICAL OBJECTS, tools and weapons make powerful symbols of the inner or spiritual world. In myth, their obvious functions take on symbolic meaning. Gods are often associated with the implements they use, and while these may appear purely functional, they always symbolize concepts such as fertility, death, and war. Sometimes the implement itself denotes the god. Weapons generally represent power, protection, and destruction. In the hands of the gods, they symbolize the defeat of ignorance and thus liberation. Weapons also stand for the state of conflict that the god or hero overcomes.

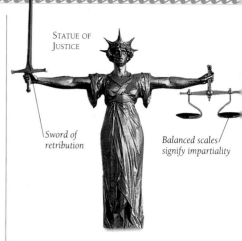
STATUE OF JUSTICE
Sword of retribution
Balanced scales signify impartiality

SCALES OF JUSTICE
A pair of balanced scales represents justice and judgement, both in court and in the afterlife. In the Egyptian Hall of Judgement, the heart of the deceased was weighed against the feather of truth before the god Osiris, who passed judgement. In Roman art, Justice personified holds a sword and a pair of scales. The archangel Michael weighs the souls of the dead before Christ.

LADDER
The ladder represents our urge to climb from ignorance into the light. In Egypt, an image of a ladder was placed inside the tomb with the dead. In the Bible, Jacob dreamed of angels ascending and descending a ladder reaching up to heaven. Buddhists believe the Buddha climbed a ladder to preach to his mother in heaven.

ANVIL
The anvil is often seen as the feminine, receptive counterpart of the hammer with its masculine associations. Together they represent the opposing but complementary forces of the active and the passive.

SCYTHE
Because it is a harvesting tool, the scythe symbolizes death, the moment when life is cut short. It also stands for the liberation of the soul. The figures of Father Time and Death, the Grim Reaper, are both depicted carrying a scythe.

THOR'S HAMMER

HAMMER
Widely seen as a symbol of thunder, the hammer is an attribute of the Norse god Thor, whose hammer always hit its target and came back to him. The Greek god Hephaestos, the blacksmith, also wielded a hammer. In Japan the hammer is an attribute of Daikoku, god of riches. Along with the nail, the hammer is a symbol of the Passion of Christ.

HAMMER & SICKLE
The sickle lends its name to the new moon because of its shape. It therefore symbolizes time and death, but also the annual cycle of renewal. The Greek goddess of agriculture, Demeter, carries a sickle. The hammer and sickle were brought together in the symbol of the former Soviet Union. That symbol now represents the Communist movement.

CRETAN AXE

AXE
The axe is an emblem of sky gods such as Zeus. It is a symbol of power, associated with many deities, for example, Shiva and Agni in India, and the Yoruba storm god of West Africa. In China, it represents justice, authority, and punishment. The axe is also symbolic of death ordered by a wrathful deity. For Hindus and Buddhists, the axe removes ignorance and thus severs the cycle of birth, death, and rebirth.

SIMON AND ANDREW, GABRIEL LOIRE, 1975

NET
The net symbolizes the power of the gods to bind and hold humans helpless in the mesh of life. In Christian art, a net with fish represents the church. St Peter (originally the fisherman Simon) was a "fisher of men", and St Andrew (also a fisherman) carries a net.

ROPE
Rope represents bondage and captivity. It also connects heaven and earth, acting like a cosmic umbilical cord. In the form of a noose, it is a symbol of death and despair. In Christianity, it is a symbol of the betrayal of Christ who was bound by his captors.

PLOUGH
The plough is usually an attribute of Greek pastoral gods such as Demeter and Dionysus. As a phallic symbol, it represents impregnation of the earth by the gods, the furrow being feminine and receptive. It also represents the act of Creation when primal matter broke up into different life forms.

SPINNING WHEEL
The spindle is an attribute of goddesses concerned with destiny. They are often shown as three spinners who govern birth, life, and death. The turning wheel is a symbol of the universe. The loom is the loom of life, with masculine, active threads and feminine, passive threads united in harmony. According to Buddhism, the loom weaves the fabric of illusion.

GUN
The gun is a symbol of masculine power and aggression. Because of its projectile capabilities, the gun is commonly associated with virility, along with other firearms and missiles. In Freudian thought it is a phallic symbol, an association echoed in gangster movies, where guns have become linked to male prowess.

MUSLIM KRIS

DAGGER
The dagger is generally a phallic symbol and stands for masculinity. It is an attribute of military gods such as Mars and Mithras. To Muslims the sacred kris represents the word of Allah and absolute truth. The kris, with its characteristic undulating form, is usually beautifully decorated, often with words from the Koran.

SWORDS
In all cultures, the sword stands for power and strength. A sword taken from an enemy is a symbol of victory, and to receive a sword – when knighted, for example – is to be given authority. The sword divides good from evil and cuts through ignorance. Many gods, heroes, and saints, including St George, hold a sword.

ASANTE SWORD
This late 19th-century sword of the Asante kingdom of Ghana has an unsharpened iron blade as it was used for ceremonial purposes only. The gilded wooden beads on the handle are symbols of wealth and fertility.

SAMURAI SWORD
In Japan the sword is a symbol of courage and strength. For the Samurai, the aristocratic warriors of Japan, the sword was the chosen symbol of honour. It represented the noble cause and the fight for truth and justice.

CROSSED SWORDS
The arms of Saddam Hussein hold the crossed swords of the Martyrs' Monument in Baghdad, Iraq. The arch faces East (for birth) and West (for martyrdom).

KNIGHTING
The custom of knighting is very ancient. By touching both shoulders with the blade, the monarch confers authority. The sword is a symbol of purification, and so also cleanses the soul.

EMPEROR SIGISMUND DUBS HEINRICH OF ULM, 1473

Double-edged sword of truth and justice

Curved sword for God's power

Quoit – round throwing weapon

SIKH EMBLEM
The Nishan Sahib, the emblem of the Sikhs, contains a two-edged sword, symbolizing truth and justice, and two crossed swords for God's spiritual power. In the centre is a chakra, a circular throwing weapon or quoit.

SHIELD
The shield protects and has come to symbolize feminine power and chastity. In some cultures, however, it personifies the power of a male god or ancestor and can also represent a hero. It is an attribute of the Greek goddess Athena.

Indian shield decorated with mythological figures

SPEAR
With its elongated, phallic shape, the spear represents war, power, and fertility. In Christian art, an animal impaled on a spear or lance represents a vice overcome. For this reason, figures personifying virtue often carry a lance. Because of the spear thrust into Christ's side when he was on the cross, it is also a symbol of the Passion. The spear can be a symbol of the earth's axis as well.

BOW & ARROW
With its crescent shape and powerful function, the bow is both feminine and masculine and represents the moon and the arc of heaven. With the arrow, a penetrative, masculine symbol, it is an attribute of Diana and Apollo. To Chinese Taoists it is "the Way", the Tao.

SEE ALSO

HAMMER ☞
ODIN, THOR, FREY 15;
GOD OF WEALTH 27;

LADDER ☞ STAIRS 95;
FREEMASONRY 109

ROPE ☞ THREAD 97

SHIELD ☞ HERALDIC
SYMBOLS 114

SPINNING WHEEL ☞
CATHERINE'S WHEEL 19;
WHEEL OF LAW 22;
WHEEL OF FORTUNE 112;
HINDU WHEEL 104;
WHEELS WITHIN 103

SWORDS ☞
SWORD DANCE 76;
CHINESE COIN SWORD 78

DEATH & MOURNING

THE CERTAINTY OF DEATH unites us all, whether rich or poor and regardless of culture or faith. The many different rites and rituals surrounding death and mourning illustrate how each society deals with its fear of the unknown. Ancient beliefs speak of the body being reunited with Mother Earth, or the soul rejoining the cosmic ocean or entering heaven; in other words, life returning to a state of oneness with nature. For others death can be the door into another future that will be favourable if the deceased was devout in this life. A source of great fear and an occasion for both sorrow and joy, death is laden with symbolism. Many death rituals are symbolic enactments to aid the soul's journey into the afterlife as well as to console the bereaved.

DAY OF THE DEAD
SCULPTURE

DAY OF THE DEAD
On November 1, Mexicans celebrate the Day of the Dead. They make images of Death in the form of skeletons, light candles in graveyards and set out offerings of food to welcome the dead back to earth. The rituals are a symbolic way of maintaining a link with the past.

RAVEN
Although viewed in many cultures as an auspicious symbol of wisdom, fertility, and creation, the prophetic raven is seen in the Christian tradition as a bird of ill-omen. It heralds evil, warfare, and death. This is probably due to its black colour, associated with the night. The raven is thought to haunt graveyards and foretell death and destruction.

CHINESE PAPER FOR RITUAL
BURNING AT A FUNERAL

LUCK FOR THE DEAD
At Chinese funerals it is the custom for mourners to burn auspicious squares of coloured paper on the funeral pyre to bring good luck to the soul of the deceased on its journey to the afterlife.

DANCE OF DEATH, AFTER HOLBEIN, 1786

DEATHLY DANCE
The *Danse Macabre* was used to illustrate the concept that death is the great leveller. A procession of figures representing the various classes – from Pope to peasant – each alternating with a skeleton, is led towards a grave, showing that all are ultimately linked by death. Another popular medieval belief, the Dance of Death, held that the dead rose at midnight and danced about in the graveyard. The two themes were often intermingled.

HEARSE
This magnificent hearse is from a bygone era. The hearse and the horses were always black, symbolic of mourning, as was the livery. Modern funerals are more streamlined, but such old-fashioned formalities are still preferred by some for the solace that tradition provides.

TAROT CARD
In the Tarot, Death is not the last card but marks a transition from one state to another. This might signify the end – or death – of one phase of life and the beginning of a new one. Either phase would be accompanied by profound inner changes. Death is shown carrying the scythe, with which he mows down the living.

Black livery of horses extends to dyed ostrich plumes

Black stove-pipe hat with crêpe band

Black gloves and black formal attire

Black trappings on hearse

Black pall to cover horses' hindquarters

HORSE-DRAWN HEARSE

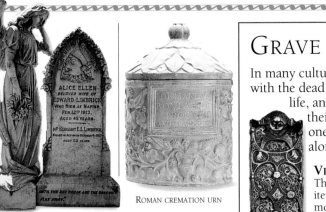

ROMAN CREMATION URN

HEADSTONE, 1913,
NAPIER, NEW ZEALAND

GRAVESTONE
The site of a Christian burial is marked by a memorial stone, often accompanied by symbolic reminders such as a wreath, a Bible, or an angel. An angel is an intermediary between heaven and earth and so symbolizes the passage of the soul to the heavenly realm.

FUNERARY URN
After a cremation the ashes of the deceased are often placed inside a funerary urn. As a large round-bodied vessel of containment, the urn is a symbol of the feminine. The urn with a lid is a good luck emblem, symbol in Chinese Buddhism of supreme intelligence that triumphs over birth and death.

GRAVE GOODS

In many cultures precious goods are buried with the dead as a sign of their prestige in life, and also to accompany them on their journey to the afterlife. At one time even slaves were buried along with their dead owner.

VIKING GOLD
TREASURE

VIKING GOLD
The Vikings buried items of gold, the most precious metal, in the graves of important men.

Steering oar

Rigging up for the afterlife

Helmsman

FOOD OFEERINGS
Bowls containing food were a common offering in many cultures. They symbolize the spiritual nourishment of the soul after death. These Japanese funerary bowls date from the 3rd century.

SHIP OF DEATH
There is a widespread association of death with a journey across water. Model ships buried in a grave were believed to carry the deceased to the afterlife.

EGYPTIAN
SHIP OF DEATH

RITUAL MOURNING
Mourners at a Taoist funeral in Gansu province in China are completely covered, out of respect for the dead. The chief mourners wear white robes, and the principal mourner carries a green sash. Hessian veils are used, as it would be disrespectful to use fine cloth. For the first two or three years after the death, mourners eat only the humblest of foods.

ETERNAL FLAME
At the tomb of the unknown soldier a flame burns continually as a constant reminder of all those who have died nameless in battle. The unknown soldier is a particularly poignant reminder of the indiscriminate slaughter of war.

ETERNAL FLAME, MOSCOW

TAJ MAHAL, AGRA, INDIA

FLAG AT HALF MAST
The custom of flying a flag halfway down the pole as a sign of mourning began as a naval custom in the 17th century. The top of the mast was left empty for an invisible flag of death. The custom continues as a public sign of mourning.

Flag hoist at half mast in mourning

WHITE LILY

LILY
The white lily, the flower of the Madonna, is traditionally associated with purity in the West, and this may explain why it has become customary to place lilies on the grave at a funeral. Death is seen as a return to a pure state – white as opposed to the black of death.

POPPY
WREATH

WREATH OF RED
Red poppies have become a symbol of lives lost during the two World Wars. The association stems from a poem written by Canadian John McCrae: "In Flanders fields where poppies blow/ Between the crosses row on row …" The poppy is also a symbol of sleep and dreams.

AIDS
RIBBON

RIBBON
The red ribbon, devised in New York in 1991 by a group called Visual AIDS, has become a world-wide symbol of the fight against AIDS. Wearing the red ribbon symbolizes support for the fight against the disease and the need for continuing research towards a cure.

MAUSOLEUM
The Taj Mahal is the tomb of the wife of the Indian emperor Shah Jehan. Built in the 17th century, it was planned as the most magnificent memorial on earth, a symbol of the emperor's great love for his wife. His own tomb across the river was never finished so he was buried beside her.

SEE ALSO

DEATH ☞ CYPRESS 45; RAVEN 64; SKELETON 74; SCYTHE 90

MOURNING ☞ MOURNING JEWELLERY 85; BLACK, WHITE 106

RAVEN ☞ RAVEN 64

RED WREATH ☞ POPPY 50

TAROT CARD ☞ THE LANGUAGE OF THE TAROT 111

ARCHITECTURE

THE SYMBOLIC MEANING OF A BUILDING and its components can be very complex, especially with religious buildings. Stepped terraces may represent heavenly levels and a spire points symbolically to heaven, while a dome represents the vaults of heaven itself. Differently shaped buildings represent differing symbolic ideals: skyscrapers, for instance, represent status and achievement in the material world, while modern, environmentally sensitive buildings symbolize union with nature. Separate elements have their own symbolism: doors and windows often mark boundaries between worlds.

OCULUS

WINDOW
Just as the eye is known as the "window of the soul", the window is the "eye of the soul", symbolic both of consciousness and of the individual's perception of the world. A round window is appropriately called an oculus or ox-eye window. Since it lets in light the window also symbolizes the light of truth entering the soul.

INDIAN BALCONY

BALCONY
The balcony represents mystery and ambivalence due to its partly concealing, partly revealing nature and also its position, both inside and outside a building. Enclosed balconies add to the mystery. In colder countries bay and oriel windows act as enclosed balconies.

Angel at top protects church and those who enter

Mythical beasts symbolically keep evil at bay

ENGLISH CHURCH DOORWAY, 12TH CENTURY

KNOCKER
Door knockers in animal shapes protect the house and keep evil spirits at bay. The ominous knock at the door has long been a symbol in literature – and music – of inexorable fate or death.

DOORWAY
The doorway marks the passage between sacred and profane, between safety and danger. It also symbolizes the transition from one stage of life to another or the passage from life to death. Temple doorways in particular are often carved with guardian spirits and fabulous beasts to dispel evil and offer protection.

REACH FOR THE SKY

Humankind has always been fascinated by tall buildings that reach upward to the sky, building them both for religious reasons and for reasons of power. Whether ancient pyramids or modern skyscrapers, such buildings represent man's need to reach up to the heavens and also to gain supremacy over his surroundings.

PYRAMIDS
For the ancient Egyptians the pyramid stood symbolically as a world axis at the centre of the universe. Its apex represents the highest level of spiritual attainment. A stepped pyramid signifies the stages of consciousness through which the soul must pass on its ascent.

102nd floor observatory

WALL
The wall encloses and protects the sheltering interior of a building or a garden, suggesting strength, privacy, and containment. In the case of the Berlin Wall, above, it may be divisive, signifying the separation of East and West.

THE BERLIN WALL

SKYSCRAPER
The Empire State building in New York was for decades the tallest building in the world. It stands as an obviously phallic symbol of man's achievement, instantly recognizable by people all over the world.

THE TOWER OF BABEL, PIETER BRUEGHEL THE ELDER, 1560

TOWER OF BABEL
The fabled tower of Babel was a ziggurat, or stepped pyramid, in ancient Babylonia. It is a symbol of man's arrogance. In the Bible the Babylonians were determined to build such a tower to reach the heavens. God divided the speech of the builders into many languages so that they could not understand each other, and the tower was never completed.

BRIDGE OF SIGHS, OXFORD

BRIDGE
The bridge is a symbolic link between heaven and earth. It is the passage from life to death, and from death to immortality. The original Bridge of Sighs in Venice led from the courtrooms to the dungeons.

THE PARTHENON, ATHENS

CLASSICAL TEMPLE
Temples in Greek and Roman times were believed to be the house of gods. They could be square, polygonal, or round. Round has been considered the perfect shape because the circle itself is a symbol of the cosmic mind and nature's perfection. Classical temples were erected in commanding locations, for example, the Acropolis in Athens, site of the Parthenon.

CATHEDRAL, FLORENCE

DOME
The dome is a symbol of the heavens. Religious buildings often incorporate a dome which may be decorated on the inside with paintings of the sun, moon, and stars as well as angels.

NOBLE HOUSE, INDONESIA

ROOF
The roof symbolizes the feminine, sheltering principle. Some societies hang treasures and powerful hunting trophies in the roof space to increase its protective power.

STAIRS
A staircase represents the steps in spiritual development. Its symbolism is related to that of the ladder and the stepped pyramid. One can either ascend towards Enlightenment or descend into darkness and ignorance. A winding staircase, with its upper or lower end unknown and hidden from view, symbolizes the mysterious.

ARCH
The arch symbolizes passage from one state to another. Victorious Roman armies marched through triumphal arches. In initiation rites, to pass under an arch is to be reborn.

ARCH OF CONSTANTINE, ROME

THE NATURE SANCTUARY BUILDING, FINDHORN, SCOTLAND

EARTH DWELLING
In many countries people live in houses made entirely of natural materials found around them, from adobe huts in Africa to igloos in the Arctic. This keeps them, literally, in touch with nature and more in tune with their surroundings. A modern earth-integrated house, roofed with turf, represents a return to this more natural way of life with its related symbolism of union with nature.

CHARLES D'ORLEANS IN THE TOWER OF LONDON, FLEMISH, c.1650

Holding place at top of tower to prevent rescue or escape

Castellated tower

LIGHTHOUSE
A lighthouse provides a beacon of light to guide ships to safety. It is a symbol of the teachings of Christ, which guide the soul to the safety of faith and understanding.

NATURE HOUSE, SWEDEN

GLASS HOUSE
Mainly built of glass, this house provides full access to the natural elements and all their associated symbolism – a window to the world. The glass lets in the maximum amount of light and stores heat. The garden is visible and fresh air from it is scented by flowers and plants.

TOWER AND CASTLE
The tower is a symbol of inaccessibility and protection. With its castellated towers, moats, and drawbridge, the castle is a symbol of territorial power and security, and is often a heraldic symbol. A castle is also seen in fairy tales as an enchanted place that houses a giant or demon. In order to release the captive princess or treasure inside (symbols of spiritual knowledge), the giant (the burden of ignorance) has to be defeated.

SEE ALSO
ARCH ☞ SQUARE WITHIN SQUARE 104

CLASSICAL TEMPLE ☞ TEMPLE 21; SIGN LANGUAGE 109

TOWER AND CASTLE ☞ PRINCE & PRINCESS 89

STAIRS ☞ LADDER 90

EVERYDAY OBJECTS

IN THE WORLD OF FAMILIAR OBJECTS, many do not fit easily into obvious categories but are so much part of our everyday life that they have become imbued with symbolic meaning. These range from different types of containers, associated with the feminine, secrecy, or protection, to objects connected with human frailty and the passage of time. Items linked to fire or light are also rich in meaning, signifying enlightenment, as are keys, which unlock secrets or mark a coming of age.

KEY
The key has the power to open and close. It gives access to another realm, and so symbolizes wisdom, maturity, or success. Many keys dangling from a key chain symbolize status, since they denote the ownership of valued property. Keys are the attribute of St Peter, as the guardian of the gates of heaven.

BASKET
The basket is an attribute of the four seasons, and, when full, it symbolizes fertility, fruition, and abundance, therefore also life. In Buddhism the "three baskets" are the scriptures of the Buddhist canon.

FAN
The fan is a common symbol of high rank or royalty. It is also thought to ward off evil spirits. To Taoists it represents the flight of a bird and release into the world of the Immortals. In addition, the fan has long been thought of as a symbol of femininity and flirtation.

PANDORA OPENS THE BOX

EGYPTIAN DRINKING CUP

CUP
Because they are containers, cups, like bowls, are symbols of the receptive, feminine realm. In this Egyptian example, the lotus pattern shows the flower's relationship to water, and thus adds to its links with the feminine.

BOX
The box is a feminine symbol. When closed, it symbolizes the unconscious, and when opened, it may unleash a storm of devastation, disease, and death upon the world, as did Pandora's box.

Gold and silver coins, symbols of wealth and greed

MONEY PURSE
The purse represents worldly vanity and the transience of wealth. In Christian art, a purse is an attribute of Judas Iscariot and of St Matthew, the tax collector. Coins spilling out of a purse are a symbol of worldly attachment and greed.

THE SWING, JEAN-HONORE FRAGONARD, 1767

SWING
The swing is associated with fertility because its movements represent the rhythms of the seasons and the rising and setting of the sun and moon, as well as the rhythms of love-making. In this charming 18th-century French painting, the swing, with its backward and forward motion, is a playful symbol of amorous flirtation. A stone Cupid presides over the secluded corner of the garden, while the lush vegetation provides a fertile backdrop for the lovers' games.

MEASURING TIME

People have always been fascinated by the concept of time, and have linked its many related objects to their own mortality. Thus the ageing process may be seen as "time marching on", and heart problems as a failure of the "old ticker".

LAMP

The flame of the oil lamp represents life and the light of the spirit, wisdom, and immortality. Through the stories of the Arabian Nights the lamp has become associated with the genie who lives within it and grants wishes to the person who sets him free. Aladdin's lamp is thus a symbol of magic as well as of good fortune.

LIGHT BULB

Invented *c.*1880, the light bulb has become the archetypal symbol of a bright idea. Cartoon characters often have one "flashing" over their head to signify a moment of inspiration.

HOURGLASS

This simple instrument for measuring time operates on the principle of sand filtering down over a period of an hour under the force of gravity. The process has given rise to the notion of life being like "sand ebbing away".

WATCH

Like the clock, the watch is a symbol of the passing hours and a reminder of the brevity of life. "Time stands still for no man".

SUNDIAL

The sundial shows the time using the shadow cast by the sun. In ancient times this was thought to be the shadow of a sun god as he moved through the heavens.

EARLY HOURGLASS

18TH-CENTURY SUNDIAL

ANCHOR

The anchor is a symbol of safety, stability, and hope. Christ is often referred to as an anchor in the sea of life. An anchor depicted with a dolphin is a symbol of Christ on the cross, and to be anchored means to be rooted.

MIRROR

Since thought is reflection, the mirror indicates truth, clarity, and self-knowledge, as well as vanity. To break a mirror brings bad luck because it is a form of harming oneself. To Taoists a mirror is the calm of the sage, and the reflection of the universe.

CANDLE

A candle is a symbol of the individual soul and the flame that lights the darkness of ignorance. It is the sun and spiritual illumination, and an extinguished candle can signify death. Candles play a part in many religious rites and in Christianity the lighted candle represents Christ as the resurrected light of the world.

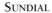

OPEN BOOK

Books are symbols of knowledge and the wisdom of the universe. An "open book" is a person or subject that can be easily understood, whereas a closed book remains a mystery.

THREAD

A thread is a symbol of life and of human destiny spun by a divine power. In Greek myth, Ariadne gives Theseus a ball of yarn by which to escape from the labyrinth. In Hinduism a thread connects this world with the next, and high-caste Hindus wear a sacred thread.

LIPSTICK

Bright red lipstick is a symbol of sexuality. It accentuates the erogenous zone of the lips, and, with its winding, upright mechanism, combines male and female imagery.

COMPASS

The compass points out the four primary directions North, South, East, and West, and the four secondary directions, echoing symbolically the directions of the cosmos. Egyptian pyramids are built on an east/west axis, with the entrance facing the Pole Star.

French fleur-de-lis

PEN AND INK

Like the brush used in Chinese calligraphy, the pen is a symbol of learning and the intellect, and it marks out destiny on the blank sheet of life. It is also a masculine symbol, dipping into the bowl-shaped ink-well to derive its power.

SILVER SPOON

In Europe, a silver spoon is often given to a baby at the time of its christening and symbolizes nurture and life. The expression that someone is "born with a silver spoon in their mouth" indicates that they were born into a life of privilege.

SEE ALSO

CANDLE ☞ MOTH 57

COMPASS ☞ COMPASS 25; FENG SHUI COMPASS 78; FOUR 102

LAMP ☞ MOSQUE LAMP 25

MIRROR ☞ MIRROR 78

MONEY PURSE ☞ MONEY CURES 78; EGYPTIAN COINS 86

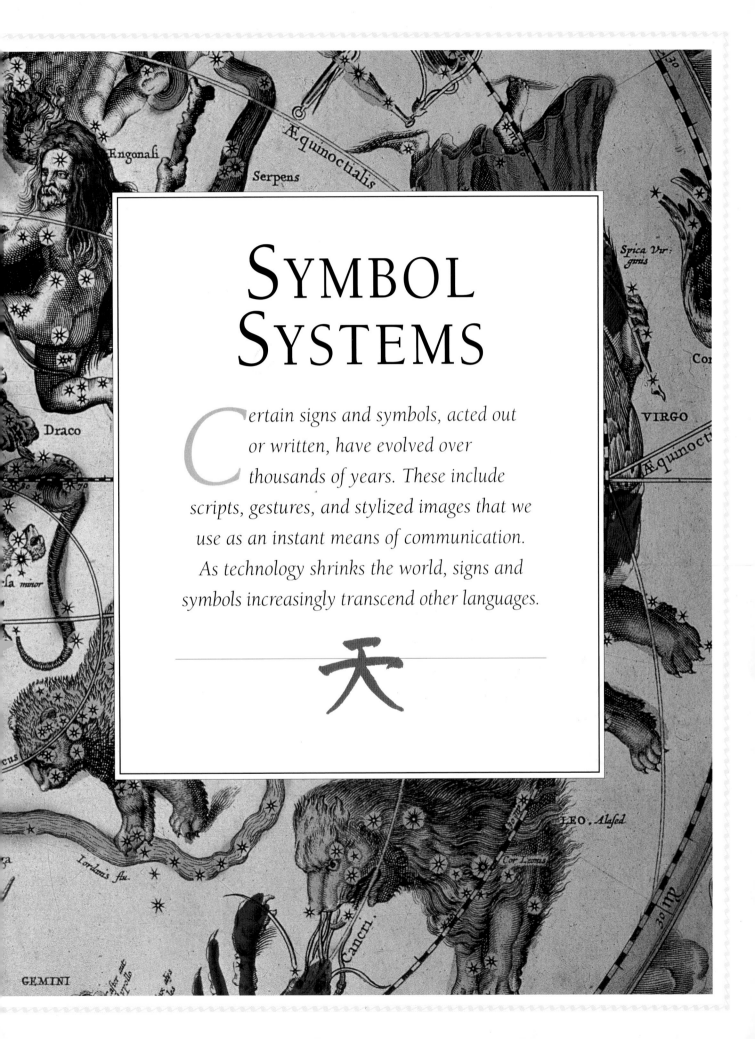

SYMBOL SYSTEMS

Certain signs and symbols, acted out or written, have evolved over thousands of years. These include scripts, gestures, and stylized images that we use as an instant means of communication. As technology shrinks the world, signs and symbols increasingly transcend other languages.

PICTURE WRITING

IN CULTURES THROUGHOUT THE WORLD, picture writing represents the earliest attempt at setting down words in a non-verbal, non-gestural form of communication. Picture writing differs from drawing in that it uses a standardized set of picture signs, or "pictograms". These picture signs came to represent particular objects which were then easily recognized by the reader. As the need for more complex forms grew, signs which represent actual word sounds were introduced, and in addition, simple signs were combined to create a more complex script.

IDEOGRAMS

These Hittite ideograms are a more abstract development of pictograms. A picture of a foot, for example, may mean the verb "to walk".

CITY   KING

STOOL   GOD   OX   GREAT

CLAY TOKENS

These Sumerian tablets date from c.3000 BC. Large numbers of representational clay tablets have been unearthed in modern Iraq and Iran. Some 1,500 different symbols have been decoded, most of them relating to agricultural and commercial matters.

 COW

 DOG

 HEART, WOMB

 STONE VESSEL

 WOOL

 SEAT

 OIL

 GRANARY

ONE

PICTOGRAMS

These particular pictograms are quite modern, dating from the early 1900s. King Njoya of Bamum, in a remote area of Cameroon, set about creating a written language for his people. Bamum has only single-syllable words and so each picture sign is also just one syllable. The meanings of the symbols are fairly easy to decipher.

NO

HOUSE

PLATE

TO GO

TO GIVE

THREAD

CHILD

EGYPTIAN HIEROGLYPHS

Hieroglyphs, literally "sacred writings", originated long before 3000 BC, but were not deciphered until the 19th century, when the Rosetta Stone was discovered in Egypt. This had inscriptions in three scripts, one of them Greek, which could be translated and compared with the hieroglyphs. Hieroglyphs are a combination of pictograms – mostly stylized drawings of animals, plants, and flowers – and "phonograms" or signs representing sounds. This script was therefore a true form of writing in the modern sense.

Brush holder

Water pot for mixing pigments

Palette

SCRIBE SYMBOL

LUCKY EYE

The "wadjet eye" or Eye of Horus (sky god) was thought to have magical powers. Scribes often included this symbol in their writing for good luck.

K L E O P A T R A

CARTOUCHE

The names of Egyptian kings and queens were always enclosed in oval borders, known as cartouches. The cartouche was a symbol of the ruler's power, signifying that he or she reigned over "all that the sun encircles". It was a French Egyptologist, Jean-François Champollion, who in 1822 cracked the code of these particular royal hieroglyphs.

This stela, or carved stone, contains symbols that act as clues to the meaning of the writing

FUNERARY STELA, c.2250 BC

The owl indicates the flow of the text

Four lines of inscription detailing the King's funerary offering for the priest Merra

OWL

 WATER   SNAIL

 REEDS   LION

READING THE STELA

A hieroglyphic text can be read from left to right, right to left, or top to bottom. The symbols of animals or people tell you which way to read. Here the faces point to the right, so the text is to be read from right to left.

CHINESE

The Chinese script, the oldest script still in use today, is over 4,000 years old. Earliest examples were inscribed onto tortoise shells or carved into ox bones. Some pictographic elements remain but the Chinese characters also include phonetic components, and an added element to characterize the word.

HEART   TO GO

JUICE   ICE

FISH   LETTER

HOUSE   GOLD

TO RECEIVE   COME

TINY   DEAR

SCOLD   DRAGON

日 + 月 = 明

SUN + MOON = BRIGHT

Some Chinese words are compounds, being the sum of two other words.

ONE   GO UP

LITTLE   SKY

SUN   MOON

CHEROKEE

Cherokee script was invented in 1821 and shows the influence of the Latin alphabet. It is a phonological system, that is, there is a clear relationship between the written symbol and the sound, shown here with phonetic symbols.

G wa   B yʌ

4 se   ꞷ ya

Ᏺ sa   Ꮖ gwa

W la   G nah

ß ye   f ga

MAYAN

Mayan script is made up of compounds of signs and is a mixture of pictograms and phonetic elements. It is written in double columns from left to right, and top to bottom. The hieroglyphs below are phonetic-syllabic – they each contain several elements and sounds, and yet are still representational.

BURDEN

OPEN

SOUTH

WEST

TURKEY

VULTURE

LIMESTONE LINTEL PANEL FROM MEXICAN TEMPLE, C. AD 725

The inscription records the names and dates of Mayan rulers

MAYAN STORY

This panel comes from the temple of Yaxchilan, close to the present border between Mexico and Guatemala. It depicts the sacrificial offering of blood to bring forth ancestral spirits. Lady Xoc, the wife of Lord Shield Jaguar, is gazing up at Yat-Balam, a spirit who has emerged from the jaws of a huge, double-headed serpent.

CUNEIFORM

This form of writing was used for over 3,000 years throughout the Near East by Sumerians, Assyrians, Babylonians, and Hittites. It developed from a system of pictograms and changed gradually to a more complex phonological system. The script is made up of wedge-shaped signs created with a stylus. At first, symbols were written vertically, as shown in the table to the right, but later many symbols were reversed and became more abstract.

MEANING	3000 BC	2400 BC	650 BC
BIRD			
HAND			
HEAD			
REED			
WALK OR STAND			
WATER			

SEE ALSO

CALLIGRAPHY ☞ CALLIGRAPHY, KORAN 25; PEN AND INK 97

CARTOUCHE ☞ PERSONIFICATION OF SUN AND MOON 34; SUN KING 39; ROYALTY 88-89

EGYPTIAN HIEROGLYPHS ☞ EGYPTIAN 14; PHARAOH 88; PYRAMIDS 94

LUCKY EYE ☞ ISIS AND HORUS 14; LUNAR EYE 72

MAYAN STORY ☞ ANCESTOR & NATURE SPIRITS 26-27; DOUBLE-HEADED SERPENT 28

PICTOGRAMS ☞ COWRIE SHELLS 55

NUMBERS

NUMBERS HAVE LONG BEEN SEEN as expressions of cosmic order, possibly deriving from ancient Babylonian observations of regular cosmic events, such as night and day, the phases of the moon, and cycles of the year. In most cultures numbers are laden with symbolic meaning, and the practice of numerology is the study of their influence on the future. Viewed symbolically, numbers represent more than quantities; they also have qualities. To the Greek mathematician Pythagoras, even numbers were feminine, divisible into two equal parts, and passive; odd numbers were masculine, and active.

NUMBER SYSTEMS

DEVANAGARI
Most Western languages use Arabic numerals. These derive from the classical Indian language Sanskrit, written in the Devanagari script that is still used for many North-Indian languages.

९	२	३	४	५
ONE	TWO	THREE	FOUR	FIVE
६	७	८	९	०
SIX	SEVEN	EIGHT	NINE	ZERO

ROMAN
The Roman system uses seven alphabetical signs: I, V, X, L, C, D, and M. Numbers are formed by adding (6 = V+I = VI) or subtracting (4 = I less than V = IV). Larger numbers come from Latin words, for example C=*centum*=100; M= *mille*=1,000.

I	II	III	IV	V
ONE	TWO	THREE	FOUR	FIVE
VI	VII	VIII	IX	X
SIX	SEVEN	EIGHT	NINE	TEN
L	C	D	M
FIFTY	HUNDRED	FIVE HUNDRED	THOUSAND

HEBREW
Numerals in Hebrew (read from right to left) correspond to the alphabet. One is the first letter, aleph; two, the second; and so on. After the tenth letter, the value of each letter goes up in tens.

FIVE (HE)	FOUR (DALETH)	THREE (GIMEL)	TWO (VETH)	ONE (ALEPH)
TEN (YOD)	NINE (TETH)	EIGHT (HETH)	SEVEN (ZAYIN)	SIX (VAV)

0 Zero was invented in ancient India. Represented by the continuous circle, it signifies non-being and eternity. To Pythagoras it was the perfect form which contains all and from which all is created. In Islam it is limitless light and the Divine Essence.

1 To be number one is to be the best. Spiritually, one stands for the state before the creation of the myriad forms of life. It also symbolizes the oneness to which all living things must return. It is God but also the individual.

FLEGMAT SANGVIN

MELANC COLERIC

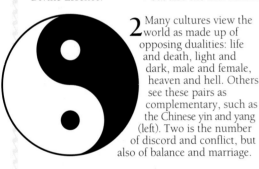

2 Many cultures view the world as made up of opposing dualities: life and death, light and dark, male and female, heaven and hell. Others see these pairs as complementary, such as the Chinese yin and yang (left). Two is the number of discord and conflict, but also of balance and marriage.

4 Four is the number of the square; the four elements, earth, fire, water, and air; and the cardinal points of the compass. It is associated with the Earth and with completeness. In medieval Europe human nature was characterized by the four humours (seen above): phlegmatic, sanguine, choleric, and melancholic.

THREE

3 Sacred to most religions, the number three combines the numbers one and two and so includes all life and experience. It is birth, life, and death; mind, body, and soul; past, present, and future; man, woman, and child.

Brahma *Vishnu* *Shiva*

HINDU TRINITY
In India Brahma, Vishnu, and Shiva form a powerful trinity of gods. Between them they create, sustain, and destroy life in an endless cycle of birth and rebirth.

TREFOIL OF THE TRINITY
Three geometric shapes coming together can express the Christian Trinity, one God in three persons: the Father, the Son, and the Holy Spirit. Thus the architectural device of the trefoil is often found in churches.

NEPTUNE'S TRIDENT
The trident is a symbol of the Roman sea god, Neptune, possibly representing the past, the present, and the future. The trident of the Hindu god Shiva stands for his function as creator, preserver, and destroyer. Satan also holds a trident.

5 As the sum of two, a feminine number, and three, a masculine number, five is important in many cultures. It is a symbol for man. On a figure of a man, a line joining head to outstretched arms and legs forms a pentagram, and also there are five human senses. Muslims pray five times a day and there are five pillars of piety in Islam.

THE CREATION, FRENCH BIBLE, 14TH CENTURY

6 According to the Bible, God created the world in six days and rested on the seventh. Six represents balance, love, health, and also luck, as it is the winning throw at dice.

BUDDHIST WHEEL OF LIFE

8 As the first cubic number (2 x 2 x 2), eight is considered the perfect number. Chinese life is ruled by eight: at eight months a child has milk teeth; at eight years he loses them; at twice eight he reaches maturity; and at 64 (8 x 8) he loses the power of procreation. The Buddhist wheel of life has eight spokes, for the eight-fold path to Enlightenment.

SYMBOL FOR NINE

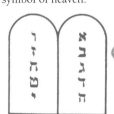

9 Nine is the sacred number: three multiplied by itself to give eternity, completion, and fulfilment. The Norse god Odin hung for nine days and nine nights on the tree Yggdrasil to win the secret of wisdom for mankind. In China it is the number of celestial power: the nine-storeyed pagoda is a symbol of heaven.

COMMANDMENT TABLETS

10 As the number of the fingers, ten is the foundation of most counting systems including the decimal system. Ten also figures strongly in the Bible: there are ten commandments and ten Egyptian plagues. According to some theories, in the decimal system, ten is symbolic of the return to unity.

THE LAST SUPPER, LEONARDO DA VINCI, 1495-98

13 In Christian countries 13 is an unlucky number because there were 13 at the fateful Last Supper. In Leonardo's fresco above, Jesus has just announced that one of the disciples will betray him. In ancient South America there were 13 Mayan heavens and the Aztec calendar was divided into 13-day periods.

21 Originally the age at which a citizen was entitled to vote (though now lowered in many countries), 21 is still considered a major landmark in life. A symbolic key signifies entry into adulthood. In many countries this is the age at which a person is allowed to buy and drink alcohol.

40 Representing wholeness, the number 40 is especially important in the Bible. Moses' sojourn on Sinai lasted 40 days, as did that of Christ in the wilderness, and Noah's ark floated in the Flood for 40 days and 40 nights. Forty was also significant in terms of years – the Jews spent 40 years in the wilderness, and the reigns of David and Solomon were both 40 years.

50 This is the number of joy and celebration. It marks the completion of 7 x 7-year cycles and signifies new beginnings.

60 This marks the division of the minute and the hour, and so is associated with time. In Egypt it represented a long life.

SEVEN

7 Seven is a sacred number, representing the union of divinity (number three) and earth (number four). Each of the four phases of the moon lasts seven days and there are seven days in the week.

MENORAH
The branches of the Jewish candlestick indicate the seven days of the week as well as the sun, moon, and five principal planets. The three U-shaped arms represent wisdom, strength, and beauty.

WHEELS WITHIN
In Hindu philosophy there are seven *chakras*, or wheels, in the body. These stand for levels of consciousness, ranging from the lowest for physical survival to the highest for spiritual enlightenment.

SEVEN DEADLY SINS
The seven deadly sins (*clockwise from top*) – gluttony, sloth, lust, vanity, anger, envy, avarice – are the counterparts of the three theological and the four cardinal virtues.

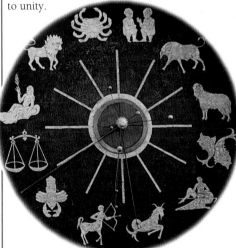

12 As the multiple of the masculine three and the feminine four, 12 represents both spiritual and earthly order. There are 12 signs of the zodiac, 12 months of the year, 12 hours of day and night. There are also 12 knights of the Round Table, 12 days of Christmas, 12 disciples, and 12 tribes of Israel.

SEE ALSO

TWO ☞
CHINESE CLOUDS 37;
CROW 65; I CHING 111;
SOUTH KOREA 115

THREE ☞
TRACING BOARD 109

SEVEN ☞
ORPHEUS' LYRE 81

TEN ☞ THE BIRTH OF
JEWISH LAW 17;
PLANETARY RULERS 113

SHAPES & PATTERNS

MANY SHAPES AND PATTERNS are universal. For example, similar patterns may decorate objects separated by thousands of kilometres and thousands of years. Symmetrical shapes appeal to our need for order, intricate shapes, such as puzzles and knots, appeal to an urge to unravel mysteries, and labyrinths can express the need to find a true path despite obstacles. Shapes may be mystical symbols. They may also be used symbolically in architecture, the square temple surmounted by the circular dome, for instance, where the square is the solidity of the earth and the dome represents the sky.

YANTRA OR MANDALA

A sacred Hindu diagram, the *yantra* is used as a focus for meditation. Concentrating on the geometric shapes draws the mind into the diagram and beyond, into ultimate reality. Yantras often form the basis for the ground plans of temples. The mandala is a circular yantra, usually enclosing a square.

DOORS OF PERCEPTION
The four projections from the middle of each side of the inner square are the "doors" of the yantra, through which the mind may enter or leave the centre during contemplation.

SQUARE WITHIN SQUARE
The square represents the earth, solidity, order, and safety. It also represents the four compass directions and the balance of opposites. The immense Grande Arche in Paris seems to embody these qualities by its location, size, and function. Where one square sits inside another, the outer square symbolizes awareness of the physical world and the inner square the unconscious.

STONE CIRCLE
Certain stone-age peoples have left behind huge standing stones as monuments. The original function of the stone circle at Stonehenge in England is still a mystery. It was probably a form of temple, maybe representing the eye of the Great Goddess.

STAR
The star symbolizes light in darkness and wisdom shining through ignorance. To many people stars are the spirits of the dead, set in the sky. To "reach for the stars" is to set the highest goal. In the US the star became a badge of honour.

SHRI YANTRA, NEPAL, C. 1700

WHEEL
This wheel, which is one of twelve from the base of the Sun Temple at Konarak, India, symbolizes *samsara*, the endless round of existence. The wheel in Buddhism is a symbol of the Buddhist law, or doctrine, set in motion in the Buddha's first sermon.

LONGEVITY
This is *shou*, one of the three ways of representing the Chinese symbol for longevity or immortality. It is often seen with other symbols of longevity, such as the pine or the tortoise. When paired with a peach, it is a wish for a long and happy marriage.

CIRCLE
The enclosing circles serve to unify the opposing triangles. They are made up of lotus petals to signify the unfolding of reality, as perceived by meditating on the yantra.

TRIANGLE
The upward-pointing triangles represent the male principle, and the downward-pointing triangles the female principle. They interlock to show the creative activity of the cosmos.

SWASTIKA
The swastika is a very ancient and auspicious sign with complicated symbolism. It is found in most parts of the world but is especially popular in India. However, in the West it is now a symbol of evil because of its association with Adolf Hitler and the Nazis.

FLEUR-DE-LIS
Emblem of French monarchy, the fleur-de-lis may be a stylized iris. Legend also claims an angel gave a lily to Clovis, King of the Franks, in AD 496 when he accepted Christianity.

ALMOND
Also known as the mandorla, the almond-shaped halo is formed from two intersecting circles. It is used to symbolize Christ's ascension to heaven.

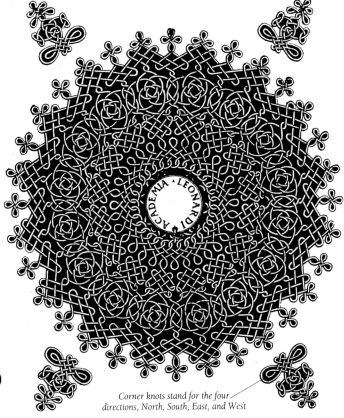

Corner knots stand for the four directions, North, South, East, and West

KNOT
This engraving by Leonardo da Vinci is, like a yantra, a contemplative diagram. It is a knot made from a single thread which, if followed, will lead to one's inner being. The knot binds but also holds the promise of release. A knot can be tied for protection, and to "tie the knot" means to get married.

THRESHOLD STONE, NEW GRANGE, EIRE, 3RD/4TH MILLENIUM BC

SPIRALS
Energy was once believed to flow in spiral form. The spiral symbolizes both masculine and feminine energy and that of the sun and moon. It is the great swirling force of the whirlwind and the movement of the heavens. It is a manifestation of the energy in nature, and is related to the powerful imagery of the serpent. The spiral also symbolizes the circlings of the soul, which eventually returns to the centre, or truth.

MAZE
The maze, or labyrinth, has appeared in the art of the Egyptians, Indians, Celts, and Mediterranean peoples. Some mazes have a clear path leading to the centre, where truth lies; others are puzzles, with the path constantly dividing. Such mazes often occur in dreams, representing indecision. The labyrinth is difficult to enter but also difficult to leave, and only those with wisdom can find their way through it.

Pillar of the god Osiris

ANKH
The ankh is an ancient Egyptian symbol. By combining the Tau cross of the god Osiris and the oval of the goddess Isis, it signified life. It was later adopted by the Coptic Christian church in Egypt.

TRISKELE
This Chinese drum bears the triskele symbol, which, like the swastika, was originally a symbol of good fortune. It may represent the movement of the sun across the heavens.

SEE ALSO
MAZE ☞
MINOTAUR 28; MAZE 43
STAR ☞
STAR OF DAVID 16;
SEAL OF SOLOMON 108
SWASTIKA ☞
SWASTIKA 21; FOOTPRINT 22
TRIANGLE ☞
ALCHEMICAL SYMBOLS 108
YANTRA ☞ ROSE WINDOW
51; EYE OF WISDOM 72

COLOUR

WE ARE SURROUNDED BY COLOUR, and its immediate visual effect on our senses has powerful emotional and symbolic overtones. Red is equated with blood, for instance, and green with grass. The two colours traditionally associated with death are black and white. Though it differs from culture to culture – and even from person to person – colour symbolism is among the most universal. Certain colours, such as red, advance, and are considered lively and stimulating; others, such as blue, retreat, and tend to be soothing. Rainbows, which contain the full spectrum, are viewed as lucky.

ORANGE

Like red, orange symbolizes flames but also luxury and splendour. In China and Japan it is equated with love and happiness.

RED

Red is the colour of life – of blood, fire, passion, and war. It is worn by brides in India and China as a symbol of good luck and fertility. Christian calendars marked holy days in red, hence red-letter days. But red is also the colour of danger, and warnings are often marked in red.

WHITE

White symbolizes purity and perfection, also the absolute. It is the colour most associated with sacredness: sacrificial animals are often white. In the West brides traditionally wear white, but it is the colour of mourning in much of Asia. Ghosts are thought to be white because it is a colour that conceals nothing. A white flag signals truce, and therefore peace.

BLACK
In the West, black is the colour of death, mourning, and the underworld. It also has associations with evil magic. In Hinduism, Kali, the terrible goddess of destruction, is black. In China it represents the north and winter.

JET EARRINGS

SAFFRON ROBES
These young initiates wear the saffron-coloured robes of Buddhist monks to indicate that they have taken vows of humility and renunciation.

RED FLAG
Symbol of revolution and the Communist party, the red flag was first raised during the French Revolution. It was adopted during the Paris Commune in 1871, and then by the Russian communists.

RED DEVIL
Since medieval times, Satan, or the Devil, has been depicted with red clothes or skin. Red is the colour of hell fire and damnation and also of unbridled passion and lust.

BROWN
Brown symbolizes the earth and autumn. It is also, as the colour of the earth, humility, and degradation.

JET BLACK
Jewellery made of jet, a black, semi-precious stone, was commonly used by those in mourning in Victorian times. Queen Victoria, in perpetual mourning after her husband's death, thought that displaying bright jewellery showed a lack of respect for the deceased, and this led to a fashion in jet jewellery.

HOLY RED
To celebrate a mass commemorating martyrs, a Christian priest wears a red chasuble, the colour symbolizing shed blood. Red is also the colour of Christ's Passion.

MONK IN BROWN HABIT

MONK
In the Middle Ages brown was the colour of mourning. Several Christian orders adopted it to signify retreat from the world.

ECCE ANCILLA DOMINI (ANNUNCIATION), ROSSETTI, 1849-50

LILY WHITE
Sometimes called the Madonna Lily, the white lily is a symbol of purity and the Virgin Mary. The angel Gabriel is traditionally depicted with a white lily when he announces to Mary that she is to bear the son of God. In the Christian church, white is associated with the priesthood, baptism, and first communion.

STATUS-SYMBOL RED
The association of red with virility, danger, and sexual excitement makes it one of the most popular colours for flashy sports cars – the ultimate symbol of masculine success in wealthy countries.

YELLOW

Yellow is gold, light, and the sun. In Islam golden yellow represents wisdom and good advice while pale yellow is deceit and betrayal. In Egypt yellow is the colour of envy and disgrace, and in Europe it is associated with cowardice; in China yellow was the colour of royalty. It is the most visible colour and is used internationally for warning.

TREACHEROUS YELLOW
Since the Middle Ages yellow has come to signify, in Europe, betrayal and treachery. Here Judas envelops Jesus in his yellow cloak as he identifies him with a kiss, a sign to the chief priests that they should arrest him. The colour symbolism would have been evident to Renaissance viewers.

BETRAYAL OF CHRIST, GIOTTO, 1305-6

IMPERIAL YELLOW
In China yellow is symbolic of the masculine principle, yang, and the power of the sun. During the Ch'ing dynasty (1644-1911), only the emperor could wear yellow. This 18th-century imperial throne cushion is decorated with dragons, also the emblem of the emperor.

FESTIVE YELLOW
During the Somavati Amavasya festival in India, pilgrims scatter vast amounts of turmeric powder over the god Khandoba. The yellow powder represents the power of the sun. The festival marks the conjunction of the sun and moon – the new moon – when it falls on a Monday.

GREEN

Green is the colour of life, spring, and youth. It represents hope and joy. It is the sacred colour of Islam, and in Christianity it is the colour of the Trinity. Today, green represents a concern with ecology. However, it also represents decay and jealousy.

FLAG OF PAKISTAN

ISLAMIC GREEN
Pakistan's flag declares the nation's faith. Green, Islam's sacred colour, is combined with white for purity. The crescent became a symbol of Islam in the 14th century and the star was later added as a symbol of sovereignty.

GREEN FOR GO
Green is used universally as a sign giving the go-ahead. Along with red and amber, it was originally used for railway signalling before it was adopted on the road.

VEGETARIAN SOCIETY LOGO

COLOUR OF LIFE
Chlorophyll gives plants their green colour. A stylized seedling forms the V of the Vegetarian Society. Its logo is increasingly used in the Western world to draw attention to manufactured foods suitable for vegetarian consumption.

BLUE

As the colour of the sky and water, blue symbolizes calm, reflection, and the intellect. It is also the infinite, and the void from which all life develops.

BLUE STONE
Ground lapis lazuli produced a pigment highly prized in Mesopotamia for decorating temple ceilings. The colour signifies divine favour.

BLUE-SKINNED GOD
Rama, an incarnation of the Hindu god Vishnu, is usually depicted with blue skin, as is Krishna, another much-loved incarnation. Blue is an appropriate colour for Vishnu, as it represents the enormity of the heavens.

BLUE DOME
The blue dome of this Russian church with its gold stars represents the heavens, with the cross above indicating that Christ's dominion encompasses all life.

Gold stars in blue heaven

PURPLE

In the West, purple signifies royalty and imperial power as it did in ancient South America. It represents pride and grandeur and also justice.

DYED PURPLE
In ancient Greece purple dye, extracted from molluscs, was a luxury which only the rich could afford. Thus the colour now symbolizes wealth.

PURPLE HEART
In 1782 George Washington created the first US military medal, a heart-shaped badge of purple cloth. It was revived in 1932 as the Purple Heart, awarded to those wounded or killed in battle.

PINK

In western traditions, pink is the colour of flesh, and hence sensuality. A softer tone of red, it is primarily associated with the feminine.

BABY PINK
More muted than red, pink probably suggests sensuality in a less aggressive way. Pink is the traditional colour for young girls. Baby girls are still often dressed in pale pink, in contrast to the traditional pale blue for boys.

GREY

Grey is associated with gloom and depression. But as a balance between black and white it is the colour of mediation. Things that are not certain are considered grey areas. In Christianity grey represents the immortality of the soul and is worn by religious groups.

SEE ALSO

BLACK ☞
JET 38; MOURNING JEWELLERY 87; RAVEN, HEARSE 92

BLUE ☞ LAPIS LAZULI 40

LILY WHITE ☞ THE LILY AND CHRISTIANITY 53; 93; RITUAL MOURNING, LILY 93

RED ☞
GOLDFINCH 66; ROBIN 67; INDIAN WEDDING 83

SAFFRON ROBES ☞ BUDDHIST MONKS 23

ALCHEMY

ALCHEMY, THE MEDIEVAL FORERUNNER OF CHEMISTRY, was a richly symbolic tradition that united scientific practice with a mystical view of nature. The goal of alchemists was to discover the Philosopher's Stone or the Elixir of Life, which would create gold from base metals. This was known as transmutation, but could also be understood as a quest for spiritual perfection. One way of achieving this was to unite opposing elements such as water and fire, earth and air, the four primary elements. The fifth element or essence, "quintessence", symbolized the spirit.

UROBOROS

ALCHEMISTS IN LABORATORY

THE TAIL OF THE DRAGON
In alchemy a dragon or serpent eating its own tail is known as the uroboros. The dragon was a symbol of the god Mercury and the circle a powerful symbol of the eternal cycle of nature. Because the uroboros recreates itself by feeding on its own body, it is a symbol of transforming matter, and so of alchemy itself.

CADUCEUS
According to alchemical lore, Mercury, messenger of the gods, cast his magic wand between two warring serpents. They coiled themselves around it, forming what is called the caduceus, a symbol of opposing forces held in balance.

EARLY ALCHEMISTS
Alchemists were philosopher-chemists. Their goal was to distil an elixir that would transform common metals, such as lead, into gold. Through their ceaseless laboratory experiments they forged a path for modern chemistry.

ALCHEMICAL SYMBOLS
Alchemists believed all matter was made up of earth, fire, water, and air. The symbol for water flows down like water; the symbol for fire rises up like flames. Sulphur and mercury are often paired together as masculine and feminine symbols repectively. The sun was the symbol of gold and the moon of silver.

WATER

FIRE

MERCURY

SULPHUR

MOON

SUN

OPUS MEDICO-CHYMICUM, AFTER J. D MYLIUS, 1618

SEAL OF SOLOMON
This six-pointed star, one of the most powerful magical symbols of all time, combines the alchemical signs for fire and water. As the water descends and the fire ascends, air and earth are created. The seal, therefore, represents the union of the four elements in the quest for the Philosopher's Stone.

SEAL OF SOLOMON

IMMORTALITY
Because of fear of persecution, alchemists developed a complex vocabulary of symbols to record and pass on their knowledge. This diagram shows how to arrive at the Philosopher's Stone, the key to immortality. The alchemist brings together the four vital elements around him – water and fire, earth and air.

PHOENIX
This mythical bird is the alchemical symbol of rebirth through fire. In medieval legend, the phoenix lives in Arabia but flies to Egypt, the home of alchemy, to undergo its ritual death and regeneration. Here it cradles the all-powerful elements of water and fire under its wings.

SEE ALSO

CADUCEUS ☞ DIAMOND BROOCH 40; ROD OF AESCULAPIUS 59

EARLY ALCHEMISTS ☞ GOLD, LEAD 39

PHOENIX ☞ PHOENIX 31

SEAL OF SOLOMON ☞ STAR OF DAVID 16; ISRAEL 115

FREEMASONRY

FREEMASONRY IS THE WORLD'S OLDEST association of men. Its members, masons, belong to a lodge presided over by a master and wardens. The craft, as freemasonry is called, is concerned with "building" good men. Initiation rites, or degrees, concern the biblical Temple of Solomon and use the stone mason's tools as symbols of personal or spiritual growth.

APRON OF GRAND MASTER

MASONIC EMBLEM
As essential tools of the stone mason, the square and compasses have become the main symbol of freemasonry. Together they help to create better citizens.

LEVEL
The level is used to lay bricks horizontally. It is the symbol of the Senior Warden and signifies equality.

SQUARE
This is the emblem of the Master of a lodge. It is an instrument that gathers scattered elements into order and so represents a moral code.

PLUMB RULE
Builders use the plumb rule to obtain true verticals. For Masons it is a symbol of rectitude, indicating their upright behaviour. It is the emblem of a Junior Warden of a Lodge.

APRON
The apron harks back to the original lambskin aprons worn by stone masons. Masonic aprons are richly decorated emblems of office. That of the Grand Master bears the sun – as the sun rises in the East announcing the day, so too the Grand Master opens the lodge, sitting in the East.

TRACING BOARD
The principles of freemasonry are explained to new members using tracing boards covered with symbols. This board with its pillars of wisdom, strength, and beauty, represents the first degree of initiation into the fraternity.

Jacob's ladder
This connects the pathway between heaven and earth, with the three principal rungs of Faith, Hope, and Charity

Compass points
The cardinal points of the compass are shown on the border

Pillar
The three pillars stand for the "Rule of Three": the wisdom, beauty, and strength displayed in the building of the Temple of Solomon

Ashlar
The rough ashlar, or masonry block, represents unformed man; the complete ashlar (opposite it), perfection itself

Chequered pavement
The black and white squares represent the struggle between good and evil

The sun, representing the day

The all-seeing eye, with rays of light, an ancient symbol of God

Moon and stars, representing night

FIRST DEGREE
TRACING BOARD

TROWEL

SIGN LANGUAGE
Solomon's Temple is full of symbols, with winding stairs representing the individual's inner journey. On either side are the key to man's secrets and an ear of corn signifying plenty. The trowel "cements" brotherhood.

Pyramid and all-seeing eye

American eagle

US ONE-DOLLAR BILL

US DOLLAR BILL
America's first president, George Washington, was a mason. He adopted freemasonry symbols such as the pyramid (to denote knowledge and wisdom), and the all-seeing eye of God, as emblems of the new American nation.

SEE ALSO

SIGN LANGUAGE ☞
DOME OF THE ROCK 25
TRACING BOARD ☞
PERSONIFICATION OF SUN AND MOON 34;
SUN KING 39; LADDER 90;
STEPS 94
US DOLLAR BILL ☞
PYRAMIDS 94

DIVINATION

TO SEE INTO THE FUTURE AND PREDICT the course of events is a desire that has preoccupied humankind from time immemorial. In some countries, animal entrails and shoulder blades are still examined for signs or answers to questions, as are the feeding habits of chickens. In the West, the richly symbolic divinatory system of the Tarot with its pictorial representations of situations or states of mind has retained its popularity, and the medieval art of casting runes has re-emerged. The ancient art of palmistry, in which the lines etched on the human palm stand for areas of human life, continues to flourish everywhere.

PENDULUM
A pendulum can be used for dowsing – discovering metal objects or water beneath the earth's surface. In especially skilled hands, a pendulum can even be suspended over a map to locate lost items.

AFRICAN DIVINING BOWL AND STIC

DIVINATION BOWL
Among the Yoruba of Nigeria, a bowl is fille with sand and then tapped with a stick. The resulting sand formation can be interpreted by the diviner in answer to questions such as where to locate water or when the tribe can expect rain.

CRYSTAL BALL

CRYSTAL BALL
Crystal spheres can concentrate the rays of the sun and so have come to represent divine light and celestial powers. In Europe the crystal ball is often used in divination and is now a classic symbol of fortune telling. A medium gazes into the ball and sees "pictures", usually of the future.

OUIJA BOARD
The ouija board is a means of getting in touch with the dead, and has come to represent contact with the spirit world. While many see this as a harmless pastime, others use it seriously to contact those they have lost or to ask questions about the future. A group of people sit together lightly touching a planchette and by their concentration call down a spirit which uses it to spell out particular answers.

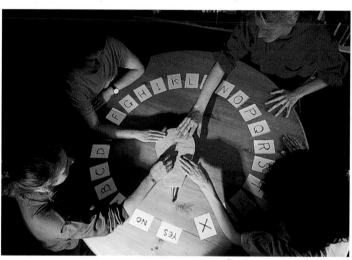
DIVINATION USING A OUIJA BOARD

ROMAN DIVINATION DEVICE

ROMAN DIVINATION
In Roman times, sacrec chickens were used as messengers of the gods They were placed in specially constructed coops and observed. The way they scratched at their food and ate was thought to show whether or not the gods approved a particular plan. A similar form of divination is still practised in parts of the world today.

READING HANDS

The idea that the lines of the hand reveal a person's character is very old. Different forms of palmistry appear in ancient Chinese and Jewish texts. As well as the lines, the shape of the fingers and of the "mounts" all play a part in the diagnosis.

A developed mount of Saturn is the sign of a hardworking personality

The mount of Mercury reveals a person's ability to communicate

One of the two mounts of Mars which denotes aggressiveness

Mount of the Moon relates to imagination

Mount of Jupiter stands for ambition and success

A developed mount of Venus indicates a kind-hearted person

OIL IN HAND
In Arab countries, the traditional method of looking into the future is by reading the formation of a pool of black ink or oil in the palm of the hand.

PALMISTRY
According to palmistry, one's character and future life is written in the lines of the hand. The palm contains numerous lines, three of which – the head line, the heart line, and the life line – are deemed particularly important. The strength and length of these major lines indicate health, relationships, and overall character, as well as destiny.

GYPSY READING TEA LEAVES

TEA LEAVES
It was once common practice in England to have one's fortune told by means of tea leaves. The "reader" would drink the tea until just one teaspoon remained in the cup. The cup would then be rotated three times before the liquid was poured into the saucer. The patterns created by the leaves that were left behind formed the basis of the reader's interpretation.

CHINESE THROWING STICKS
In Chinese temples it is common to see men and women shaking cylindrical pots of sticks until one stick clatters to the ground. In this type of divination, cryptic messages are attached to the sticks. The one which falls first is all-important, and books provide detailed interpretations.

DIVINATION STICKS WITH BOOK FOF TELLING FORTUNES

the Middle Ag... ...ome back into vogue. There are ... symbolic meaning, plus a bl... ...own. The order in which the run... ...meaning.

The Tarot cards probably originated in the East and entered Europe over 500 years ago. The cards consist of 22 major arcana or trump cards and 56 minor arcana, the two sets possibly originating separately. Together they present a picture of our personality and symbolize the soul's journey along four parallel paths towards spiritual enlightenment.

STRENGTH	SEPARATION	PARTNERSHIP
THE SELF	PROTECTION	DEFENCE
FERTILITY	GROWTH	HARVEST
JOY	JOURNEY	FLOW

THE FOOL SYMBOLIZES NAIVE WISDOM, OR AN UNPLANNED INCIDENT OR ENDEAVOUR

XIIII — TEMPERANCE	XV — LE DIABLE.	VI — L'AMOUREUX.
TEMPERANCE	THE DEVIL	THE LOVERS

XVII. — L'ÉTOILE	XVIII — LA LUNE	XX — LE JUGEMENT	XVI — LA MAISON DE DIEU
THE STAR	THE MOON	JUDGEMENT	THE TOWER

PENTACLES	SWORDS	CUPS	WANDS

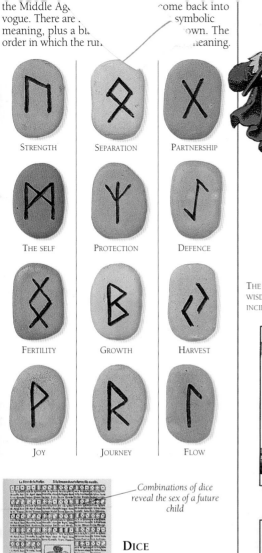

FRENCH 16TH-CENTURY TABLE

Combinations of dice reveal the sex of a future child

DICE

Dice have been thrown in divination since ancient times, and are common symbols of luck or chance. In this method of looking into the future, three dice are thrown. When they fall, the numbers that they reveal and the order in which the dice lie are checked against a table of meanings. This in turn provides answers to or interpretations of the questions raised.

I CHING

The I Ching is an ancient Chinese divinatory text in which answers to questions are set out in the form of "trigrams". Each trigram consists of three whole (male) or broken (female) lines. There are eight basic patterns which can be combined to provide a choice of 64 hexagrams of 6 lines, each giving a different meaning.

	FIRE, LIGHTNING OR THE SUN	HEAVEN, THE SKY
	WATER OF CLOUDS OR STREAMS	THUNDER

	HILLS OR MOUNTAINS
	WATER OF A LAKE OR MARSH
	THE WIND, WOOD
	THE EARTH

BACK OF I CHING CARD

The complementary forces of yin and yang are central to the I Ching

FRONT OF I CHING CARD

This hexagram of the earth over the earth relates to fertility

SEE ALSO

CRYSTAL BALL ☞ CRYSTAL 39

DICE ☞ DICE 79

I CHING ☞ CROW 65; TWO 102

PALMISTRY ☞ HAND OF THE FUTURE 75; PLANETARY RULERS 113

PREDICTION ☞ SNAIL 57; NEWT 58

ROMAN DIVINATION ☞ COCKS AND HENS 64

THE LANGUAGE OF THE TAROT ☞ TAROT CARD 92

ASTROLOGY

THE IDEA THAT THE MOVEMENT of the Sun, the Moon, and the planets through the heavens influences our lives goes back thousands of years. As early as 3000 BC, the ancient Mesopotamian civilizations recorded the movement of the Sun, the Moon, and the planets, and endowed their gods and goddesses with the power and attributes of the heavenly bodies. The Greeks saw them as representations of their own deities, and the Romans gave the five known planets – Mercury, Venus, Mars, Jupiter, and Saturn – the names that we still use today.

ASTROLOGICAL WHEEL

shows 12 "houses", each representing one-twelfth of the heavens at the time of birth. The outer ring shows the signs; the inner ring shows the element assigned to each. Fire signs are energetic and forceful; water signs are emotional and intuitive; air signs are objective and logical; earth signs are practical and reliable.

EVERYTHING UNDER THE SUN

THE SUN SPENDS ONE MONTH IN EACH ZODIAC SIGN

Our Sun sign is the astrological sign of the zodiac that the powerful Sun is passing through at the time of our birth. Using symbolic language, the Sun sign in astrology describes how we express ourselves most naturally. The Moon in astrology is the feminine counterpart of the Sun. It represents our emotional responses and our links with the past.

THE MOON PASSES THROUGH EVERY SIGN EACH MONTH

ARIES 21 MAR–20 APR

 ARIES
Courageous, passionate, enthusiastic, and assertive, Aries people are inclined to rush into things. This fire sign is associated with spring – a time of renewed growth, and energy.

TAURUS 21 APR–21 MAY

TAURUS
Those born under this earth sign are said to be practical and reliable, yet with a stubborn streak. Sensuous Taureans have a love of beauty, and some have beautiful voices.

GEMINI 22 MAY–21 JUN

 GEMINI
Versatile and quick-witted, those born under the sign of the twins can also be changeable. Geminis are communicative people and need to know what is going on around them.

CANCER 22 JUN–22 JUL

 CANCER
Cancerians are said to be sensitive, home-loving types who will retreat into their shell if upset. This water sign is associated with the family, and many Cancerians have very close family ties.

LEO 23 JUL–23 AUG

 LEO
The typical Leo likes to be the centre of attention and can have a powerful personality with a touch of the dramatic. Warm and loyal, Leos have a generous and friendly nature.

VIRGO 24 AUG–23 SEPT

 VIRGO
Cautious and quite private, the practical Virgoan pays attention to detail and likes to be well prepared. Virgoans may take a special interest in their health and diet.

LIBRA 24 SEPT–23 OCT

LIBRA
The symbol of the scales indicates that justice and fairness are important to Librans. Charming and diplomatic, Librans need harmony and are upset by discord.

SCORPIO 24 OCT–22 NOV

SCORPIO
Intense and passionate, with a love of mystery and secrets, Scorpios are loyal and private people. Not known for their moderation, they react strongly, especially when threatened.

SAGITTARIUS 23 NOV–21 DEC

SAGITTARIUS
Enthusiastic, direct, and adventurous, Sagittarians love to learn. With a great desire for freedom, Sagittarians can become restless if life becomes routine, and many enjoy travelling.

CAPRICORN 22 DEC–20 JAN

CAPRICORN
Cautious and disciplined, those born under the sign of the goat are hard-working and have a marked urge to succeed in life. They prefer the tried and tested and can resist change.

AQUARIUS 21 JAN–19 FEB

AQUARIUS
Independent and with a reformist streak, Aquarians are individualists who rarely subscribe to conventional views. Champions of new causes, their opinions can appear dogmatic.

PISCES 20 FEB–20 MAR

PISCES
The typical Pisces is imaginative and intuitive and has a very compassionate nature. Pisces' fish symbolism reflects the rather slippery and changeable quality of the sign.

PLANETARY RULERS

In astrology, the ten planets (the Sun and Moon are treated as planets, although technically a star and a satellite) represent basic drives or characteristics that are common to everyone. The sign the planet occupies at birth, its position, and the aspects it makes, colour the expression of its energies. Below are the main symbols and associations for each planet.

SUN
The central creative force in the zodiac, the Sun has masculine attributes and is linked with rulers and fathers. It is associated with the heart and its metal is gold. The Sun rules the sign of Leo.

MOON
Associated with mothers, the body, and childhood, the Moon is the Sun's feminine counterpart. Linked to the stomach and womb, its metal is silver. The Moon rules the sign of Cancer.

MERCURY
Fast-moving Mercury represents the mind and the urge to understand and communicate. Linked with the shoulders, arms, and nervous system, Mercury rules Virgo and Gemini.

VENUS
The planet of love, attraction, beauty, and co-operation, Venus also represents what we value in life. It is linked to the kidneys and is the natural ruler of Taurus and Libra.

MARS
Named after the god of war, Mars symbolizes direct energy and getting what we want. Ruler of Aries and Scorpio, Mars is associated with the head, and with iron and steel.

JUPITER
The largest known planet, Jupiter represents expansion, exploration, and the search for knowledge and meaning. Jupiter's associated body part is the liver, and it rules Sagittarius and Pisces.

SATURN
Once the farthest known planet, Saturn represents order, limitation, and responsibility. It is associated with the skeleton and the skin, and rules Capricorn and Aquarius.

URANUS
Discovered only in the late 18th century at a time of revolutions and social unrest, Uranus represents individual freedom, new ideas, and dramatic change. It is the ruler of Aquarius.

NEPTUNE
Neptune, discovered in the middle of the 19th century, symbolizes the intangible and the extraordinary. The planet of fantasy and dreams, Neptune rules the sign of Pisces.

PLUTO
Pluto represents powerful, hidden forces beyond our control, and is named after the Roman god of the underworld. It is associated with life, death, and renewal and rules Scorpio.

THOSE BORN UNDER THE OX ARE STRONG AND STUBBORN

CHINESE ASTROLOGY

The Chinese system is based on the year of birth. Each of the twelve animal signs occurs every twelve years according to a lunar calendar that begins around January/ February. The signs are further defined by the elements wood, fire, air, metal, and water.

THE COCK IS DISCIPLINED BUT FUNNY

RAT
(e.g. 1948) The rat is ambitious, hard-working, and liable to accumulate money. Rats may be reserved and shy.

OX
(e.g. 1973) The intelligent and hard-working ox can be stubborn. Once aroused, however, his feelings are deep.

TIGER
(e.g. 1962) The tiger takes risks but is usually born lucky. Tigers have a sensual nature and often act on impulse.

RABBIT
(e.g. 1987) The rabbit is artistic, thoughtful, intelligent, and lucky. He often pursues a comfortable lifestyle.

DRAGON
(e.g. 1940) Dragons are strong-willed and fiery. They are usually successful, and either marry young or stay single.

SNAKE
(e.g. 1953) Snakes are pleasure-loving, with a tendency to be secretive. They are as energetic and self-reliant as dragons.

HORSE
(e.g. 1990) Freedom-loving, good-humoured, and generous, the horse is a popular and rather unpredictable character.

BOAR
(e.g. 1959) Those born in the year of the boar tend to be sociable, loyal, and reliable, with a passionate nature.

DOG
(e.g. 1934) Dogs are intelligent, affectionate, honest, and loyal. They are objective but can be inflexible.

COCK
(e.g. 1957) Disciplined and good at organizing others, the cock can be eccentric but has a sense of humour.

MONKEY
(e.g. 1992) The charming and conceited monkey can be promiscuous when young but is more settled later.

SHEEP
(e.g. 1943) Those born under this sign tend to feel easily hurt. Their compassionate nature makes them popular.

NEPALESE ZODIAC, EARLY 20TH CENTURY

A WHEEL OF YEARS
This Nepalese zodiac displays the 12 images of the Chinese system in the outer circle and the 8 sacred Buddhist symbols in the central circle.

SIGNS OF THE ZODIAC FROM HARMONIA MACRO COSMICA, 1708

MAPPING THE SKIES
As men and women gazed up at the night sky, the patterns created by the stars suggested familiar objects or animals. They named the stars according to what they saw – Leo for lion and Gemini for twins – and included these images in their early maps.

SEE ALSO
CHINESE ZODIAC ☞ CHINESE DRAGON 30
HINDU ZODIAC ☞ MAKARA 29; HINDU WHEEL 104
PLANETS ☞ SUN AND MOON 34-35; PALMISTRY 110
WHEEL ☞ WHEEL OF LAW 22; WHEELS WITHIN 103; HINDU WHEEL 104

HERALDIC EMBLEMS

ONE OF THE MOST COLOURFUL and attractive uses of symbols is in heraldry. There is no limit to the variety of devices used – plants, animals, humans, mythical beings, geometric shapes, colours, and inscriptions are grouped in a coat of arms or as a flag to represent a family, business, or nation. The practice of heraldry began in medieval times when symbols were used to identify knights on a battlefield or jousting in tournaments. It soon became a highly complicated system that had to be strictly regulated. This was done by the king's messengers, the heralds, which is why it is called heraldry.

VIVID LANGUAGE

Heraldic devices are described in a language called "blazon". It uses terms such as "shield", "charge" (a symbol on the shield), and "supporter" (a figure on either side of a shield).

TRAPPINGS OF CHIVALRY
Knights and their horses dressed sumptuously for battle or jousting. They wore their heraldic symbols on their shield, armour, and surcoat – the garment worn over the armour – from which we get the term "coat of arms".

SPANISH PLATE, 15TH CENTURY

MIXED SIGNALS
The "charges" on this "shield" are a castle, denoting the Spanish city of Castile, and a lion, for the city of Leon. The surrounding decoration is of Islamic origin, reflecting Spain's Moorish heritage.

LION
The so-called king of beasts is a natural symbol of royalty.

BEAR
In Central European heraldry the bear, standing for strength, often replaces the lion.

EAGLE
The double-headed eagle is of Byzantine (late Roman) origin.

DOG
Symbol of faithfulness and loyalty, a dog may signify a Crusader.

CRESTED EAGLE
Crests were originally heraldic symbols mounted on helmets. An eagle, symbol of German power, crowns an early 20th-century Prussian officer's helmet.

CADENCY MARKS
On English coats of arms, these symbols represent the rank of each son within the family.

2ND SON

3RD SON

1ST SON

4TH SON

5TH SON

STATUS SYMBOLS
Since coats of arms are ultimately granted by the "fount of all honour", the Crown, they have come to represent power and authority – royal, inherited, or civic.

ARMS OF HENRY VIII
At the time of Henry VIII, the British royal coat of arms bore the English lion and the Welsh dragon. The unicorn of Scotland was not represented as Scotland was then a separate kingdom.

ARMS OF THE SWINTON FAMILY
Dating from the 12th century, the Swinton family arms have evolved from a single boar "rampant" or upright into a herd of six, acquiring along the way the mottos "I hope" and "I think".

ARMS OF THE CITY OF LIVERPOOL
Neptune and a merman, the "supporters", refer to Liverpool's long history as a port, as does the ship. The liver bird (rather like a cormorant), is a visual pun, a device in heraldry called "canting".

ORIENTAL BADGES OF HONOUR

Japan is the only nation that shares a similar system of heraldry to that of Europe, and it also developed in the 12th century. Japanese heraldic symbols are called "mons", and are usually circular. The red sun on the Japanese flag is the mon of the Land of the Rising Sun. Symbolic patterns were also used on Chinese court dress to denote rank.

16-PETALLED CHRYSANTHEMUM

IMPERIAL FLOWER
The chrysanthemum is the national flower of Japan and a symbol of long life and prosperity. The 16-petalled flower is the crest of the emperor; other imperial males use a 14-petalled mon.

OFFICIAL'S DRESS
Each round pattern on this Chinese court coat is made up of good luck symbols. The Manchurian crane was a symbol of longevity, and was supposed to carry the immortals through the air. White cranes were embroidered on the court robes of civic officials of the fourth grade. Here they are encircled by clouds and tiny bats, the bats being symbols of happiness.

Clouds indicate sky

Crane, symbol of long life

Wave pattern, for water, symbol of purity

CHINESE COURT ROBE, 19TH CENTURY

PAULOWNIA, THE NATIVE FLOWERING TREE, PRIVATE MON OF THE IMPERIAL FAMILY

MON WITH EIGHT ARROWS

FIVE-SICKLED WHEEL

ENCIRCLING CENTIPEDES

FLAGS

Using a range of colours, forms, emblems, and designs, flags represent a wide variety of different peoples, but probably the best known flags are those of nation states.

PIRATE ENSIGN
A red flag meant no mercy would be shown to the victim. The winged hourglass, arm and sword, and skull-and-crossbones all signified death.

SRI LANKA
The lion emblem comes from Kandy, heart of the island's Buddhism. It is the largest animal on any national flag.

CANADA
The maple leaf, representing the local red maple, is the largest plant symbol on a national flag.

MALAWI
The sun appears on many flags, sometimes representing royalty. The rising red sun in the top band of Malawi's flag is taken from the arms of the former colony of Nyasaland.

ZAIRE
The hand holding a blazing torch is the emblem of the MPR (Movement of the Revolution). Now incorporated on the national flag, it is a symbol of the struggle for independence.

SOUTH KOREA
The "yin-yang" symbol in the centre represents the two universal opposing forces of Taoism. The four trigrams of the *I Ching* represent sun, moon, earth, and heaven.

ISRAEL
The Star of David is a religious symbol. The six points represent the six days of creation; the centre, the Sabbath. The blue stripes come from the prayer shawl. Blue stands for heaven; white, for purity.

BHUTAN
The dragon – similar to those that appeared on Chinese flags – is a reminder that this Himalayan kingdom's name in its own language, "Druk Yul", means "Land of the Thunder Dragon".

KENYA
The sword and crossed spears symbolize the Masai, an ancient warrior-hunter tribe. The colours are those of the main political party at the time of independence; the red is known as Kenya red.

USA
The Stars and Stripes is the most modified flag in the world. The 13 stripes stand for the original states of the union, but the number of stars increased as each new state joined. The 50th, for Hawaii, was added in 1960.

International Signs

PEACE SIGN

THE NOTION OF A PICTURE BEING WORTH "a thousand words" is borne out by the vast number of signs and symbols that now represent words and phrases throughout the world. Take, for example, the no smoking sign. The red circle with its diagonal line over a smouldering cigarette is as instantly recognizable in New York as it would be in Kathmandu. This sign, like traffic signs or the CND peace symbol above, has been designed to communicate immediately and effectively; other signs, such as mathematical and musical notation, have evolved over centuries as virtual languages in their own right.

Organizations

The Red Cross
The International Red Cross was founded in Geneva in 1863 to provide medical relief to all during wartime. Its emblem was formed by reversing the colours and symbol of the Swiss flag.

The Olympic flag
The Olympic emblem of five interlocking circles was created to represent five continents – Europe, Asia, Africa, Australia, and the Americas.

The United Nations
The United Nations was founded in 1945 and adopted as its emblem a polar view of the world encircled by two olive branches of peace.

The European flag
The European Union (EU) flag was formally adopted in 1986. The 12 five-pointed gold stars represent perfection according to heraldic code.

Mathematical symbols

ADD
The plus sign first appeared in Germany in 1489 in *Mercantile Arithmetic* by John Widman.

SUBTRACT
The symbol for the minus sign, like the plus sign, was first used in John Widman's book.

DIVIDE
The division symbol was invented in 1668 by John Pell, a professor of mathematics from Cambridge, England.

MULTIPLY
The symbol for multiplication first appeared in William Oughtred's *Clavis Mathematica*, published in 1631.

EQUALS
The equals sign was invented by Robert Recorde, who used it in an algebraic text published in 1557.

PER CENT
The per cent sign derives from the formula $x/100$. The term is from the Latin, *per centum*.

INFINITY
The earliest recorded use of the infinity symbol was in 1665, in *De Sectionibus Conicis* by John Wallis.

SQUARE ROOT
Coined in 1557, the square root sign is a modified form of a division sign.

Musical notation
The present system of representing music has evolved over hundreds of years. At the end of the Roman period a system was devised using the letters A-G to represent the 7-note scale. The standardization of the 5-line stave, used to determine pitch, came about in the 17th century.

Treble clef

Middle C

Bass clef

Note values
The duration of notes and rests – the sounds and the silences – is indicated by symbols of different shapes. Semibreves represent a whole note or rest, minims a half, crotchets a quarter, quavers an eighth, semiquavers a 16th, and demisemiquavers a 32nd. The clef signs determine the range of the staves, or parallel lines.

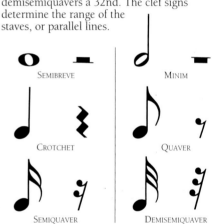

SEMIBREVE | MINIM

CROTCHET | QUAVER

SEMIQUAVER | DEMISEMIQUAVER

Quality control marks

The system of stamping precious metals as proof of their purity came into being in the 13th century. Silver had to have at least 92.5 per cent silver content in order to be considered sterling. Countries adopted different signs to denote purity, and cities also had individual stamps so that pieces could be located accurately.

Silver marks

SILVER PROOF OF 92.5 PER CENT SILVER CONTENT

SWEDEN FROM 1752 (STATE CONTROL MARK)

ITALY (PURITY OF 900/1000; BELOW STERLING)

FRANCE 1798-1809 (PURITY OF 950/1000)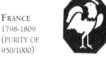

LONDON LEOPARD'S HEAD, IN USE FROM 1327 (STERLING)

MUNICH GERMAN CITY MARK, C.1700

REGISTERED TRADEMARK OWNED BY IWS DENOTING PURE NEW WOOL AND QUALITY ASSURANCE

SYMBOL OF PURE COTTON | SYMBOL OF REAL LEATHER

WARNING SIGNS

Highway "sign language" has been devised for maximum impact. It involves a clear system of colours and shapes that can be understood instantly. Red, for example, indicates prohibition; yellow, caution; and green, safety. Similarly a triangle is a warning sign and a red circle, with or without crossbar, is a prohibition sign.

WARNING TRIANGLE
A triangular black band on a yellow background colour is a cautionary sign.

GENERAL WARNING

TOXIC/POISONOUS

RADIOACTIVE

FLAMMABLE

BEWARE CAMELS!

SLIPPERY ROAD

PROHIBITION
Circles with red outer bands, with or without crossbars, indicate prohibition.

NO ENTRY

NOT SUITABLE FOR DRINKING

NO SMOKING

NO CYCLING

NO FOULING

PUBLIC INFORMATION

The standardization of public symbols has been in operation since the early 1900s, reflecting the growth of international travel. Most signs are self-explanatory.

WOMEN'S ROOM

MEN'S ROOM

DISABLED ACCESS

TELEPHONE

TOURIST INFORMATION

POST

WASHING LABELS
An international labelling scheme exists to promote the aftercare of clothes and textiles. Words are intentionally kept to a minimum. A cross through any symbol means "do not".

WASHING TEMPERATURE

DO NOT WASH

HAND WASH ONLY

IRONING TEMPERATURE

DO NOT IRON

DO NOT TUMBLE DRY

DO NOT BLEACH

DRY CLEAN

RECYCLE
Our ever-increasing awareness of the harmful effects of toxic waste and the vanishing ozone layer has prompted a return to things natural, or "eco-friendly". The recycling sign with its constantly revolving arrows is now a familiar sight on biodegradable products.

DIRECTION
The sign indicating direction has varied over the years, from the graphic hand with outstretched finger of Victorian times to the more stylized arrow used today.

SYMBOLIC GESTURES

"ACTIONS SPEAK LOUDER THAN WORDS", and this is particularly true of gestures. The various postures that we assume, both consciously and unconsciously, are highly revealing although just what they reveal will depend on whether or not the action is intentional, and the context in which it occurs. Some gestures, however, transcend cultures, so that hands clasped together and held out to another are a symbol of entreaty the world over.

THINKING
People adopt this posture unconsciously. It is a modified prayer with a reassuring touching of the lips.

TEETH FLICK
This gesture of thumbnail flicked against front teeth is common in Mediterranean countries where it denotes anger.

HANDS

FINGERS CROSSED
This widespread symbol of protection or good luck is a modified form of the Christian cross.

THUMBS UP
Meaning "okay", this stems from Roman times when spectators would make a similar gesture, covering their thumbs (symbols of swords), to spare a gladiator's life.

V FOR VICTORY
Originating in Britain, this sign is now known worldwide. It was a trademark of Winston Churchill, used first to indicate victory over the Nazis, and later any form of victory.

HORNS
This sign of protection against evil or bad luck is often combined with a backwards and forwards rotation of the hand.

PRAYING HANDS
This familiar symbol of prayer is also one of respect and greeting in India and Southeast Asia. Originally it signified hands bound together in a symbolic offering of oneself to God.

PLEADING HANDS
This is a prayer directed at another person, usually begging for assistance.

LOOSE SCREW
This gesture indicates that the other person is crazy, that he needs to tighten the loose screw in his head.

STUPIDITY
Common in Saudi Arabia, this implies "I can see clearly that you are a fool."

QUERY
In Italy this gesture of fingers and thumb pressed together with the hand twitching up and down asks "What do you want?" or "What do you mean?"

OKAY
Here the thumb and forefinger form a circle and move back and forth to indicate that something is good.

MOCKERY
"Cocking a snook" or holding a thumb to one's nose is a playful insult, familiar to all different ages and nationalities.

JEALOUSY
This gesture has various, related meanings, and is generally an insult. In Mediterranean countries it represents the horns of a cuckold; in Japan, it denotes an angry or jealous woman.

GREETINGS

WAVING
This gesture can be either a "hello" or a "goodbye". The hand raised with palm upwards is a classic way of drawing attention to oneself.

NOSE RUBBING
Although rare in the West, the rubbing of noses in greeting is practised in other cultures, notably by Polynesians.

HANDSHAKE
The clasping of hands is a common gesture both on meeting and parting. Unlike a bow or a curtsey, it signifies a certain equality of status.

JUDO CEREMONIAL BOW

BOWING
This form of greeting is practised mainly in Asia and is a common sign of respect. Performers also bow to their audience to acknowledge applause. In the West bowing still sometimes accompanies the handshake, signifying humility, the person bowing being symbolically "smaller" than the other.

ARMS

TRIUMPH
Arms straight in the air are a sign of success: the person feels this big.

PRAISE
In this gesture, palms, and head are turned heavenwards.

HAIL
Depending on the stiffness of the arm, this is a friendly gesture or a Fascist salute. It goes back to Roman times and was adopted by Hitler in the 1930s.

SURRENDER
A recognized gesture of submission, this arms-raised posture shows that the person is not reaching for a weapon.

REJOICING
This gesture which combines jumping in the air with the slapping of right hands, is a spontaneous display of joy. It is most common in the field of team sports.

FOOTBALL PLAYERS CELEBRATING A GOAL

HEAD

NO
"No" can be expressed by turning the head from side to side, or as in North Africa, with a single, sharp turn to one side and back.

YES
Although shaking one's head generally means "no", in India and Pakistan this wobbling from side to side means "yes".

MOUTH

CHILDHOOD INSULT
Children the world over stick their tongues out as a rude gesture – perhaps their first learned insult.

BE QUIET
An easily recognized symbol of silence, the lips are sealed.

I DON'T KNOW
This gesture involves pulling down the corners of the mouth – a facial equivalent of shrugging shoulders.

ANGER
Biting one's lower lip while shaking one's head from side to side shows barely contained anger.

EYES

EXASPERATION
A familiar sign of exasperation, the eyes are turned heavenwards, as though invoking divine assistance.

WINKING
A wink has various meanings, from sexual approval by a potential partner, to collusion between two people in the know.

SCEPTICISM
Raising just one eyebrow is a common gesture of disbelief. The two sides of the face are at odds, registering a state of confusion.

ANXIETY
Eyebrows raised and furrowed is an instinctive response to extreme anxiety. It is a natural expression, common to all cultures.

KISSING

CHEEK KISS
This is a friendly gesture practised in the West, in which both people kiss each other on one or both cheeks.

HAND KISS
This gesture is a symbol of repect and courtesy, which was once commonly performed by a man greeting a woman.

THE KISS, GUSTAV KLIMT, 1907-8

LOVERS' KISS
An erotic image of a kiss, in which two people are fused together in total intimacy.

BLOWING A KISS
A symbol of love, often from a mother to a child, or to a friend too distant to embrace.

FOOT KISS
A gesture symbolizing humility and respect, performed by the Pope during Holy Week.

SEE ALSO
ARMS ☞ DURGA, SHIVA *20*; BODHISATTVA *23*; ARMS *75*

FINGERS CROSSED ☞ JESUS CHRIST *18*

HANDS ☞ HAND OF GOD *24*; HANDS *75*; CLASSICAL INDIAN DANCE GESTURES *77*; HENNAED HANDS *83*

KISSING ☞ LIPS *82*

MOUTH ☞ TONGUE *72*; TEETH *73*

GLOSSARY

In references to Greek and Roman mythology in the book, we have generally used the Roman names for the gods in preference to their Greek counterparts, as they tend to be more familiar. The Roman gods are given here with their Greek equivalents.

Absolute, the A term for God or the state of cosmic unity.

Adonis In Greek and Roman mythology, a beautiful youth loved by Venus. He was killed while boar-hunting.

Agni Hindu fire god.

Ainu Aboriginal inhabitants of the Japanese island Hokkaido.

Aladdin The main character in *The 1001 Nights*, a poor boy who has a magic lamp.

Alchemy The chemistry of medieval scientists, who tried to find a way to turn ordinary metals into gold.

Allah Islamic name for God.

allegory A story in which the characters and events are interpreted symbolically.

amulet A charm, often inscribed with a magic formula, to protect one against evil.

Annunciation The angel Gabriel's visit to the Virgin Mary to tell her that she would give birth to Jesus.

Apollo Greek and Roman sun god, and god of prophecy.

Ariadne Daughter of Cretan King Minos in Greek mythology, who helped Theseus only to be later abandoned by him.

Aristotle Ancient Greek philosopher advocating reason and moderation.

Asante People from central Ghana.

asceticism Denying oneself physical pleasure for religious reasons.

Assyrians Ancient peoples who inhabited what is now Iraq, and who conquered a vast empire.

auspicious Bringing good luck.

avatar Incarnation; one of the Hindu god Vishnu's ten incarnations on earth.

Aztecs An American Indian people who inhabited ancient Mexico.

Babylonians Inhabitants of ancient Iraq.

Bacchus (Greek Dionysus) Roman god of fertility and wine.

Bodhisattva Future Buddha; one who postpones Nirvana in order to save others.

Brahma The four-headed god who created the universe and who with Vishnu and Shiva forms the Hindu trinity.

Buddha Religious leader, founder of Buddhism, who taught that enlightenment is achieved by meditation and detachment.

Cernunnos Celtic horned god, lord of nature and fertility.

Cherokee Native American people.

Churchill, Winston British Prime Minister during the Second World War.

CND Campaign for Nuclear Disarmament.

Comanches Native people of North America.

cosmos, cosmology Universe; study of the universe as an ordered whole.

Crucifixion The execution of Christ by nailing him to a cross.

cuckold Man whose wife is unfaithful to him.

Cupid (Greek Eros) Roman god of earthly love, son of Venus.

David Second Hebrew king, father of Solomon.

Diana (Greek Artemis) Roman goddess of hunting, protector of women.

Donar Teutonic god of thunder.

Dreaming, the In Australian Aboriginal thought, the spiritual and natural order incorporating legends of the ancestors.

Durga A terrifying form of the Goddess in Hinduism.

elixir A liquid giving everlasting life.

erogenous zone Area of body susceptible to erotic stimulation.

Eve Biblical first woman who lived with her husband Adam in the Garden of Eden.

Exodus The escape of the Jews from slavery in Egypt.

Fates Atropos, Clotho, and Lachesis, Greek goddesses controlling destiny.

Flood, the According to many religious traditions, an ancient disaster which drowned all humanity except for a chosen few.

four elements Earth, air, fire, and water, believed in medieval times to be the basic ingredients of the universe.

four humours The four fluids (blood, phlegm, yellow bile, and black bile) that, according to medieval belief, shaped the personality depending on how much of each was present in the body.

Freud, Sigmund (1856–1939) Austrian psychologist who invented psychoanalysis.

Freya In Norse mythology, Odin's wife and goddess of love, marriage, and fertility.

Furies Avenging goddesses in Greek mythology.

Gabriel Archangel in Christian and Muslim belief; God's messenger.

Gandhi, "Mahatma" (1869–1948) Indian nationalist leader, famous for heading a non-violent freedom struggle.

Garuda Fabulous bird, mount of Vishnu.

Great Goddess An embodiment of the feminine principle. May take different forms. In Hinduism, may be benign or terrifying.

griffin A mythical beast with a lion's body and eagle's beak and wings.

Hanukkah The Jewish festival of lights.

harbinger Forerunner, precursor.

Hathor Egyptian goddess of love and beauty.

Hercules (Greek Herakles) Hero of Roman mythology famous for his strength.

heresy A belief that contradicts authorized religious teaching.

Herod Herod Antipas, governor of the Jews in Jesus' time.

Hittites Inhabitants of ancient Anatolia and Syria.

Homer Blind Greek poet of the 8th century BC, author of the epics *Iliad* and *Odyssey*.

Horus Egyptian hawk-headed sun god, son of Isis and Osiris.

I Ching Ancient Chinese book of divination.

initiation ceremony A rite of admission, often marking the entry into adulthood.

Inuits Inhabitants of Greenland and the Arctic region of North America; Eskimos.

Isis Chief goddess of ancient Egypt, sister-wife of Osiris.

Israelites Descendants of the patriarch (Jacob); the Jews.

Jacob Hebrew patriarch, whose twelve sons were ancestors to Israel's twelve tribes.

Jonah Biblical figure who was swallowed by a great fish.

Judas Iscariot Disciple who betrayed Christ to the Jews.

Judea Southern division of ancient Palestine.

Jung, Carl (1875–1961) Swiss psychologist and colleague of Freud who originated Analytical Psychology.

Juno (Greek Hera) Queen of the Roman pantheon, protector of women.

Jupiter (Greek Zeus) King of the gods in Roman mythology, god of thunder.

Koran The Muslim sacred texts as revealed to the prophet Mohammed.

Krishna Incarnation of the Hindu god Vishnu.

mandala Pictorial symbol of the universe, a Buddhist aid to meditation.

Mars (Greek Ares) Roman god of war.

martyrdom Dying for one's belief.

Mary, Virgin The mother of Jesus Christ.

Maya An ancient Indian people who lived in Central America and Southern Mexico.

Mecca The birthplace of Mohammed.

Medusa In Greek mythology, a female monster with snakes for hair, whose glance turned people to stone.

Mercury (Greek Hermes) Roman messenger god, god of travellers.

Mesoamerica Central America, between Northern Mexico and Panama.

Mesopotamia The ancient name for part of modern Iraq.

microcosm The world or universe in miniature.

Minerva (Greek Athena) Roman goddess of wisdom and war.

Minoan Of prehistoric Crete.

Mithras Ancient Persian god of light worshipped by Romans.

Moghul emperors North Indian Muslim dynasty 1526–1857.

Mohammed (c.570–632) The prophet and founder of Islam.

monotheistic Believing in one god only.

Moses Hebrew law-giver and judge who led his people out of Egypt.

mysticism A way of directly experiencing the Divine through ecstatic or heightened spiritual awareness.

Navaho Native American people of North America.

Nefertem Human-headed Egyptian god of the setting sun.

Neptune (Greek Poseidon) Roman god of the sea.

Nirvana Extinction of individuality and absorption into the cosmos, never to be re-born; goal of Buddhism.

Noah Biblical character who, at God's command, built an Ark to save his family from the Flood.

Odin Chief deity of Norse mythology, sky god.

Orpheus Mythical Greek poet and musician, with the power to enchant all living creatures.

Osiris Egyptian god of the dead.

Ottoman Belonging to the Ottoman Empire, ruled by the Turks AD 1300–1920.

Pan Greek god of shepherds and hunters, with a goat's horns and hoofs. His pipes had a hypnotic effect.

pantheon All the gods of a mythology collectively.

Parsee Descendant of eighth-century Zoroastrian emigrés to India.

patriarchs The founding fathers of a nation or religion.

Phaeton Son of Apollo, who drove the chariot of the sun for one day, nearly set the earth on fire, and was killed by Jupiter's thunderbolt.

phoenix Fabulous Arabian bird re-born from the flames of its own destruction.

Pluto (Greek Dis) Roman god of Hades, the Underworld, kingdom of the dead.

primordial Existing from the beginning; primeval.

Promised Land Canaan (present-day Israel), which the Jews believed had been promised them by God.

Quetzalcoatl Aztec god of learning and of priestly functions, usually depicted as a feathered serpent.

Rama Vishnu's seventh incarnation, the mythical hero of India's war with Lanka.

Ramadan The ninth month of the Islamic calendar, when Muslims fast by day.

Re Egyptian sun-god, father of Osiris and Isis.

Renaissance The transitional period between the Middle Ages and modern times; literally the "rebirth" of arts and learning.

Samurai Japanese aristocratic warriors, equivalent of England's knights.

Sanskrit The ancient literary language of India.

Saturn The second largest planet. Its influence is believed by astrologers to give rise to a cold, melancholy temperament.

satyrs Half-goat and half-human woodland gods in Greek mythology.

Selket Human-headed Egyptian scorpion-goddess.

shaman Priest-doctor who works directly with the spirit world.

Shiva The Destroyer, one of the three great gods of Hinduism.

Sinai Mountain in Egypt where Moses received the Ten Commandments.

Sioux A Native American people of North America.

Solomon, King Hebrew king, son of David, famed for wisdom.

Soviet Union The former Union of Soviet Socialist Republics.

stylus Pointed implement for writing on wax tablets.

Taoism Chinese philosophical system teaching harmonious interaction with nature.

Theseus Hero of Greek mythology, who killed the minotaur.

Thor Norse god of thunder.

Thoth Ibis-headed god of wisdom and learning in Egyptian mythology.

totem An object or creature regarded as sacred by a clan. Often an ancestor figure.

transcendence The surpassing of all limitations of human knowledge and experience.

tribe of Judah Descendants of Judah, son of Jewish patriarch Jacob.

Trojan War Legendary siege of the city of Troy by the Greeks.

tzars Emperors of pre-Revolutionary Russia.

Ulysses (Greek Odysseus) Hero of Roman and Greek mythology, who fought the Trojans and was famous for his courage and ingenuity.

Venus (Greek Aphrodite) Roman goddess of beauty and love.

Venus, sphere of In medieval thought, the earth was encased in nine invisible rotating spheres of increasing size, each holding a planet.

Virgin Birth The birth of Jesus to the Virgin Mary after her insemination by God.

Vishnu The Preserver. With Shiva, one of the most important Hindu gods.

yin and yang Chinese opposing yet complementary principles, *yin* being negative, feminine, and dark, while *yang* is positive, masculine, and bright.

Yoruba People of south-west Nigeria.

Zoroastrianism Pre-Islamic Persian religion.

INDEX

FURTHER READING

Alexeiev, Basil, *The Chinese Gods of Wealth*, School of Oriental and African Studies, London 1928

Ayo, Yvonne, *Africa, Eyewitness Guides*, Dorling Kindersley, London 1995

Baquedano, Elizabeth, *Aztec, Eyewitness Guides*, Dorling Kindersley, London 1993

Bechert, Heinz & Gombrich, Richard, *The World of Buddhism*, Thames and Hudson, London 1984

Becker, Udo, *The Element Encyclopedia of Symbols*, Element, Dorset 1994

Becket, Sister Wendy, *The Story of Painting*, Dorling Kindersley, London 1994

Black, Jeremy & Green, Anthony, *Gods, Demons & Symbols of Ancient Mesopotamia*, BMP, London 1992

Blurton, Richard, *Hindu Art*, BMP, London 1992

Campbell, Joseph, *The Masks of God, vol 1: Primitive Mythology; vol 2: Oriental Mythology; vol 3: Occidental Mythology; vol 4: Creative Mythology*, Viking, New York 1959-68

Chetwynd, Tom, *Dictionary of Symbols*, Aquarian/Thorsons, London 1982

Child, Heather & Colles, Dorothy, *Christian Symbols*, Bell & Hyman, London 1971

Chiron Dictionary of Greek and Roman Mythology, Chiron, Illinois 1994

Christie, Anthony, *Chinese Mythology*, Hamlyn, Feltham, UK 1968

Cirlot, J.E., *A Dictionary of Symbols*, Routledge, London 1993

Cooper, J.C., *An Illustrated Encyclopedia of Traditional Symbols*, Thames & Hudson, London 1992

Cooper, J.C., *Symbolic & Mythological Animals*, Aquarian Press, London 1992

Crossley-Holland, Kevin, *The Norse Myths, Gods of the Vikings*, Penguin, London 1980

De Rola, Stanislas Klossowski, *The Secret Art of Alchemy*, Thames & Hudson, London 1973

Dreyfuss, Henry, *Symbol Sourcebook*, McGraw-Hill, New York 1972

Eberard, Wolfram, *A Dictionary of Chinese Symbols, English edition*, Routledge & Kegan Paul, London 1986

Ferguson, George, *Signs & Symbols in Christian Art*, Oxford University Press, London 1961

Foley, John, *The Guinness Encyclopedia of Signs & Symbols*, Guinness Publishing, UK 1993

Fontana, David, *The Secret Language of Symbols*, Pavilion Books, London 1993

Freud, Sigmund, *The Interpretation of Dreams*, Pelican ed., London 1979

Gordon, Matthew S., *Islam*, Facts On File, New York 1991

Graham-Campbell, James & Kidd, Dafydd, *The Vikings*, BMP, London 1980

Guerber, H.A. *The Myths of Greece & Rome*, Harrap & Co., London 1963

Haeffner, Mark, *Dictionary of Alchemy*, Aquarian, London 1991

Hall, James, *Subjects & Symbols in Art*, John Murray, London 1995

Hamill, John, *The History of English Freemasonry*, Lewis Masonic Books, Surrey 1994

Herder Symbol Dictionary, The, Chiron Publications, Illinois 1991

Honour, Hugh & Fleming, John, *A World History of Art*, Lawrence King Publishing, London 1995 (revised ed.)

Hoult, Janet, *Dragons, Their History and Symbolism*, Gothic Image, Somerset 1987

Huntingdon, Susan, *The Art of Ancient India*, Weatherhill, New York 1995

Hutt, Michael, *Nepal, a Guide to the Art and Architecture of the Kathmadu Valley*, Kiskadale, Stirling 1994

Ibbot, Selena, *Folklore, Legends and Spells*, Ashgrove Press, Bath 1994

Japan, An Illustrated Encyclopedia, 2 vols., Kodansha, Tokyo 1993

Jean, Georges, *Writing, the Story of Alphabets and Scripts*, Thames and Hudson, London 1992

Jenson, Hans, *Sign, Symbol and Script*, George Allen & Unwin, London 1970

Jung, Carl G., *Man and his Symbols*, Aldus Books, London 1964

King, Francis X., *Mind, Magic & Mystery*, Dorling Kindersley, London 1992

Knappert, Jan, *Indian Mythology, Encyclopedia of Myth and Legend*, Aquarian Press, London 1991

Knappert, Jan, *Pacific Mythology, An Encyclopedia of Myth and Legend*, Aquarian Press, London 1992

Knappert, Jan, *The Encyclopedia of Middle Eastern Mythology and Religion*, Element, Dorset 1993

Kruger, Anna, *Herbs, Their Medicine and Magic*, Dragon's World, London 1992

Kunz, George Frederick, *The Curious Lore of Precious Stones*, Dover Publications, New York 1971

Larousse Dictionary of Beliefs and Religions, Larousse, Edinburgh 1994

Lundquist, John M., *The Temple, Meeting Place of Heaven and Earth*, Thames and Hudson, London 1986

Lurker, Manfred, *The Gods and Symbols of Ancient Egypt*, Thames & Hudson, London 1994

Morris, Desmond, *Bodytalk*, Jonathan Cape, London 1994

New Larousse Encyclopedia of Mythology, Hamlyn, London 1959

Oxford Companion to Music, Oxford University Press, London 1967

Parker, Julia & Derek, *Parkers' Astrology*, Dorling Kindersley, London 1994

Philip, Neil, *The Illustrated Book of Myths*, Dorling Kindersley, London 1995

Rawson, Philip, *Tantra, The Indian Cult of Ecstasy*, Thames and Hudson, London 1979

Sahi, Jyoti, *The Child and the Serpent, Reflections of Popular Indian Symbols*, Arkana, London 1980

Saunders, Nicholas, *The Cult of the Cat*, Thames and Hudson, London 1991

Stutley, Margaret & James, *A Dictionary of Hinduism and its Symbols*, Routledge & Kegan Paul, London 1977

Theroux, Alexander, *The Primary Colours*, Picador, London, 1994

Thomas, Nicholas, *Oceanic Art*, Thames and Hudson, London 1995

Versluis, Arthur, *Native American Traditions*, Element, Dorset 1994

Villiers, Elizabeth, *The Good Luck Book*, Studio Editions, London 1994

Wangu, Madhu Bazaz, *Buddhism*, Facts On File, New York/Oxford 1993

Wangu, Madhu Bazaz, *Hinduism*, Facts On File, New York 1991

Werner, E.T.C., *Myths and Legends of China*, Sinclair Browne Ltd, London 1984

Williams, C.A.S., *Outlines of Chinese Symbolism and Art Motives*, Charles E. Tuttle Company, Rutland 1981

Witkower, Rudolf, *Allegory and the Migration of Symbols*, Thames and Hudson, New York 1977

World's Religions, The, Lion Publishing plc, Oxford, UK (revised) 1994

Yarwood, Doreen, *The Encyclopedia of World Costume*, Batsford, London, 1986

Zaehner, R.C., *The Concise Encyclopedia of Living Faiths*, Hutchinson, London 1971 (revised)

Zimmer, Heinrich, *Myths and Symbols in Indian Art and Civilization*, Pantheon Books, Washington 1946

Zuylen, Gabrielle van, *The Garden*, Thames & Hudson, London 1995

ACKNOWLEDGEMENTS

From the author:
I would like to thank the friends and colleagues who answered queries concerning the text. These include Richard Blurton, Heather Elgood, Anat Feinberg, Edward Gibbs, Meher McArthur and John Okell. Thank you to Alison Cole, the Western Art adviser, for her many valuable comments, and to Joanna Lane for her meticulous indexing skills. I owe a great debt of gratitude to those at Dorling Kindersley: Anna Kruger, Peter Bailey, the team of Sarah Ponder, Emma Foa, Martin Wilson, Shirin Patel, Joanna Pocock, and Ali Cobb, who all worked tirelessly on this book. An especial thank you to Sarah for her calm and assured handling of the design – and her smile, and to Emma, Editor Extraordinary, for her expertise, good advice and good humour. Thanks also to Harriet Griffey, and to my friends at Tolli's for all their encouragement; and lastly to Robert, Jessica and Jonathan, for their uncomplaining support through every crisis. I dedicate this book to them.

The publishers would like to thank:
Laraine Newberry, our Australian consultant; Julian Perry and John Hamill for all their help regarding Freemasonry; Hugh Myers for the loan of his precious chess set; Bentley & Co., the Bond Street Jewellers, for their advice and use of their many transparencies; Past Times for access to their historical gift collection; and Spink and Son Ltd for all their assistance.
Special thanks to: Sue Unstead, for her continuing support and encouragement.
Additional design, editorial, and picture research: Caroline Brooke, Louise Cox, Sarah Crouch, Robert Graham, Anderley Moore, Fergus Muir, Caroline Potts.
Specially commissioned photography: Andy Crawford, Steve Gorton, Ellen Howden at the Glasgow Museum, and Geoff Thompson at the Manchester Museum.
Specially commissioned illustrations: Peter Bull, Nick Hall, Colette Ho, Malcolm McGregor, Peter Visscher, John Woodcock.
Additional photography: Max Alexander, Peter Anderson, Geoff Brightling, Jane Burton, Peter Chadwick, Tim Daly, Geoff Dann, Philip Dowell, Andreas von Einsiedel, Neil Fletcher, Lynton Gardiner, David Garner, Philip Gatwood, Paul Goff, Christi Graham, Frank Greenaway, Peter Hayman, Stephen Hayward, John Heseltine, Alan Hills, Chas Howson, Colin Keates, Dave King, Cyril Laubscher, Richard Leeney, Liz McAulay, Andrew McRobb, Kevin Mallet, Diana Miller, Ray Moller, Nick Nicholas, Martin Norris, Stephen Oliver, Gary Ombler, Roger Philips, Martin Ploner, Laurence Pordes, Kim Sayer, Karl Shone, Steve Shott, David Spence, James Stevenson, Clive Streeter, Harry Taylor, Matthew Ward, Kate Warren, Jerry Young, Michel Zabé.
Additional illustration: Christian Hook, Danuta Mayer.

The publishers would like to thank the following for their kind permission to reproduce the photographs:

l=left, r=right, c=centre, t=top, b=bottom, a=above, cb=centre below, cfr=centre far right, cfl=centre far left, clb=centre left below, crb=centre right below, bcl=bottom centre left, bcr=bottom centre right, bfl=bottom far left, bfr=bottom far right, tfl=top far left, tfr=top far right.

AKG 17tl, 19tl, 34-35, 53cr, 81tr, 94br; /Erich Lessing 15cra, bl, 19cb, 38bl, bc, 89cr, 91cr; Staatliche Antikensammlungen und Glyptothek 54tr; **Reproduced by permission of The American Museum in Britain, Bath** 70bl; **American Museum of Natural History** 63cra, 77cra, cbr, 78br, 86c; **Ancient Art & Architecture/Ronald Sheridan** back jacket, 16tl, 20cr, 96cra; **Heather Angel** 21cla; **The College of Arms** 114tr; **Ashmolean Museum, Oxford** 18tr, 20tr, 25tc, 29tl, 52cr, 103tcl, 105tc; **The Australian Museum/Nature Focus Library** 26bfr; **Bentley & Co.** 86tl, br, bcr, 87tl, cb, cr, cfr, bla, bl, br; **Bibliothèque Nationale** (01FR 143 fol 198v) 42tr; **Birmingham Museum** 49bl; **BLC** 116bfr; **The Bridgeman Art Library** 8br, 26cr, 27tr, 34ca, 42br; / Archaeological Museum, Naples 15cl; Musee des Beaux-Arts, Le Havre 36b; Bibliothèque Nationale, Paris 8b, 16tr, 27bc; Bonhams, London 2tr, 34b, 40cl; Brancacci Chapel, Santa Maria del Carmine, Florence 59br; © Brewster Arts Ltd, New York, *Tuesday*, Leonora Carrington 9cr; British Library 24c, 34l, 46c, 75bl, 98-99, 113br; Schloss Charlottenburg, Berlin 89cfr; Christies, London 29bc; Musée Cluny, Paris 3b, 28cl; De Morgan Foundation, London 78c, bc; © Fondation P Delvaux-St Idesbald, Belgium/DACS 1996, *The Temple 1949*, Paul Delvaux 6-7; Ferens Art Gallery, Hull 29cr; Giraudon 43tr /Musée des Beaux-Arts, Nantes 8t; / Musée Condé, Chantilly 103tl; /Musée Municipal, Laon, France 81tl; Index/Museo Diocesano de Solsona, Lerida 44cl; Kremlin Museum, Moscow 89trb; Museum of Mankind 26bc, 40br; National Gallery, London 73bl; Oriental Museum, Durham University 58c; Osterriches Gallery, Vienna 119cr; Prado, Madrid 10tl, 42bl, cl, Preweatt Neate Fine Art Auctioneers, Newbury 45crb; Rheims Cathedral 51c, St Peters, Leuven 49cr; Santa Maria delle Grazie, Milan 103tr; Scrovegni (Arena) Chapel, Padua 107tfl; Tate Gallery 50br, 106bl/©ADAGP, Paris and DACS, London 1996, *The Reckless Sleeper* René Magritte 10b; Galleria degli Uffizi, Florence 48bl; Courtesy of the Board of Trustees of the V & A 29tr, 60bl, 71bc, 82br (detail), 89tl; Walker Art Gallery, Liverpool 53t; Wallace Collection 96bl; Westminster Abbey, London 88tr; Woburn Abbey (detail) 88cl; **The British Library, London** 19br, 22c, 31tl, 60tl, 61bl, 62tc (Or Ms. 2748 f. 208b), 21bc (Or 11387 f.10b); **The British Museum,** London 9tl, 14tr, c, bc, cl, cfl, cfr, 15tc, tr, cr, bc, 25cl, 27tl, cl, 39cfl ,41tr, 48tr, 52cla,54br, 55bla, tc, 57br (obj no. 1900.4-7.48), 59bla, 60tr, 61bl, tl, br (obj no.1936.4-11.023), 62cl, tr (obj no. 19102-12-464), 63b, 64-65t, 65tr, 66cl, 70cl, 71br, 78cra, cr,79cl, 86bcl, 93tcl, 96cr, 105bc; **Duncan Brown** 28c, 39cr, 75tcl, 93cb, 107br; **J.Allan Cash** 77c, 93crb, 94tr, bl; **Lester Cheeseman** 21bl, 72cl, 73br; **Christie's Images** 32-33, 47tr; **Cinema Bookshop, London** 11br; **Bruce Coleman Ltd**/Christer Fredriksson 106tl; Carol Hughes 37bc; Luiz Claudio Marigo 36tr; Hans Reinhard 26bc; **Cotton Technology International** 116br; **National Museum of Denmark, Copenhagen** 4clb, 18bl, 30tr, 90cla; **James Davis Photography** 16bc; **C.M.Dixon** 35tr, 74bl, 75tl; **Museum of English Rural Life, University of Reading, Leeds** 90cfr; **ET Archive** 1, 2cl, 20l, 22tr, 31tl, 62bl, 66tr, 71cra, 72bc, 74cl, 81tc, 89tc, 101tr, 103bl; **Mary Evans Picture Library** 4b, 4cra, 9bl, 9tr, 28cfr, 31br, 37c, 45tr, 65br, 72tr, 73tr, 74tl, 75br, 79tr, 80tl, 81cfr, 84bra, 89cl, 90cl, 90bl, 92c, 95tcl, 102bl, 110crb, clb; **Eye Ubiquitous** 43c; /David Cumming 21cr; Frank Leather 27cr; **Exeter Museum** 86cl; **Chris Fairclough Colour Library** 18br, 95bl; **Forest Light/Alan Watson** 95cl; **Werner Forman Archive** 23clb/British Museum, London inside jacket, 4cla, 28tr; Philip Goldman Collection 52bl, Musée National du Bardo, Tunis 63cl; National Museum of Man, Ottawa, Ontario 63clb; Statens Historiska Museum, Stockholm 15br; University of Philadelphia, U.S. 39br; **The Garden Picture Library** 42cb,/John Bethell 73cr; Bridgitte Thomas 43clb; **Garrard, London** 39cl; **Glasgow Museums** 4crb, 5cra, 16cla, cb, br, clb, 20br, 21cra, tfr, tc, 22bc, 23tr, 25cfl, cr, tl, 26tfr, tr, tc, 59c, 64bla, 76-77cs,79tc, crb, 81bra, 82tr, cr, 89clb; **Golders Green United Synagogue** 16cr; **Ronald Grant Archive** 54bl; **Greenjackets Museum, Winchester** 80cfl; **Greenpeace**/Dorreboom 65cra; **Sonia Halliday and Laura Lushington Photographs** 19bc 37crb, 90bc, 106crb; /Barry Searle 16crb; **Robert Harding Picture Library** inside jacket, 14bl, 39c, 73bra; British Library 95cr; Alain Evrard 83tl; Paolo Koch 106ca; Kodak Ltd. 83c; T.J. Larse-Collingen 27bl; Jenny Pate 25bl; John Ross 88bl; J.H.C.Wilson 20c, 104crb; Adam Woolfitt 6tr; **Hodder & Stoughton** 89bc; **Michael Holford** 10tc, 30cl, 72br; **HMSO Crown Copyright** 89br; **Hulton Getty Picture Collection** 77br, 89crb; **The Hutchison Library**/Sarah Errington 93cl, Goy Coolea 21c; **Ikona**/Galleria Borghese 15cla; **The Image Bank**/Andrea Pistolesi 12-13; Guido Alberto Rossi 36c; F.Reginato 34c; **Images Colour Library** 77tc, 95c; /The Dawes Collection 106cra; /Charles Walker Collection front jacket, 4clb, 5t, 6tl, 7b, 23tc, 28bl, 72cb, 74tr, 79bl, 92tr, 102c, 103clb, br, 107c, 108tl, c, b, 110c, 111cl, 113tr; **Impact Photos** Christopher Bluntzer 25br; Colin Jones 21br; Rachel Morton 84cl; Homer Sykes 83tr; Rajesh Vora 107bl; **Imperial War Museum** 114bc; **Japan Archive** 63tr; **Michael Jenner** 18bc; **The Jewish Museum** 16bl, 17tr, c; **JNTO** 23cb; **Joods Historich Museum, Amsterdam** 17br; **Kobal Collection** 11tr, 73tfr; **Anna Kruger** 18c; **Museum of London** 91br; **Manchester Museum** back jacket, 4cl, 14cfl, cr, bcr, 15clb, 20tc, 28br, 29bl, 31c, 55tr, 56cl, 61cl, 62cr, 75cr, 93cra, 100cl, bc; **Mansell Collection** 47cl, 85br; **Arxiu Mas** 41bl; **Museum of Mankind** 55bl, 66bl; **Miranda Bruce-Mitford** 23cl, bc; **Museum of the Moving Image** 76bl; **NASA** 11bl, 34cr; /JPL 36tl; **National Army Museum** 66c; **The National Gallery, London** 19tc, 30br, bl, 57tl, cb; **National Maritime Museum, London** 2crb, 29br, 59bc, 72bl, cr; **National Museum of Scotland** 31tc, 93tr; **National Trust Photographic Library**/Nick Meers 43tl; **National Trust for Scotland**/Harvey Wood 48br; **Natural History Museum, London** 38br, 39tl, tr, bl, 40tl, bcl, 40bcr, c, cr, 55cr, 56cr, 79cra; **Past Times, Witney, Oxfordshire** 43cla, 79cr; **Peter Newark's Western Americana** 61tr, 76tr; **Photostage/Donald Cooper** 77tl; **Pictor** 76c; **Pitt Rivers Museum** back jacket, 18cl, 41tcl, 47tcl, 54cr, 58tr, 62br, cla, crb, 70tr, 75tr, 77cb, 78tr, 86br, 86cr, clb, 87cl, 91tl, tr; **Sarah Ponder** 93 tfl, bc; **Powell Cotton Museum** 23c, br, 70cra, 80cl; **Retna Pictures**/A&M Records 11bl; **Rex Features Ltd** 76bc, 80tr; /Tim Rooke 85bl; Simmons 106tr; **Royal Mail** 65cl; **Peter Sanders** 24bc; **Scala** 19bl, 105bl; **Sir John Soane's Museum** 46tr; **Sotheby's, London** 21tcl, 22br, 24tr, bl, 25tr, 37tl; **Spink & Son Ltd.** 30c, 37cra, 107clb, 115tc; **Frank Spooner Pictures**/Jane Taylor 91c; **Sporting Pictures (U.K.) Ltd.** 39tc, 119cl; **Statens Historiska Museum** 28cr, 93tc; **Tony Stone**/Christopher Arnesen 68-69; Kevin Miller 26br; Tate Gallery 51br; **Thames & Hudson Ltd**/Jeff Teasdale (from *Tantra* by Philip Rawson) 74cr; / John Webb 104cl, tl, bc, bl; **Trip**/H. Rogers 20bc, 21clb; **United Grand Lodge, London** 35tl, 109tr, tc, cr, bl; **US Postal Service** 70crb, bca; **V & A Museum, London** 56br; **The Vegetarian Society** 107bc; **The Wallace Collection, London** 63c, 66tl, tc, 73tl, 114bl; **Rodney Wilson** 35tc; **Westminster Cathedral** 106cb; **Elizabeth Whiting Associates** 95bcl; **Robin Wigington, Arbour Antiques** 91tfl, bc; **Wimbledon Buddhist Temple** 23tl; **International Wool Secretariat** 116bra; **Michel Zabé** 66cb; **Zefa Pictures Ltd** 95tr; /Taner 24cr

Every effort has been made to trace the copyright holders. Dorling Kindersley apologizes for any unintentional omissions and would be pleased, in such cases, to add an acknowledgement in future editions.